CRYSIS

INTRODUCTION

The world has been ravaged by a series of climatic disasters and society is on the verge of total breakdown. Now the aliens have returned, with a full invasion force bent on nothing less than the total annihilation of mankind, starting by trying to rip the heart out of Earth's most iconic city.

In New York, terrifying alien invaders stalk the streets and a nightmare plague strikes down the city's myriad inhabitants with brutal epidemic speed. The city's systems are in chaos, its streets and skyline are smashed and in flaming ruin. This is New York City like you've never seen it before.

Neither paramilitary law enforcement nor the might of the US military machine can stand against the invaders, and all who choose not to flee are dead men walking. Just to survive in this maelstrom of death will require technology beyond anything any modern soldier has ever seen.

One man will inherit that means to survive. One supersoldier, wielding the combat enhancement technology of the future with Nanosuit 2, will make the last stand to save humanity from destruction in the urban jungle that is New York City.

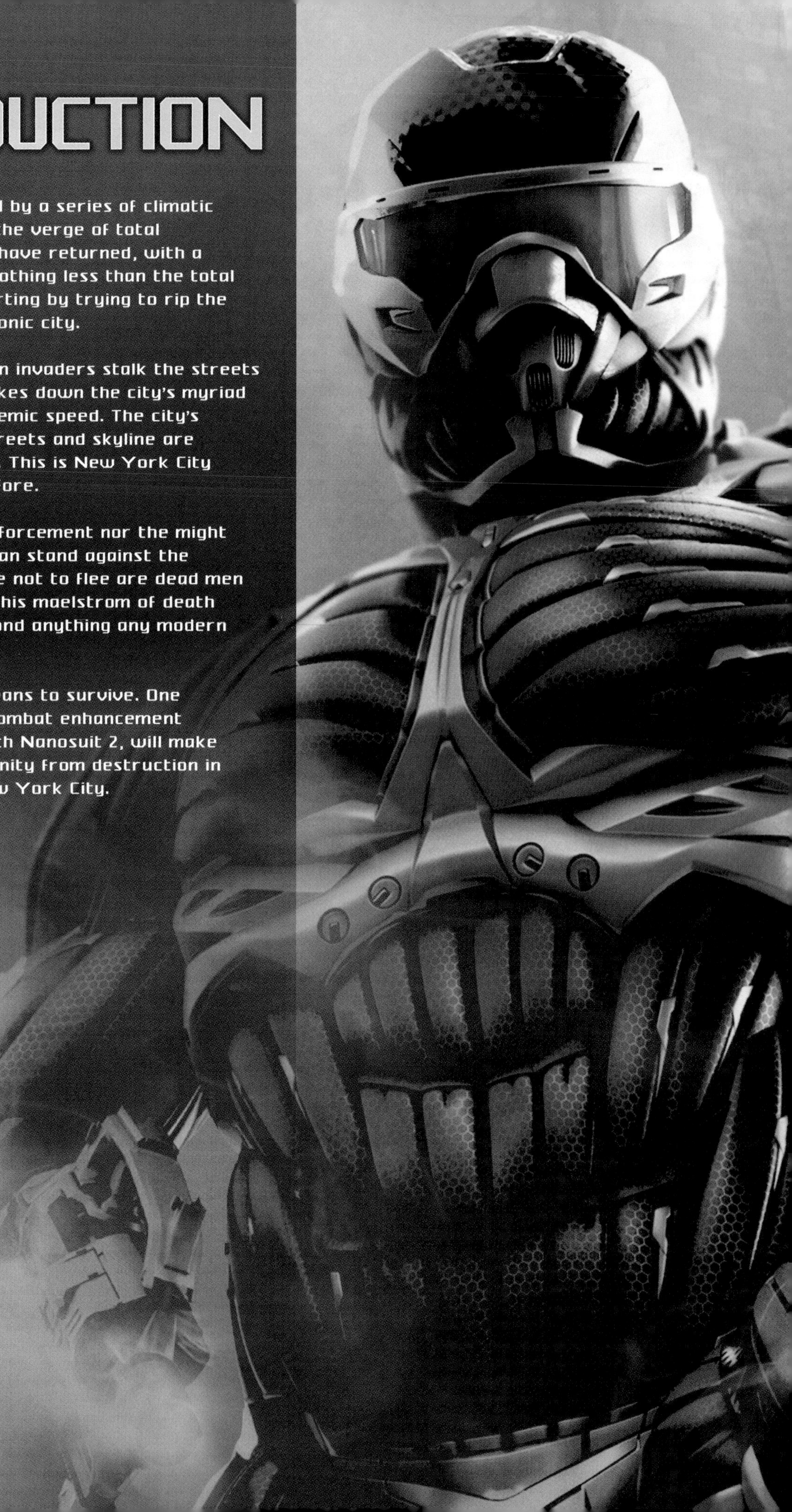

ABOUT THIS GUIDE

The Nanosuit alone isn't enough to save mankind from the terror befallen New York City, you need this guide too. The *Crysis 2 Official Strategy Guide* contains the tools necessary to train you to be the ultimate supersoldier, to get the most out of the weapons available, and understand the ways of the enemy. The comprehensive walkthrough directs provides a tactical assessment for every major encounter, directs you through each skirmish efficiently, and helps to ensure you don't miss a single collectible. The action continues with the game's robust multiplayer component and this guide's Multiplayer Training chapter provides tips and strategies for every game mode while also detailing the unlocking conditions for each of the hundreds of Dog Tags. The guidebook also includes beautifully rendered maps for each multiplayer level, including all target locations for each of the objective-based multiplayer modes.

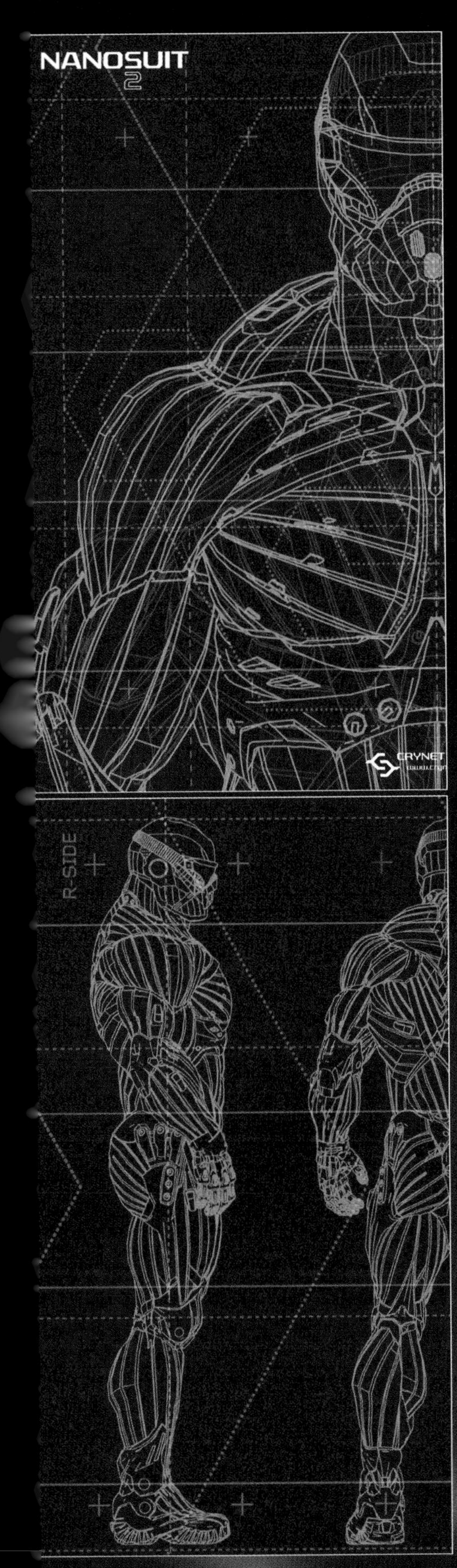

SUPERSOLDIER TRAINING

The Marines sent to New York City to investigate the deadly outbreak are in for quite a surprise. Most will end up dead, but not Alcatraz. Alcatraz finds himself in possession of a magnificent and powerful piece of weaponry known as the Nanosuit. He also finds himself on a mission to save humanity from a force far more powerful than any the Department of Defense dared envision. The battle is as long as it is arduous. Alcatraz requires some training in order to succeed. This chapter is intended to complement the helpful user's manual that accompanied your copy of Crysis 2. The following pages discuss the Nanosuit's major abilities and provides tips for getting the most out of the suit—and Alcatraz in combat.

GAME FUNDAMENTALS

CONTROLS

This guide covers all three versions of the game (Xbox 360, PS3, and PC). The controls for each are highly customizable, particularly for the PC. The following tables detail the default controls for the Xbox 360 and PS3 versions of the game. Those using the Controller-S for play on the PC (instead of a mouse and keyboard) should refer to the Xbox 360 controls.

BASIC CONTROLS

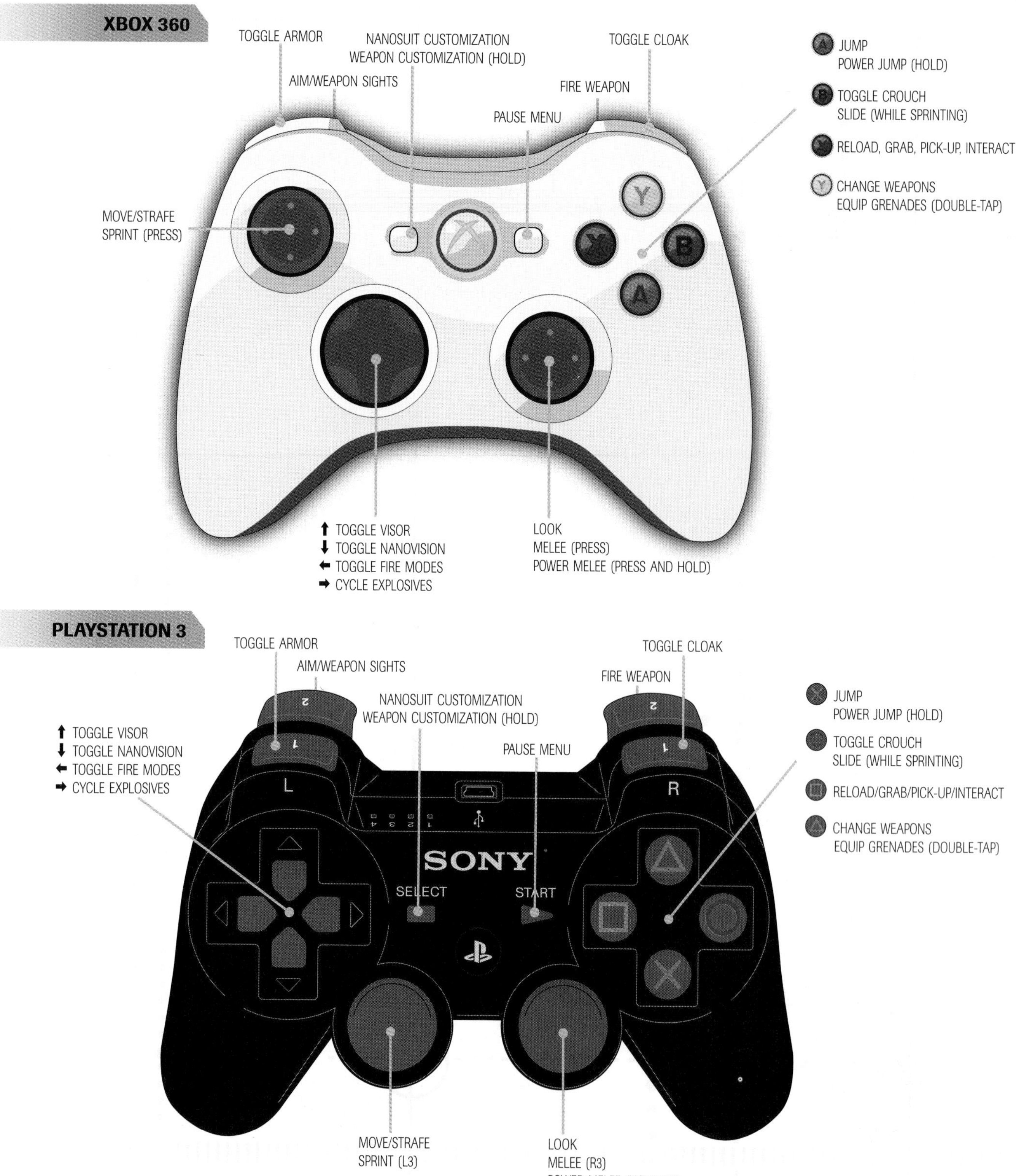

VEHICLE CONTROLS

XBOX 360

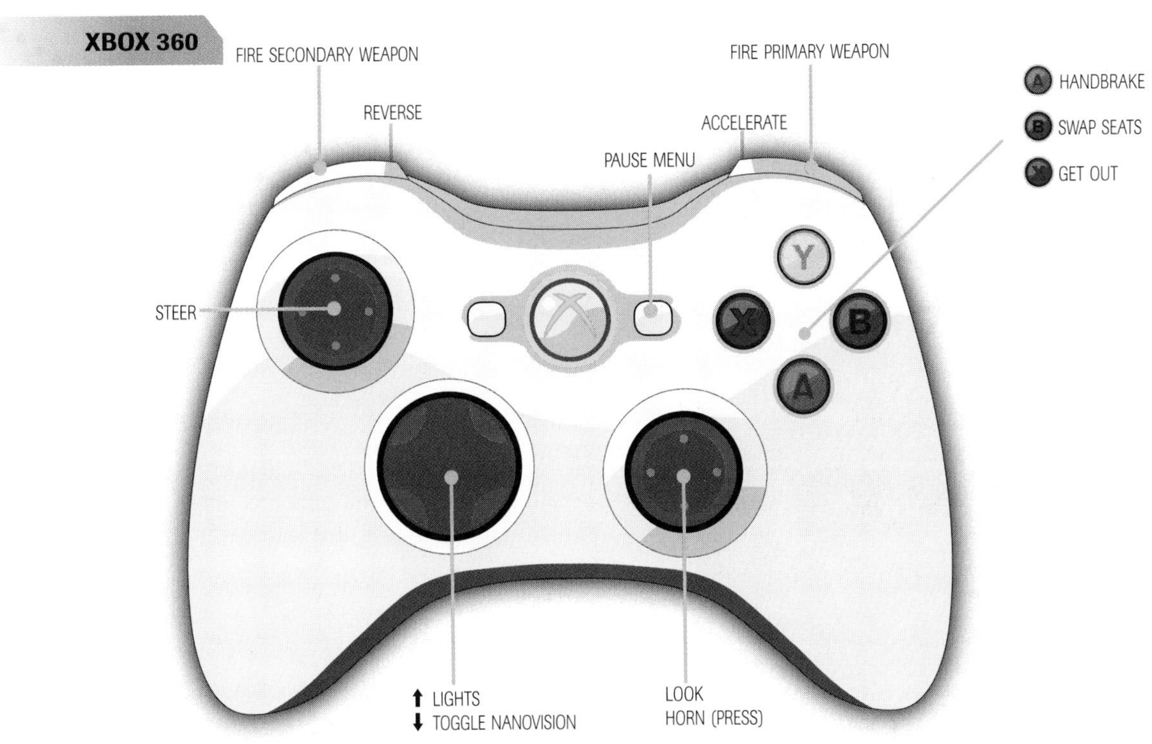

PLAYSTATION 3

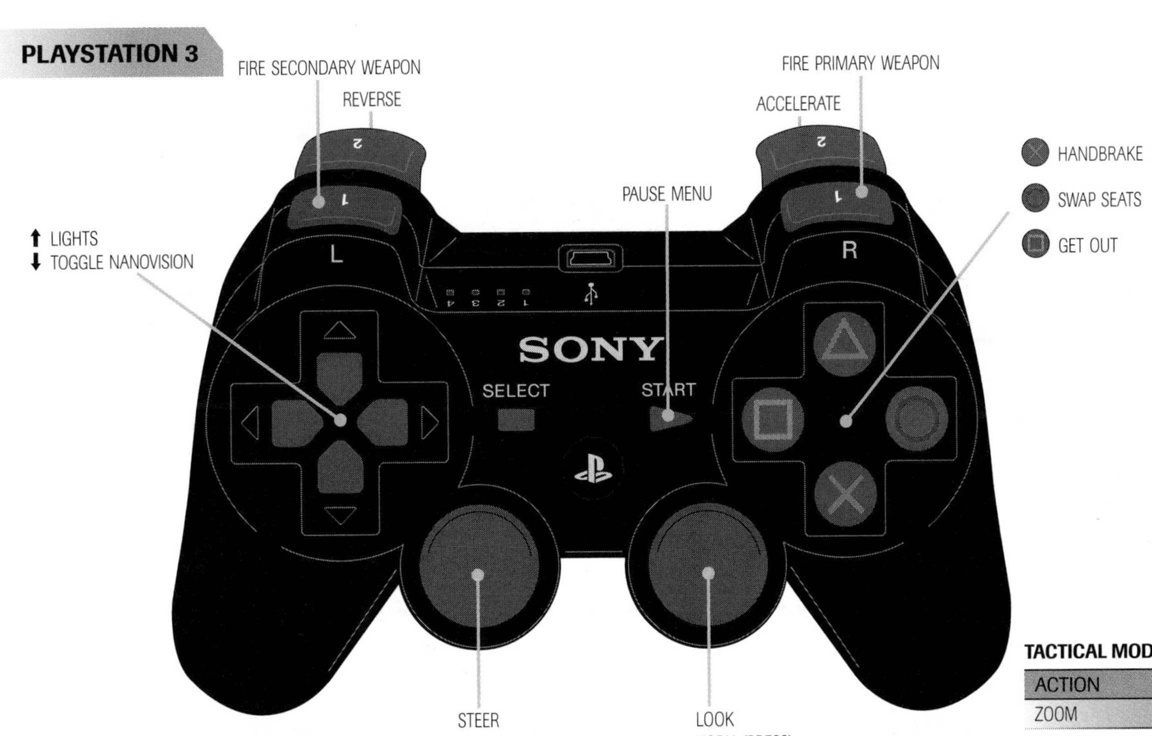

TACTICAL MODE (WHILE VISOR ACTIVE)

ACTION	XBOX 360	PS3
ZOOM	L TRIGGER	L2
HIGHLIGHT TARGET	Ⓧ	▢

DIFFICULTY MODES

Crysis 2 features the following four difficulty modes:

RECRUIT: A WALK IN THE PARK. RECOMMENDED FOR PLAYERS NEW TO THE SHOOTER GENRE.

SOLDIER: THE RECOMMENDED SETTING FOR EXPERIENCED FPS PLAYERS. TEST YOUR ABILITIES AGAINST CHALLENGING ENEMIES.

VETERAN: ENEMIES REACT FASTER WITH INCREASED LETHALITY. BE AT THE TOP OF YOUR GAME TO SURVIVE.

SUPERSOLDIER: THE ULTIMATE CHALLENGE FOR PLAYERS AT THE PEAK OF THEIR ABILITIES.

Unless you have never before played a game in the first-person shooter genre, we recommend selecting the Soldier difficulty setting. This is the mode for which this book's walkthrough is based. Enemies in Veteran and Supersoldier modes are more aggressive, inflict more damage when they attack, and are more difficult to kill. They are also much more aware of their surroundings, thus making it harder for Alcatraz to remain stealthy.

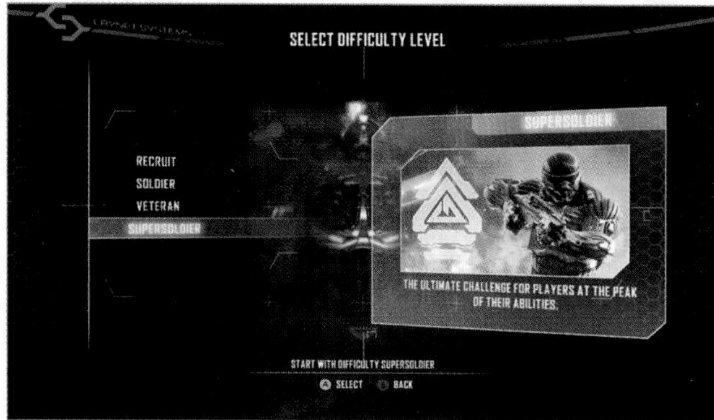

The Achievements/Trophies system and "Replay Mission" option, selectable from the Campaign menu, entice players to play each mission on multiple difficulties. Consider playing through the entire campaign on Soldier difficulty first, then use the Replay Mission option to go back and replay each of the missions on Veteran and, if your skills are up to it, Supersoldier. The best way to do this is to play a mission on Veteran, then immediately play that same mission again on Supersoldier while it's fresh in your mind.

CAMPAIGN FLOW

The single-player campaign consists of 19 missions. Each mission has a number of collectibles to locate and a small number of primary objectives. The objectives are marked on-screen with a blue hexagon to help guide Alcatraz in the right direction. Saving is done automatically each time Alcatraz reaches a checkpoint, which usually coincides with a minor objective. Each objective usually has a number of minor, sub-objectives that must be completed in linear fashion. The primary and minor objectives are shown on screen separated by a colon, always focus on the task shown to the right of the colon, as that is the immediate concern.

TACTICAL ASSESSMENT

The Nanosuit isn't just a piece of clothing or armor, it's a secret weapon with its own intelligence and satellite uplink that displays valuable tactical information. Listen for the "Tactical Assessment Available" prompt and immediately toggle the visor on. The yellow hexagons that appear on the screen represent various tactical options for the present situation. Though numbered, they do not represent sequential steps (they're not even necessary to follow), but a collection of helpful suggestions. Zoom in on each individual hexagon to see a one-word description such as "Flank" or "Resupply" and highlight it if desired.

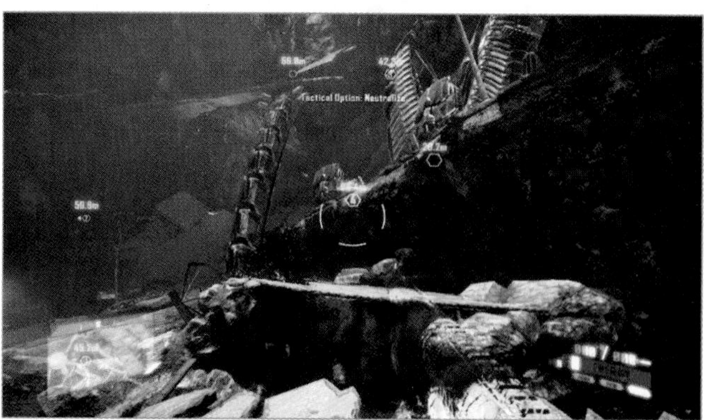

The campaign walkthrough portion of this guide takes advantage of each tactical assessment and divides the mission into encounters based on such. Each encounter describes the vital information pertinent to each tactical option; using the initial numbering sequence visible when the tactical assessment is first available. These numbers sometimes change as Alcatraz advances through the encounter. The encounter then contains a detailed strategy for incorporating the tactical options into what we feel is the most effective way of handling the given situation.

HEALTH AND DEATH

Thanks to the Nanosuit, Alcatraz can withstand quite plenty of punishment at the hands of enemy fire. Rather than contain a traditional "health meter" as part of the Head's Up Display (HUD), damage taken is relayed to the player through a reddening along the edges of the screen. The farther this dark red color extends into the center of the screen, the closer Alcatraz is to death. *Crysis 2* uses an auto-save feature that activates whenever a checkpoint is reached. Follow the on-screen prompt to reload the game at the previous checkpoint after dying. Note that any collectibles are instantly saved upon being discovered and won't need to be "found" again, even if Alcatraz dies before reaching the next checkpoint.

USING THE NANOSUIT

The Nanosuit was developed to turn an ordinary soldier into a supersoldier. Its ability to meld with the wearer's DNA on a molecular level provides increased strength, speed, and agility in addition to the Nanosuit's technological features.

PHYSIOLOGICAL BENEFITS

The supersoldier can use the Nanosuit's ever-replenishing energy stores to perform feats of super-human strength. Simply running, jumping, or grabbing hold of enemies does not consume energy, but the suit's special abilities do. Though the Energy Meter replenishes quickly, Alcatraz must be careful to not leave himself out of energy when needing it most.

STEADY AIM: PRESS THE SPRINT BUTTON WHILE AIMING DOWN THE SIGHTS OF A WEAPON TO MAKE ALCATRAZ HOLD HIS BREATH TO STEADY THE AIM OF THE WEAPON. THIS CONSUMES SOME ENERGY.

COVER & LEAN: TAKE COVER BEHIND OBJECTS IN THE GAME. ALCATRAZ WILL LEAN OUT AUTOMATICALLY TO AIM WHEN READY. FINE-TUNE HIS POSITION BY USING THE MOVEMENT CONTROLS TO MAKE HIM LEAN.

SPRINT: RUN AT A MUCH FASTER SPEED TO ESCAPE ENEMY ATTACKERS OR TO BUILD UP SPEED FOR A VERY LONG JUMP. GRADUALLY CONSUMES ENERGY DURING DURATION OF SPRINT.

POWER JUMP: CHARGE AND RELEASE A JUMP TO LEAP A CONSIDERABLE DISTANCE OR HEIGHT. THIS IS OFTEN NECESSARY TO REACH LEDGES AND REQUIRES ROUGHLY 50% OF THE ENERGY METER.

SLIDE: PRESS THE CROUCH BUTTON WHILE SPRINTING TO DROP INTO A SLIDE. ALCATRAZ CAN FIRE HIS EQUIPPED GUN WHILE SLIDING AND USE THIS TECHNIQUE TO SLIDE BENEATH TRACTOR TRAILERS, OR TO QUICKLY ESCAPE ENEMIES ON A SLOPED SURFACE. SPRINTING CONSUMES ENERGY, BUT THE SLIDE ITSELF DOES NOT. ALCATRAZ CAN ALSO KICK ENEMIES WHILE SLIDING.

POWER KICK: CHARGE UP A MIGHTY ENERGY-DEPLETING KICK TO BUST OPEN DOORS OR USE IT TO KICK A VEHICLE INTO A GROUP OF ENEMIES. THE POWER KICK CAN SEND A CAR FLYING INTO NEARBY ENEMIES FOR A NEAR-CERTAIN MASSACRE. VEHICLES MAY CATCH FIRE AND EXPLODE IF KICKED DIRECTLY INTO SOLID OBJECTS.

GRAB & THROW: USE THE NANOSUIT'S INCREDIBLE STRENGTH TO GRAB HOLD OF AN ENEMY AND THROW HIM OFF A LEDGE, OR INTO OTHER ENEMIES. THROWING ENEMIES OFF ROOFTOPS AND CLIFFS IS A BIT RISKIER THAN A STEALTH KILL, BUT ULTIMATELY REWARDING. THIS ATTACK CONSUMES VERY LITTLE ENERGY. ALCATRAZ CAN ALSO PICK UP MANNER AND SIZE OF OBJECTS AND THROW THEM AT ENEMIES, EITHER FOR DAMAGE OR TO SIMPLY DISTRACT THEM.

TECHNOLOGICAL FEATURES

The Nanosuit's main gifts to the supersoldier come in the form of several marked technological advances, the likes of which the U.S. Special Forces have never before seen. Alcatraz must familiarize himself with these abilities quickly; his chance of survival depends entirely on their frequent use.

CLOAK: THERE IS NO DENYING THE IMPORTANCE OF CLOAK. THIS ABILITY ALLOWS ALCATRAZ TO INSTANTLY RENDER HIMSELF INVISIBLE AND SHOULD BE RELIED UPON HEAVILY. CLOAK GRADUALLY DRAINS THE ENERGY METER. TAKE COVER BEHIND SOLID OBJECTS TO ALLOW THE METER TO REPLENISH. CLOAK IS CANCELLED BY FIRING UN-SILENCED WEAPONS AND ENEMIES CAN OFTEN HEAR ALCATRAZ'S FOOTSTEPS EVEN WHILE CLOAKED. CLOAK CAN HELP ALCATRAZ STEALTHILY ASSASSINATE HIS ENEMIES, AS WELL AS AID IN FLEEING AN UNWINNABLE SITUATION.

ARMOR: THE OTHER PRIMARY ABILITY IS ARMOR MODE. ACTIVATE ARMOR MODE TO STRENGTHEN THE NANOSUIT, MAKING IT MORE ABSORBENT OF ENEMY ATTACKS AND HELPING TO INCREASE ALCATRAZ'S COMBAT AWARENESS. ARMOR MODE CAN ALSO BE USED TO CUSHION THE DAMAGE FROM FALLS AND JUMP THAT WOULD OTHERWISE BE FATAL. ARMOR MODE GRADUALLY DRAINS THE ENERGY METER MUCH LIKE CLOAK DOES. THOUGH EXTREMELY HELPFUL, ALCATRAZ IS NOT INDESTRUCTIBLE WHILE ARMOR MODE IS ACTIVE. HEAVY, SUSTAINED ATTACKS CAN STILL PROVE FATAL.

NANOVISION: ENABLE NANOVISION IN DARK OR SMOKE-FILLED SITUATIONS TO GAIN A CLEARER VIEW OF THE ENVIRONMENT. NANOVISION IS ESSENTIALLY A COMBINATION OF NIGHT AND THERMAL VISION. IT PROVIDES A CRISP, GRAYSCALE VIEW OF THE SURROUNDINGS WITH ENEMIES, ALLIES, AND SUPPLIES SHOWING UP AS BRIGHTLY-COLORED SILHOUETTES, THANKS TO THEIR HEAT SIGNATURES. NANOVISION SLOWLY DRAINS THE ENERGY METER SO BE CAUTIOUS WHEN USING IT SIMULTANEOUSLY WITH CLOAK OR ARMOR.

STEALTH INDICATOR: THE NANOSUIT IS CAPABLE OF READING THE ENEMY'S ALERT STATUS AND DISPLAYS IT ON-SCREEN IN THE LOWER LEFT-HAND CORNER. A WHITE SIGNAL REPRESENTS THAT THE ENEMY IS UNAWARE OF ALCATRAZ'S PRESENCE. YELLOW INDICATES THAT THEY ARE ON ALERT AND SEARCHING FOR ALCATRAZ, AND RED SIGNIFIES THAT THEY CAN SEE HIM AND ARE ATTACKING. USING CLOAK, FLEEING THE SCENE, AND TAKING COVER CAUSES THE ENEMIES' LEVEL OF ALERT TO DIMINISH.

TACTICAL VISOR: THE VISOR ISN'T JUST FOR STUDYING TACTICAL OPTIONS AT KEY SITUATIONS. IT CAN ALSO BE USED TO "TAG" ENEMIES FOR GREATER VISIBILITY AND TRACKING. ENABLE THE VISOR AND ZOOM IN ON AN ENEMY TO HIGHLIGHT. THE ENEMY GLOWS WITH THEIR CORRESPONDING ALERT STATUS COLOR EVEN AFTER DISABLING THE VISOR. THIS IS AN EXCELLENT TOOL FOR DARK OR SMOKE-FILLED SITUATIONS WHERE IT CAN BE DIFFICULT TO SPOT ENEMIES AND CAN SAVE ALCATRAZ FROM HAVING TO USE NANOVISION. YOU CAN ALSO USE THE VISOR TO SCAN THE AREA FOR AVAILABLE AMMO AND WEAPONS.

NANOSUIT MODULES

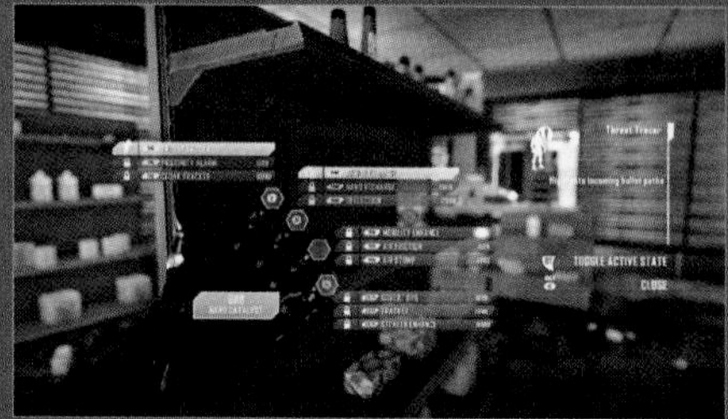

As great as the Nanosuit is, it can be made that much better through the addition of Nanosuit Modules. Every Ceph that is killed in combat yields a specific amount of Nano Catalyst. The Nano Catalyst appears as a small cloud of sparkling crystals right where the Ceph was killed (not necessarily, where their body ends up). Run to it to collect it then press the Nanosuit Customization button to see Alcatraz's current total of Nano Catalyst and the available upgrades. The 12 available Nanosuit Modules are divided into four categories of three: Tactical, Armor, Power, and Stealth. Only one module per category can be active at any given time. Modules can be purchased in any order. The less expensive modules need not be purchased in order to unlock the more expensive ones.

NANOSUIT SHOWROOM

Select the "Extras" option from the Main Menu to access the Nanosuit Showroom to witness a live preview of each module in action.

TACTICAL MODULES

MODULE	NANO CATALYST	DESCRIPTION
THREAT TRACER	100	HIGHLIGHTS INCOMING BULLET PATHS.
PROXIMITY ALARM	1200	AUTOMATIC WARNING WHEN AN ENEMY IS NEARBY.
CLOAK TRACKER	16,000	INCREASES THE VISIBILITY OF CLOAKED ENEMIES.

Threat Tracer complements the on-screen hit detection display to better reveal where enemy fire is originating, and the path it is taking. This should be one of Alcatraz's first upgrades, as it is a helpful module given its abnormally low cost. The other two modules in this category are of somewhat lower importance in single-player; they are both extremely helpful in multiplayer mode. Cloak Tracker is only necessary at the very end of the campaign, as there are no other cloaking enemies encountered save for those at the litho-ship during "A Walk in the Park."

ARMOR MODULES

MODULE	NANO CATALYST	DESCRIPTION
ARMOR ENHANCE	100	REDUCES DRAIN SPEED OF ENERGY IN ARMOR MODE.
NANO RECHARGE	8000	FASTER HEALTH AND SUIT ENERGY RECHARGE.
DEFLECTION	12,000	PROVIDES INCREASED PROTECTION FROM ENEMY FIRE BY DEFLECTING BULLETS.

Each of the three modules in this category is of value to both single-player and multiplayer modes, but only one can active at any given time. Armor Enhance should be the first module purchased during the "Sudden Impact" mission. Nano Recharge and Deflection are both even more valuable, as they don't require the use of Armor mode to be of help. This makes it possible to spend more time Cloaked while maintaining some of the benefits such as faster health recharge of bullet deflection. There's a reason Nano Recharge and Deflection are so expensive! Aim to purchase Nano Recharge roughly halfway through the campaign, then aim to acquire Deflection with the Nano Catalyst earned during "Terminus."

POWER MODULES

MODULE	NANO CATALYST	DESCRIPTION
MOBILITY ENHANCE	600	INCREASES LEDGE GRAB SPEED AND REDUCES ENERGY DRAIN FROM SPRINTING AND JUMPING.
AIR FRICTION	1600	PROVIDES EXTRA CONTROL WHEN FALLING.
AIR STOMP	4000	PERFORM A POWERFUL DOWNWARDS ATTACK WHEN IN THE AIR.

Mobility Enhance is a useful module in that it reduces the amount of energy consumed while moving about. This is especially valuable when trying to sprint to safety while Cloaked or in Armor mode. The usefulness of the other two modules in this category is highly dependent on player preference. Air Friction can come in handy in select situations, but isn't a vital upgrade in our opinion. Air Stomp, on the other hand, can be plenty of fun to employ in battles against unsuspecting enemies, but is not as useful in situations against a larger enemy force. The Air Stomp attack is quite useful in multiplayer mode.

STEALTH MODULES

MODULE	NANO CATALYST	DESCRIPTION
COVERT OPS	1000	SUPPRESSES THE SOUND OF FOOTSTEPS.
TRACKER	2000	HIGHLIGHTS ENEMY ROUTES.
STEALTH ENHANCE	10,000	FASTER TRANSITION IN AND OUT OF STEALTH, REDUCES ENERGY DRAIN IN STEALTH MODE.

Covert Ops is a valuable module that makes it easier to perform stealth kills. Essentially, it no longer requires Alcatraz to crouch to avoid making audible footsteps. It also masks the sound during sprinting which is a terrific asset. Tracker can prove useful when trying to employ guerrilla tactics against a number of enemies on patrol. Watch their footsteps to see which way they went. Nevertheless, we recommend skipping the Tracker upgrade and instead saving those Nano Catalysts for purchase of the Stealth Enhance module. Stealth Enhance is arguably the single most valuable module in campaign mode. Purchase the low-cost modules in each category, then immediately save for Stealth Enhance.

WEAPONS & ATTACHMENTS

Alcatraz has access to a wide variety of weapons including multiple assault rifles, pistols, sniper rifles, and shotguns. Many of the weapons encountered during the single-player campaign have a modified name such as "Stealth", "Demolition", "Spec Ops", or "Ranged." These names simply refer to the current configuration of attachments on the weapon. Alcatraz can toggle these attachments on and off at will, thereby turning a Scarab into a Stealth Scarab or Ranged Scarab on the fly. Equip each variety of weapon to unlock the attachments for each weapon type, even if only to set it back down and not use it.

PRIMARY WEAPONS

DSG-1

Sniper Rifle

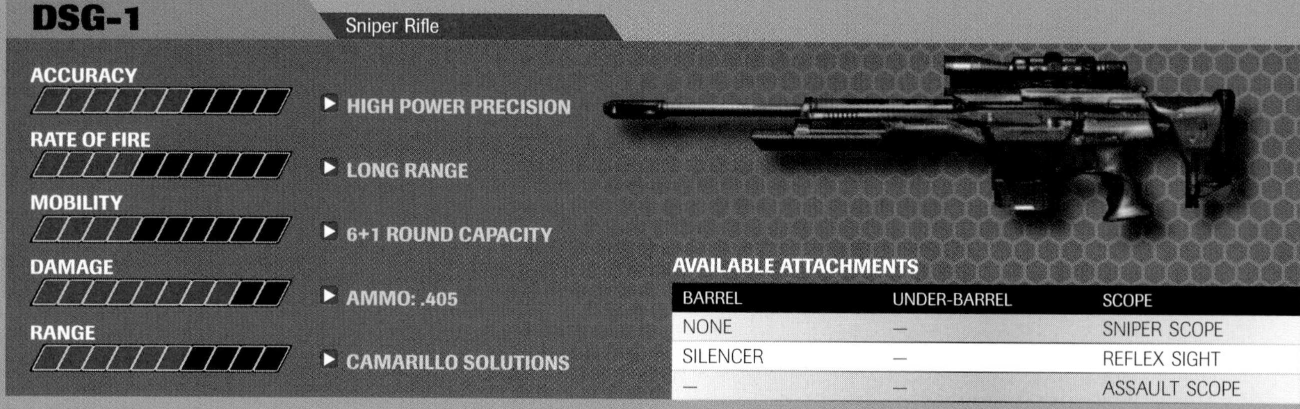

ACCURACY

RATE OF FIRE

MOBILITY

DAMAGE

RANGE

- HIGH POWER PRECISION
- LONG RANGE
- 6+1 ROUND CAPACITY
- AMMO: .405
- CAMARILLO SOLUTIONS

AVAILABLE ATTACHMENTS

BARREL	UNDER-BARREL	SCOPE
NONE	—	SNIPER SCOPE
SILENCER	—	REFLEX SIGHT
—	—	ASSAULT SCOPE

The DSG-1 is the primary sniper rifle available to Alcatraz. It has above average accuracy and range and can kill most enemies with a single headshot. Equipping the silencer lessons the effective power and range of the rifle, but makes it possible to pick enemies off while avoiding detection. The DSG-1 can take the heads right off of grunt-level Cephs, but often requires two hits to the body to deliver a fatal wound. This is one of the most commonly used weapons.

FELINE

Sub-Machine Gun

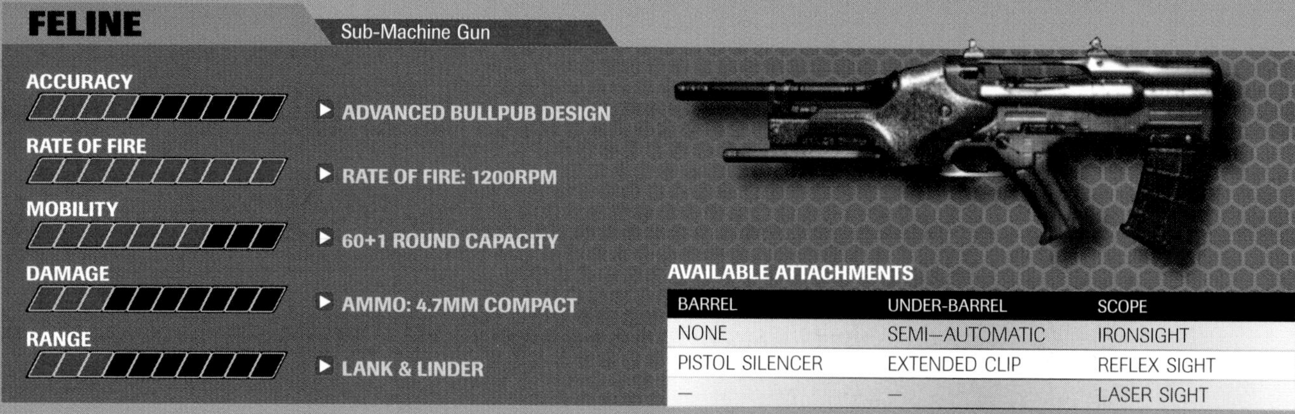

ACCURACY

RATE OF FIRE

MOBILITY

DAMAGE

RANGE

- ADVANCED BULLPUB DESIGN
- RATE OF FIRE: 1200RPM
- 60+1 ROUND CAPACITY
- AMMO: 4.7MM COMPACT
- LANK & LINDER

AVAILABLE ATTACHMENTS

BARREL	UNDER-BARREL	SCOPE
NONE	SEMI—AUTOMATIC	IRONSIGHT
PISTOL SILENCER	EXTENDED CLIP	REFLEX SIGHT
—	—	LASER SIGHT

No other weapon boasts a firing rate anywhere near as fast as the Feline, yet this tremendous firing rate comes at the expense of range and accuracy. The Feline is suitable for cutting a swath through low-level enemies in tight confines, particularly with the extended clip and reflex sight attached, but it doesn't make for a particularly useful primary weapon in open spaces. Fire in short bursts and aim for the enemy's head (or the Ceph's gelatinous backside) to maximize the damage inflicted per round.

GRENDEL

Assault Rifle

ACCURACY

RATE OF FIRE

MOBILITY

DAMAGE

RANGE

- SELECT FIRE
- HIGH STOPPING POWER
- 24+1 ROUND CAPACITY
- AMMO: 6.8MM HOLLOW-POINT
- LISUNOV ARMS

AVAILABLE ATTACHMENTS

BARREL	UNDER-BARREL	SCOPE
—	SEMI—AUTOMATIC	IRONSIGHT
—	GRENADE LAUNCHER	REFLEX SIGHT
—	LIGHT SHOTGUN	ASSAULT SCOPE

The Grendel is a versatile assault rifle with average ratings and a varied assortment of possible attachments. The Grendel's limited range and accuracy keeps it from being an adequate tool for sniping, but it excels at close- to mid-range combat. Equip the reflex sight and either the grenade launcher or light shotgun attachment for battles against groups of enemies at medium range. Fire grenades from the under-barrel attachment at groups of unsuspecting enemies, or use the light shotgun attachment to blast through enemies in narrow corridors when the Marshall or Jackal isn't available.

JACKAL

Shotgun

ACCURACY

RATE OF FIRE

MOBILITY

DAMAGE

RANGE

- SHORT RANGE
- HIGH STOPPING POWER
- 7 SHELL CAPACITY
- AMMO: 12 GAUGE SHOT
- BISHOP BALLISTICS

AVAILABLE ATTACHMENTS

BARREL	UNDER-BARREL	SCOPE
–	SEMI–AUTOMATIC	IRONSIGHT
–	EXTENDED CLIP	REFLEX SIGHT
–	–	–

The Jackal doesn't have nearly the damage and range of the Marshall, but its ability as an automatic shotgun makes up for it. With the extended clip and reflex sight attachments equipped, the Jackal is an extremely lethal weapon when advancing through narrow corridors or while trying to defend against a horde of attackers. The Jackal is best used against low-level Cephs or CELL Operators of all types.

K-VOLT

Sub-Machine Gun

ACCURACY

RATE OF FIRE

MOBILITY

DAMAGE

RANGE

- EXPERIMENTAL SHORT CIRCUIT DEVICE
- CIRCUMVENTS EMP SHIELDING
- 50 ROUND CAPACITY
- AMMO: 6MM ELECTROSTATIC PELL
- CRYNET ARMORIES

AVAILABLE ATTACHMENTS

BARREL	UNDER-BARREL	SCOPE
–	–	IRONSIGHT
–	–	REFLEX SIGHT
–	–	ASSAULT SCOPE

The K-Volt is one of the most unique weapons in that it fires electrostatic pellets that serve more to short-circuit enemy shielding than inflict harm. The K-Volt isn't particularly useful against CELL Operators or low-level Cephs. No, the K-Volt is best used against the rare Advanced Ceph Assault Unit, capable of cloaking. The K-Volt short circuits the cloaking systems and temporarily drains the enemy's energy meter, much like Alcatraz suffers when hit with enemy K-Volt pellets.

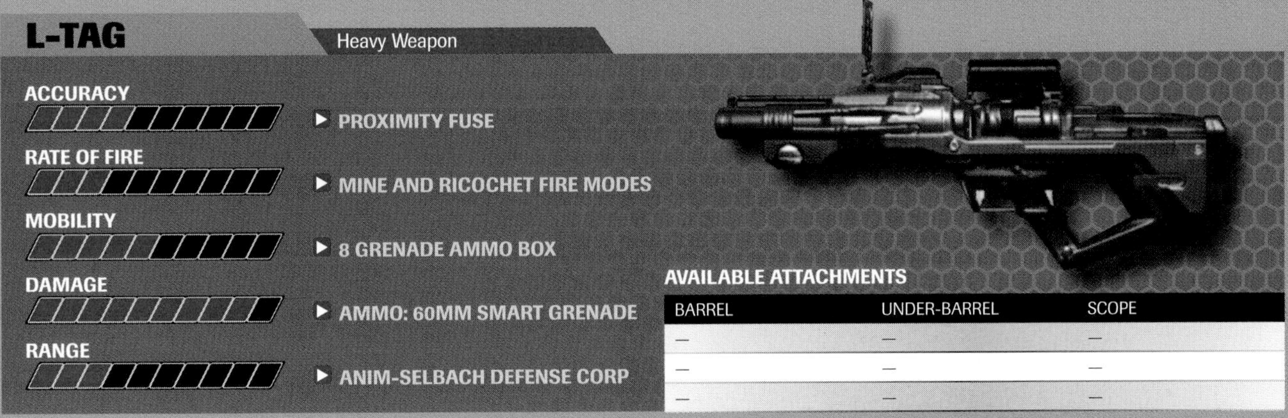

L-TAG

Heavy Weapon

ACCURACY

RATE OF FIRE

MOBILITY

DAMAGE

RANGE

- PROXIMITY FUSE
- MINE AND RICOCHET FIRE MODES
- 8 GRENADE AMMO BOX
- AMMO: 60MM SMART GRENADE
- ANIM-SELBACH DEFENSE CORP

AVAILABLE ATTACHMENTS

BARREL	UNDER-BARREL	SCOPE
–	–	–
–	–	–
–	–	–

At first glance, the L-Tag appears to be little more than a standard grenade launcher. That feeling disappears as soon as you realize that its firing mode can be toggled from ricochet to proximity mine. Launch grenades at groups of unsuspecting enemies (bounce it into the middle enemy) or lure enemies into traps pre-set with proximity mines. Aiming the L-Tag can take some getting used to, but the weapon's ammo capacity and high damage rating help to make up for any difficulty in using it. We recommend aiming a little short of the target at first, as the grenade may well bounce into it.

M20 14 GAUSS

Sniper Rifle

ACCURACY

RATE OF FIRE

MOBILITY

DAMAGE

RANGE

- HIGH VELOCITY SNIPER
- STRONG ARMOR PENETRATION
- 4+1 ROUND CAPACITY
- AMMO: 10MM SOLID SLUG
- CRYNET ARMORIES

AVAILABLE ATTACHMENTS

BARREL	UNDER-BARREL	SCOPE
–	–	SNIPER SCOPE
–	–	REFLEX SIGHT
–	–	ASSAULT SCOPE

The M20 14 Gauss is a devastatingly powerful sniper rifle capable of firing an armor-penetrating slug that can kill multiple enemies with a single shot. Equip the sniper scope and look for enemies aligned in a row and fire the slug straight through them. The M20 14 Gauss is powerful enough to deliver fatal damage to enemies even through shots fired at the enemy's torso. It can also fire through many obstacles and is capable of detonating explosive barrels with a single round.

MARSHALL

Shotgun

ACCURACY

RATE OF FIRE

MOBILITY

DAMAGE

RANGE

- SHORT RANGE
- HIGH STOPPING POWER
- 10 SHELL CAPACITY CAPACITY
- AMMO: 12 GAUGE SHOT
- CORBETTA FIREARMS

AVAILABLE ATTACHMENTS

BARREL	UNDER-BARREL	SCOPE
NONE	–	IRONSIGHT
SILENCER	–	REFLEX SIGHT
–	–	–

The Marshall will no doubt become one of your most-used weapons, thanks to its availability, stopping power, and ability to be silenced. The Marshall's 10-shell capacity is surprisingly large for a shotgun and though the weapon is only effective at short range, it pairs wonderfully with the Scarab or DSG-1. Monitor the mini-map and switch to the Marshall whenever an enemy gets a little too close for comfort. The Marshall can obliterate most low-level enemies with a single blast at close range, and even higher level enemies struggle to withstand more than two or three shells from the Marshall.

MK.60 MOD 0

Heavy Weapon

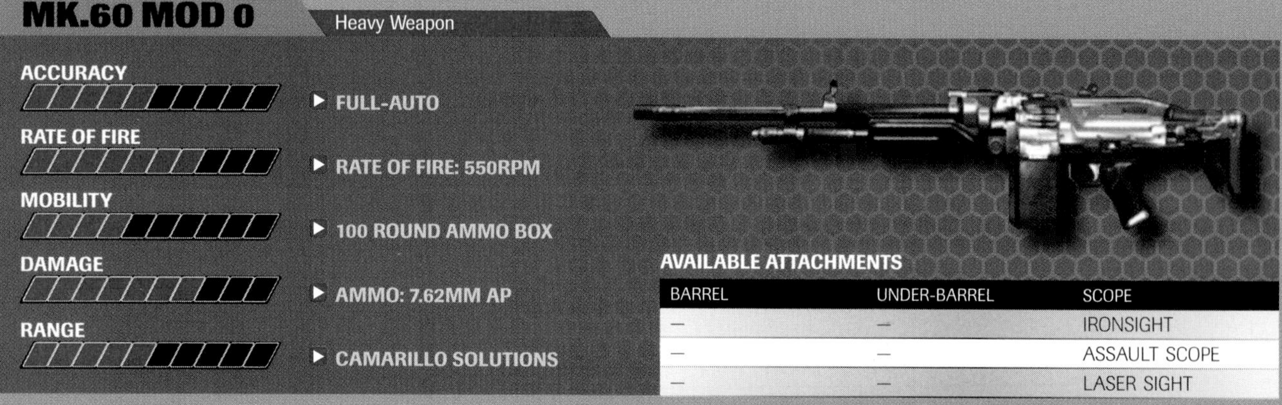

ACCURACY

RATE OF FIRE

MOBILITY

DAMAGE

RANGE

- FULL-AUTO
- RATE OF FIRE: 550RPM
- 100 ROUND AMMO BOX
- AMMO: 7.62MM AP
- CAMARILLO SOLUTIONS

AVAILABLE ATTACHMENTS

BARREL	UNDER-BARREL	SCOPE
–	–	IRONSIGHT
–	–	ASSAULT SCOPE
–	–	LASER SIGHT

The MK.60 is a high-capacity heavy machine gun that can be equipped just like any other weapon, a distinct advantage over the HMG. Its enormous ammo box allows for up to 100 bullets to be fired between reloads, which is important given the extremely lengthy reloading process that accompanies this weapon. The MK.60 isn't the most accurate of weapons, but equipping the laser sight and firing in short bursts helps to offset this drawback. The MK.60 is an excellent weapon for mid-range combat and battles against numerous foes thanks to its power, rate of fire, and ammo capacity.

SCAR

Assault Rifle

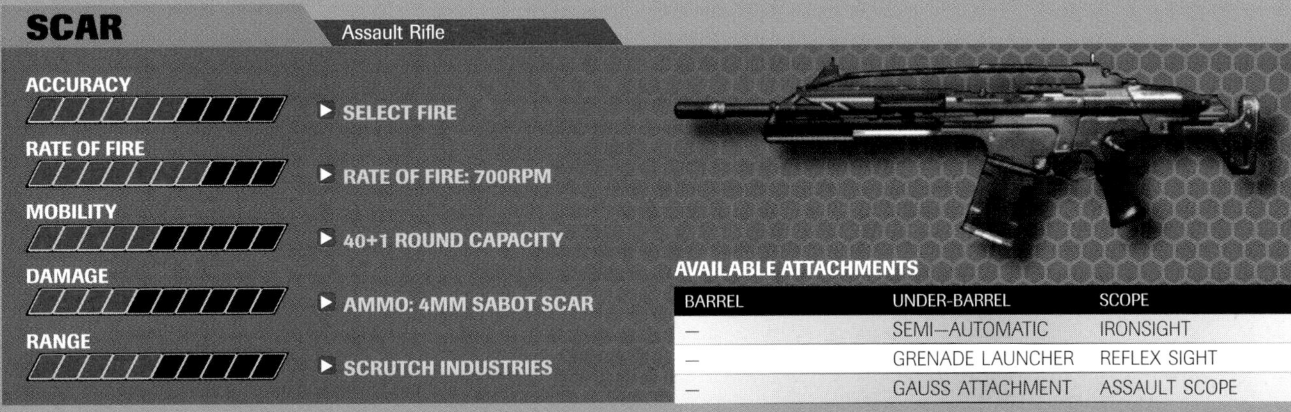

- SELECT FIRE
- RATE OF FIRE: 700RPM
- 40+1 ROUND CAPACITY
- AMMO: 4MM SABOT SCAR
- SCRUTCH INDUSTRIES

AVAILABLE ATTACHMENTS

BARREL	UNDER-BARREL	SCOPE
—	SEMI—AUTOMATIC	IRONSIGHT
—	GRENADE LAUNCHER	REFLEX SIGHT
—	GAUSS ATTACHMENT	ASSAULT SCOPE

The SCAR sits between the Scarab and Grendel in terms of raw power, range, and accuracy, but its ability to be outfitted with a grenade launcher and gauss attachment help it stand out from the crowd. Combine the gauss attachment with the assault scope for a zoom-free sniping weapon capable of firing a solid slug through multiple enemies. The grenade launcher attachment is another valid attachment for those times when Alcatraz is plain out of frag grenades.

SCARAB

Assault Rifle

- SELECT FIRE
- RATE OF FIRE: 900RPM
- 40+1 ROUND CAPACITY
- AMMO: 4MM SABOT SCAR
- SCRUTCH INDUSTRIES

AVAILABLE ATTACHMENTS

BARREL	UNDER-BARREL	SCOPE
NONE	SEMI—AUTOMATIC	IRONSIGHT
SILENCER	EXTENDED CLIP	REFLEX SIGHT
—	LIGHT SHOTGUN	LASER SIGHT

Though it lacks the damage capability of the Grendel, the Scarab exceeds the Grendel in every other category. Of the three primary assault rifles, the Scarab gets our vote for most useful. Equip the silencer, semi-automatic, and laser sight attachments to transform the Scarab into a medium-range sniper rifle, or opt for the light shotgun and reflex sights to have a multi-purpose assault rifle and shotgun in one. Keep the Scarab's limited damage rating in mind when battling tougher foes and equip the extended clip attachment when using it in full-auto mode.

X-43 MIKE

Heavy Weapon

- EXPERIMENTAL DEVICE
- DEPLOYS WEAPONIZED MICROWAVES
- KEEP BEAM ON TARGET
- BATTERY POWERED
- CRYNET INDUSTRIES

AVAILABLE ATTACHMENTS

BARREL	UNDER-BARREL	SCOPE
—	—	—
—	—	—
—	—	—

The X-43 Mike (short for "microwave") is the most unique of the weapons at Alcatraz's disposal. This experimental weapon emits a beam of weaponized microwaves that rapidly accelerate the internal molecules within the target until its insides bubble and burst. The X-43 Mike is particularly effective against the Ceph and is capable of quickly killing grunts and command units alike. The X-43 Mike can even be used to finish off a Devastator Unit, provided Alcatraz can keep the beam fixed on it long enough.

SECONDARY WEAPONS

AY69

Machine Pistol

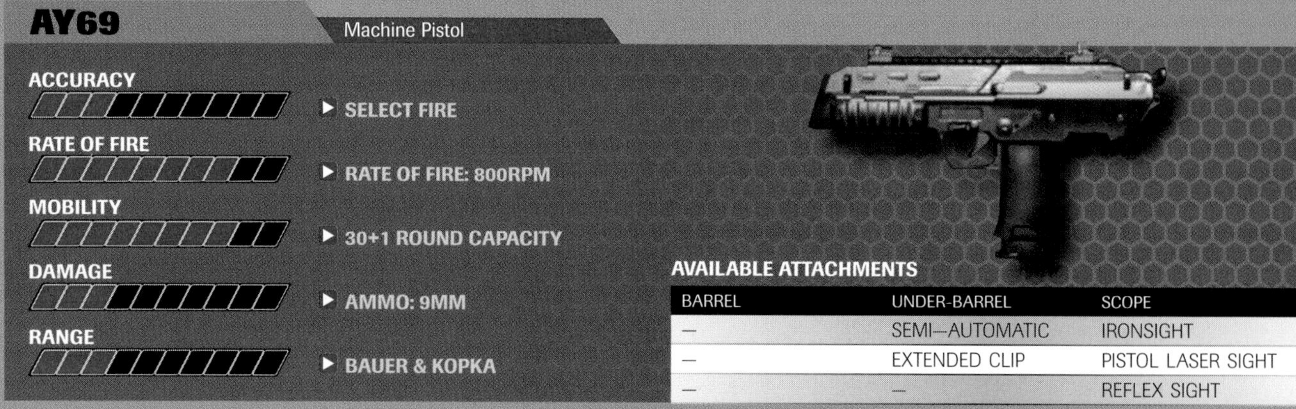

AVAILABLE ATTACHMENTS

BARREL	UNDER-BARREL	SCOPE
—	SEMI—AUTOMATIC	IRONSIGHT
—	EXTENDED CLIP	PISTOL LASER SIGHT
—	—	REFLEX SIGHT

The AY69 is a fully-automatic machine pistol that can burn through ammo—and low level enemies—with surprising speed. Equip the extended clip and pistol laser sight or reflex sight for maximum effectiveness and use it to run-and-gun through encounters with CELL Operators and Ceph grunts. The AY69 should never be Alcatraz's main weapon, but it's a useful backup should he run out of ammo for his more powerful guns.

HAMMER

Pistol

AVAILABLE ATTACHMENTS

BARREL	UNDER-BARREL	SCOPE
NONE	—	IRONSIGHT
PISTOL SILENCER	—	PISTOL LASER SIGHT
—	—	—

The Hammer is a surprisingly effective pistol, capable of providing Alcatraz with a medium-range sniping option should he need it. Attach the pistol silencer and pistol laser sight and take aim on an enemy's head for what should be a one-shot kill. The Hammer will never replace the DSG-1 or Scarab as a sniping weapon, but it can be a useful complement to the MK.60 or Marshall in situations where Alcatraz can eliminate a few isolated enemies before dealing with numerous foes at close range.

M 12 NOVA

Pistol

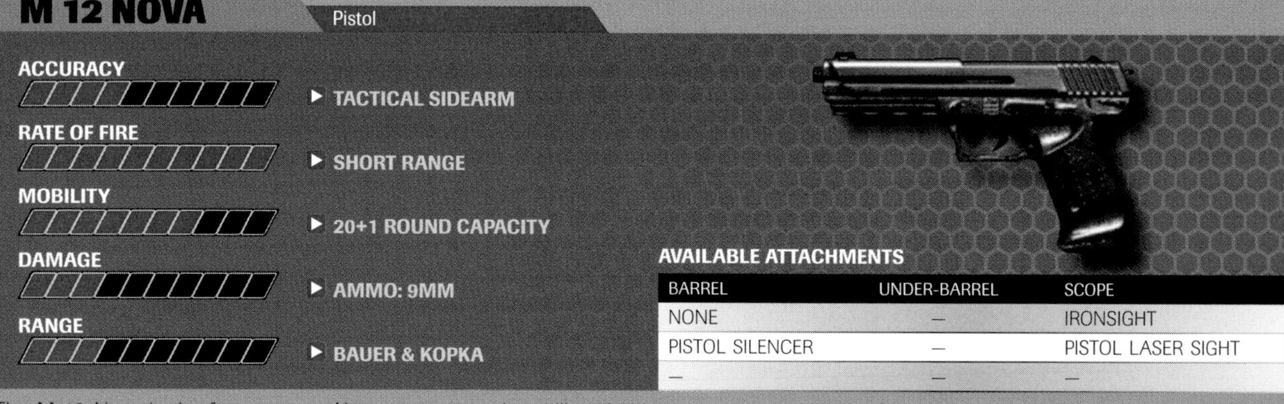

AVAILABLE ATTACHMENTS

BARREL	UNDER-BARREL	SCOPE
NONE	—	IRONSIGHT
PISTOL SILENCER	—	PISTOL LASER SIGHT
—	—	—

The M 12 Nova is the first weapon Alcatraz acquires, but will probably receive very little use. The pistol's low damage, range, and accuracy are offset to an extent by its large ammo capacity and incredibly high rate of fire (for a pistol). The M 12 Nova can be fired in quick succession to deliver lethal damage to a low level enemy, particularly if aimed at the head. Use the pistol silencer and pistol laser sight attachments for pinpoint headshots in stealth situations.

MAJESTIC

Revolver

ACCURACY
RATE OF FIRE
MOBILITY
DAMAGE
RANGE

- HIGH STOPPING POWER
- SHORT RANGE
- 6 ROUND CAPACITY
- AMMO: .50 COMPACT
- HOOD ARSENAL

AVAILABLE ATTACHMENTS

BARREL	UNDER-BARREL	SCOPE
—	—	IRONSIGHT
—	—	ASSAULT SCOPE
—	—	—

The Majestic is a one-handed cannon of a revolver, capable of blasting enemy heads clean off. Its low rate of fire and small ammo capacity limit its effectiveness in larger scale firefights, but it can nevertheless prove a lifesaver in close range combat. The Majestic's accuracy is reliable enough to warrant the assault scope attachment for finer aiming. Activate Armor mode as every enemy in the area inevitably comes running when they hear the Majestic's booming blast.

EXPLOSIVES & SPECIAL WEAPONS

C4

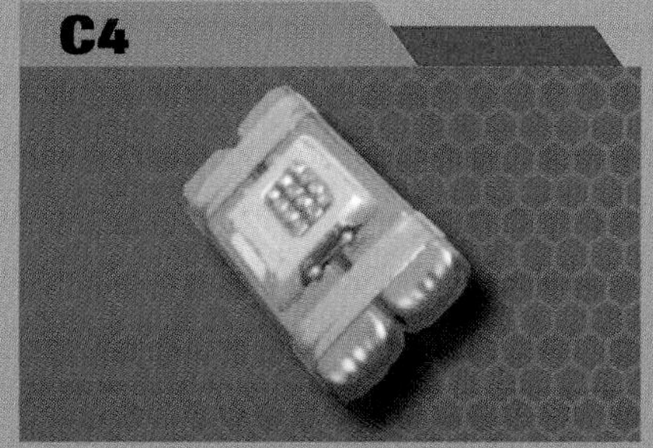

C4 is worth its weight in gold when it comes to dealing with Devastator Units and the Armored Assault Drone also known as a Pinger. Alcatraz can carry up to four pieces of C4 at once in addition to other weapons, grenades, and the JAW. Simply throw the C4 on the ground with the Fire Weapon button (can throw multiple charges) then press the Aim button to detonate all deployed C4. Alcatraz can throw the C4 a considerable distance, eliminating the need to get too close to the target. C4 can also be stuck to objects, barrels, or cars and then launched into enemies.

HMG

Turret Gun

ACCURACY
RATE OF FIRE
MOBILITY
DAMAGE
RANGE

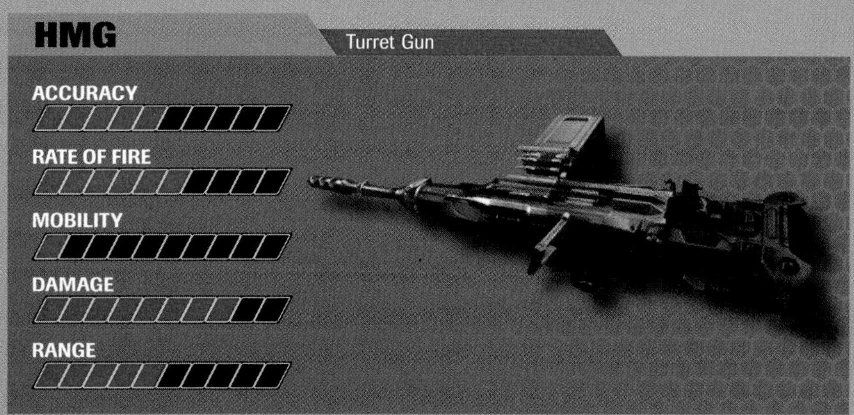

The HMG is the quintessential heavy machine gun. It is commonly found mounted to the top of a military vehicle or on a barrier for use as a turret gun. Alcatraz can rip the HMG from its mount and carry it with him in addition to his other weapons. The HMG boasts 250-round magazine, but cannot be reloaded. Carrying the HMG slows Alcatraz's mobility down considerably, but the weapon's high damage rating and rapid rate of fire enables it to cut through hordes of assailants with ease. Alcatraz must set the HMG down in order to interact with items or other objects such as elevator buttons and keypads.

JAW

Launcher

The JAW is a shoulder-mounted rocket launcher that packs a serious punch. Hold the Fire Weapon button down after launching the rocket to use its laser guidance system to continue aiming the rocket even after firing. The JAW is capable of destroying enemy helicopters with a single shot and is the weapon of choice against Devastator Units and Pingers. Alcatraz can carry up to four JAW rockets at once in addition to all other weapons, grenades, and C4. The JAW has an incredibly slow reload time. Release the aiming trigger as soon as it hits its mark to expel the spent tube, then take cover immediately after firing.

M 17 FRAG

The M 17 Frag is a standard hand-thrown grenade capable of seriously weakening or killing enemies within a moderate blast radius. For maximum results, use grenades in the vicinity of vehicles or fuel drums to magnify the explosion. Grenades are best used against groups of stationary enemies or when baiting multiple enemies into a narrow space, such as within a shop or sewer tunnel.

M34 FLASH

The M34 Flash grenade is only used during multiplayer. Unlike the frag grenade, the M34 Flash doesn't inflict direct damage, but its blinding light and ear-piercing noise effectively disorients enemies for several seconds, making them vulnerable to surprise attack.

SWARMER

Launcher

The Swarmer is a heavy multi-rocket launcher that fires a barrage of eight miniature rockets with each pull of the trigger. The rockets fly a relatively straight pattern, but aren't nearly as accurate as the JAW. The damage inflicted is also quite less. The Swarmer is perfect for use against groups of enemies at medium range or against large, slow moving targets such as a Devastator Unit or Pinger. Use the Swarmer when available as a way of conserving your JAW rockets and C4, even though the latter options may be more effective.

ATTACHMENTS

SCOPE ATTACHMENTS

Scope attachments provide increased accuracy when aiming. Most weapons come equipped with the standard ironsight attachment that consists of one sight near the stock and one at the end of the barrel. This is the most basic form of aiming device. Laser sights emit a steady red laser beam that can be used for precise aiming over moderate distances. Laser sights are best used in semi-automatic mode. Reflex sights, on the other hand, serve quite well during run-and-gun combat with fully automatic weapons. The reflex sight effectively tracks moving targets and makes it easier to hit enemies on the run. Lastly, the two optical scopes provide magnification for precise aiming. The sniper scope differs from the assault scope in that it offers two stages of zoom, the 3x offered by the assault scope and the 7.5x zoom needed for long range sniping.

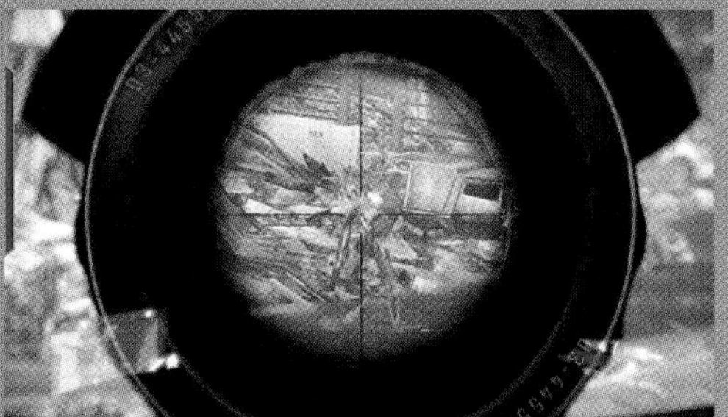

The sniper scope's two stages of zoom make long-range headshots a breeze!

The laser sight gives the shooter confidence that their bullets are going to hit the mark.

ICON	TYPE	DESCRIPTION
	IRONSIGHT	BASIC IRON SIGHT.
	ASSAULT SCOPE	ADVANCED OPTICAL 3X ZOOM.
	PISTOL LASER	SOLID STATE LASER PROJECTOR FOR ENHANCED ACCURACY.
	REFLEX SIGHT	REFRACTIVE OPTICAL RED DOT SIGHT FOR ENHANCED TARGET ACQUISITION.
	RIFLE LASER	SOLID STATE LASER PROJECTOR FOR ENHANCED ACCURACY.
	SNIPER SCOPE	ADVANCED OPTICAL 7.5X ZOOM.

BARREL ATTACHMENTS

Many pistols and assault rifles (and even the Marshall) can be equipped with the silencer (aka suppressor). This attachment muffles the noise emitted from the weapon and also serves to reduce muzzle flash. This is an invaluable attachment for situations that call for a stealthy approach, but it is not without its drawback. The silencer attachment slightly reduces the damage inflicted by the bullet at long range. Headshots with the DSG-1 will likely be fatal to lower level enemies, but greater precision is required to account for the drop in power.

The silencer attachment makes it possible to eliminate enemies without alerting others nearby.

ICON	TYPE	DESCRIPTION
	SILENCER	NOISE SUPPRESSOR FOR ENHANCED STEALTH.

UNDER-BARREL ATTACHMENTS

The under-barrel attachments make it possible to effectively carry two weapons in one. The semi-automatic attachment allows the shooter to transform an assault rifle into a medium-range sniper rifle while the extended clip reduces the frequency of reloads. The other attachments, however, essentially transform the weapon from an assault rifle into a grenade launcher, shotgun, or solid slug sniper rifle. Ammo for these special under-barrel attachments is usually quite limited, but their effects are powerful. Equipping an attachment such as the light shotgun to an assault rifle while also wielding the DSG-1, effectively gives the player three very distinct weapons.

The light shotgun attachment on this Spec Ops Scarab greatly improves the weapon's close range stopping power.

ICON	TYPE	DESCRIPTION
	SEMI—AUTOMATIC	SINGLE SHOT MODE FOR INCREASED ACCURACY.
	EXTENDED CLIP	INCREASED MAGAZINE CAPACITY.
	GRENADE	FIRES 30MM ADVANCED EXPLOSIVE ANTI—PERSONNEL PERCUSSION GRENADES.
	LIGHT SHOTGUN	A MINIATURIZED LIGHTWEIGHT SHOTGUN ATTACHMENT.
	GAUSS	A MINIATURIZED ELECTROMAGNETIC SOLID SLUG PROJECTOR.

NYC HOSTILES

Alcatraz faces enemies of two major types: the alien Ceph and the human CELL Operators. Both are well-armored, but possess fragile weaknesses. The following pages detail how best to engage each type of enemy, from both species.

THE C.E.L.L.

DESIGNATION	TYPE	RESILIENCE	COMMON WEAPONS
CELL ASSAULT	CELL OPERATOR		SUB-MACHINE GUN, ASSAULT RIFLE
CELL FLANKER	CELL OPERATOR		SHOTGUN
CELL DEMOLITION	CELL OPERATOR		GRENADE LAUNCHER
CELL SNIPER	CELL OPERATOR		SNIPER RIFLE
CELL LEADER	CELL OPERATOR		ASSAULT RIFLE

There are five different types of CELL Operators, distinguishable by their weapons and slight differences in armor. All CELL Operators can be killed with a single shot to the head from a single, well-aimed bullet, or by a close-range blast from a shotgun or explosive device. CELL Operators are aggressive in their pursuit of Alcatraz, but they aren't reckless. They often investigate stray gunfire or the sounds of their comrades calls for help, but they also take cover and attempt to flank Alcatraz whenever possible.

SNEAK UP BEHIND AN UNSUSPECTING ENEMY WHILE CLOAKED TO PERFORM AN INSTANTANEOUS STEALTH KILL.

ASSAULT RIFLES WITH THE SEMI-AUTOMATIC OPTION AND LASER SIGHTS CAN ELIMINATE CELL OPERATORS WITH A SINGLE HEADSHOT.

Alcatraz has a number of ways in which to dispatch the CELL Operators thanks to their low resiliency. The ideal method is to snipe them with a single, silenced gunshot round from afar, as this delivers a clean kill without notifying the enemy. Another option is to use Cloak to slip in behind the enemy and perform a stealth kill. Alcatraz either breaks the enemy's neck, or buries his knife under their chin. Despite their use of sophisticated CryNet body armor, their torso and limbs aren't bulletproof. Assault rifles and sub-machine guns are more than capable of dropping any of the CELL Operators with repeat shots to the torso; just don't expect to down them with a single round, unlike a shot to the head.

CELL OPERATORS

ROBOTIC HARVESTING UNITS

DESIGNATION	TYPE	RESILIENCE	NANO CATALYST
TICK	ROBOTIC HARVESTING UNIT		10

TICKERS SCAMPER ABOUT HARMLESSLY, OFTEN IN GROUPS EMERGING FROM SMALL BURROWS.

The Robotic Harvesting Unit is the lowest form of Ceph and one that is completely harmless to the living. Its sole purpose on Earth is to suck the diseased corpses dry of nutrients. Alcatraz doesn't ever need to engage them, but they do yield a small amount of Nano Catalyst. Robotic Harvesting Units can be killed with a single gunshot, by a melee strike, or even by squashing them under foot. They can be difficult to hit with an assault rifle or sub-machine gun, so opt for a melee attack unless carrying a shotgun. Even then, it's best to not waste too much ammo on them.

COMBAT UNITS

DESIGNATION	TYPE	RESILIENCE	NANO CATALYST
GRUNT	COMBAT UNIT		100
GRUNT COMMANDER	COMBAT COMMAND UNIT		300

ALWAYS ACTIVATE ARMOR MODE WHEN ENGAGING A COMBAT UNIT HEAD ON IN A GUNFIGHT.

The Ceph Combat Units is the name assigned to the most common Ceph assailant. These grunts are armed with high yield energy guns that fire a charged energy attack that. Watch for the bright light of the charging projectile and quickly dodge for cover. Though their heavy armor is quite effective, Combat Units have large patches of exposed jelly on their back. Aim for this jelly to deliver fatal damage or, as with the CELL Operators, simply snipe them in the head. Grunt Commanders are twice as resilient as the lower level unit and are therefore more deadly. It can take two headshots with a DSG-1 to drop a Commander level enemy, and as many as three or more point-blank shots from the Marshall. Commander level units are more aggressive and are seldom alone. Be aware they may have multiple other units with them close by.

ASSAULT UNITS

DESIGNATION	TYPE	RESILIENCE	NANO CATALYST
STALKER	ASSAULT UNIT		100
STALKER COMMANDER	ASSAULT COMMAND UNIT		300

CIRCLE STRAFE AROUND ASSAULT UNITS TO AVOID THEIR RAZOR-SHARP CLAWS.

Ceph Assault Units are similar in appearance to the Combat Units, but their behavior is quite different. True to their "Stalker" designation, Ceph Assault Units hunt their prey on foot and attack at close range. Their hands have been fitted with lengthy metal blades that can inflict significant damage, should they hit their mark cleanly. Assault Units tend to spring forward and attack by swiping both hands downwards in a crossing pattern. It's important to identify the Stalker and circle-strafe around their rush, else Alcatraz will no doubt suffer severe damage. Beware that they may open fire with the small projectile mounted between their blades, particularly after missing a melee attack. Assault Units can be dealt with in exactly the same manner as the Combat Units. Headshots, stealth kills, or shotgun blasts to their gelatinous backside are the most efficient ways of exterminating them.

DEVASTATOR UNITS

HEAVY	DEVASTATOR UNIT		500

LAY DOWN TWO BLOCKS OF C4 THEN DE-CLOAK TO BAIT THE DEVASTATOR UNIT TOWARDS THE EXPLOSIVES.

Few members of the Ceph instill as much fear as the Devastator Unit. This massive heavy unit is every bit as slow as it is large, but its firepower is significant. Devastator Units can attack with both rapid fire energy pellets and a rocket-like projectile. Both attacks can inflict significant damage, making the use of Armor mode and solid cover a necessity. Though it is possible to gun down a Devastator Unit with the HMG, MK.60, or X-43 Mike, it's much faster—and safer—to rely on heavy explosives. Remain Cloaked and use either the JAW or C4 to destroy this beast before it even knows Alcatraz is around. It takes three direct-hits with the JAW to destroy a Devastator Unit or, conversely, two blocks of C4 detonated in close proximity to the beast.

ARMORED ASSAULT DRONE

DESIGNATION	TYPE	RESILIENCE	NANO CATALYST
PINGER	ARMORED ASSAULT DRONE	x2	2000

SOFTEN THE PINGER UP WITH THE JAW THEN FINISH IT OFF WITH C4, WHICH DOESN'T REQUIRE NEARLY AS MUCH PRECISION.

The Armored Assault Drone, commonly called a Pinger, is the largest and most deadly of all the Ceph. This towering three-legged robotic beast has a powerful energy attack that it fires from the front of its head. The attack is powerful, accurate, and can hit Alcatraz from a considerable distance. The Pinger's other major attack is an EMP blast that drains the Nanosuit's Energy Meter in one fell swoop. Watch for the small red cylinder to rise from the Pinger's back, that's your sign an EMP blast is coming. The Pinger's one weak spot is the large red spot on the center of its lower back. Unfortunately, it can be very difficult to hit thanks to the Pinger's ability to essentially rotate in place. The L-Tag and Swarmer can be of some use against the Pinger, but it's much more effective to rely exclusively on the JAW and C4. Use Cloak to flank the Pinger and fire the JAW anywhere at it. (The JAW doesn't need to hit it in the red weak spot on its back.) Repeat until out of JAW rockets, then turn to C4. Lob a couple of C4 blocks on the ground near the Pinger then detonate it as it walks past. The explosion from the C4 is great enough to injure the Pinger, even if not directly attached to its soft underside.

ADVANCED CEPH ASSAULT UNIT

DESIGNATION	TYPE	RESILIENCE	NANO CATALYST
GUARDIAN	ADVANCED CEPH ASSAULT UNIT		5000

THESE GUARDIAN CREATURES ARE OFTEN LITTLE MORE THAN A SHADOW, EVEN WHEN SHOT WITH THE K-VOLT.

The Advanced Ceph Assault Units are the rarest of all Ceph and are only located in the area surrounding the Ceph litho-ship. These units are similar in behavior and appearance to the Assault Command Units, but have the distinct ability of being able to Cloak. It's not hard to imagine how much more difficult this makes fighting them. Invest in the Cloak Tracker Nanosuit module (16,000 Nano Catalyst) to better monitor their movements and equip the K-Volt. The K-Volts electrostatic pellets inflict little damage but short-circuit the enemy's Cloaking systems. Switch to the X-43 Mike or other more potent weapon and finish them off. The Advanced Ceph Assault Units will rely on their Cloaking ability to try and get the jump on Alcatraz and attack with lunging melee strikes, just as the Assault Command Units do. Keep one back to the cliffs surrounding the crater where they are located, and watch the mini-map closely for the telltale red blip, indicating their presence.

IN AT THE DEEP END

USS NAUTILUS | HUDSON RIVER, NY | AUGUST 23RD, 2023

FORCE RECON EXTRACTION TEAM OMEGA ONE

TARGET NAME: DR. NATHAN GOULD

You are Alcatraz, a marine assigned to the Force Recon division as part of Extraction Team Omega One. The team has been deployed via submarine to New York City to locate and rescue the bioengineer Dr. Nathan Gould. All manner of calamity has befallen the region—natural disasters, viral outbreaks, and even rumors of alien invasion—and the whole of Manhattan Island has been quarantined. Bridges and tunnels are sealed tight; nobody gets in or out. That is, unless Omega One does their job.

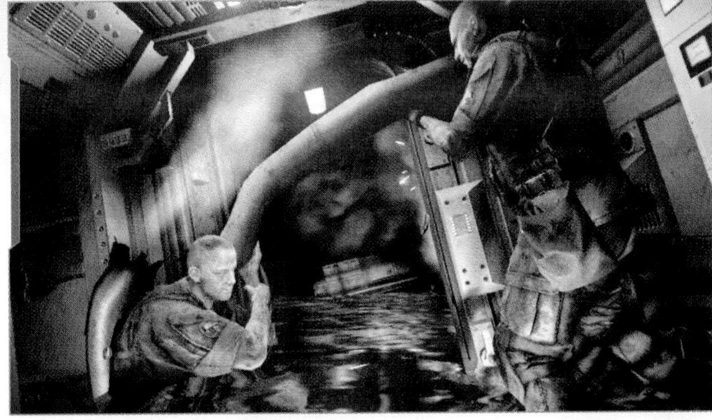

SETTING THE STAGE

This first mission is essentially a prologue designed to introduce you to the movement controls, your character Alcatraz, and the situation unfolding in New York City. Follow the on-screen prompts and use this time to invert the Y-axis if you prefer that method of control. Most importantly, relax and take it all in. With no collectibles to find or any possibility of death, even those fresh out of basic training will find it impossible to screw this up.

Use the Look Controls to nod your head when prompted. The U.S.S. Nautilus suffers a major breach just minutes from your insertion point. Follow the others down the rapidly flooding hallway and crouch to pass beneath the pipe. The sub is rocked by a second explosion and Alcatraz is thrown the length of a hallway as the sub rolls and begins to sink. Crouch to enter the opening ahead and rush to assist the other marine near the bulkhead door. Again, crouch in the water and grab hold of the door to help lift it open so the others can escape. Swim after them for as long as you can. Darkness slowly envelops Alcatraz as he blacks out from oxygen deprivation. Swim to the surface to rejoin the team—just in time to say goodbye...

ACHIEVEMENT

Can It Run Crysis?

Yes. Yes it can. Play through this opening prologue and escape the attack on the USS Nautilus to show that the fine folks at Crytek have indeed found a way to get CryENGINE 3 running on all platforms.

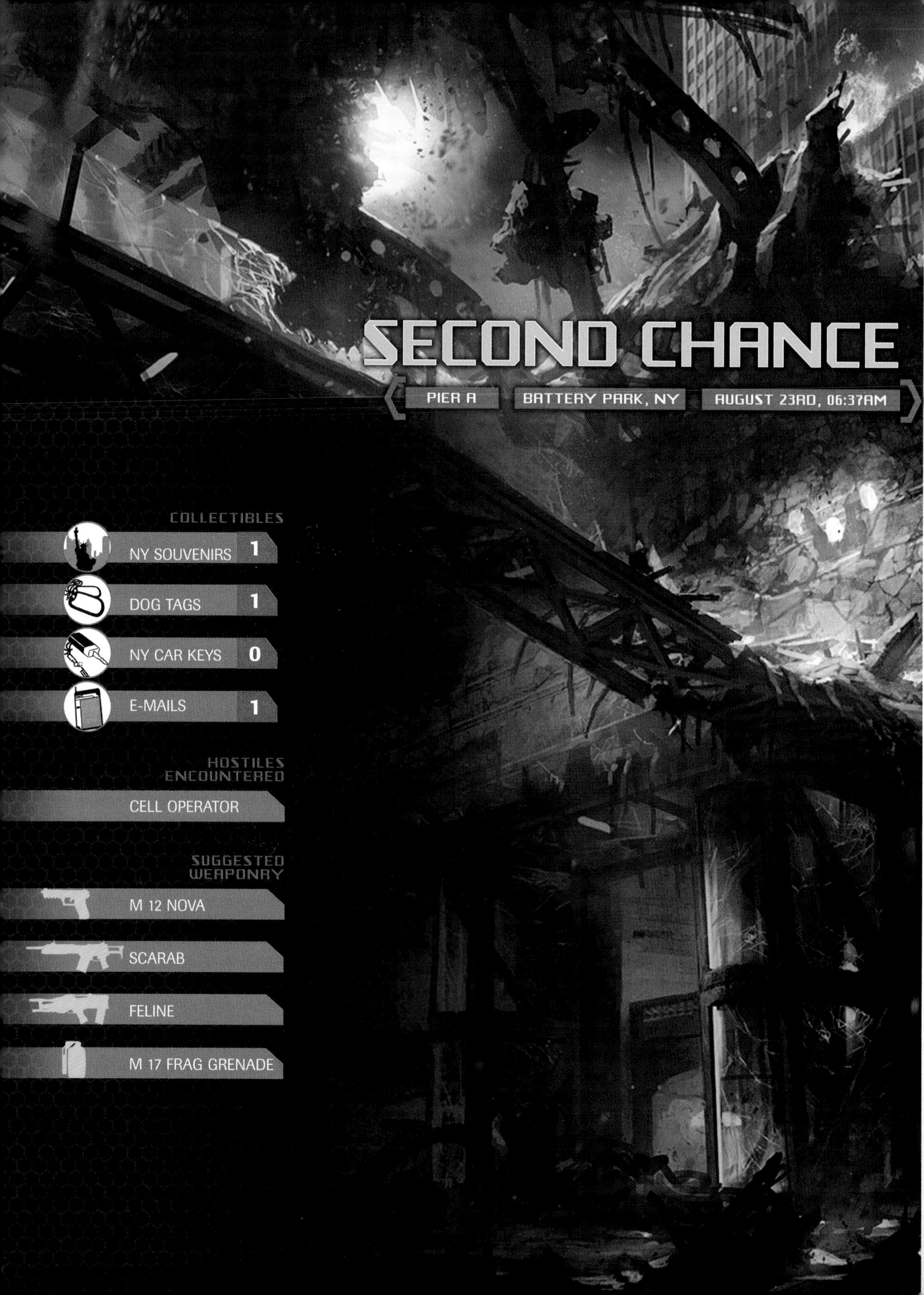

SECOND CHANCE

PIER A | BATTERY PARK, NY | AUGUST 23RD, 06:37AM

COLLECTIBLES

NY SOUVENIRS 1

DOG TAGS 1

NY CAR KEYS 0

E-MAILS 1

HOSTILES ENCOUNTERED

CELL OPERATOR

SUGGESTED WEAPONRY

M 12 NOVA

SCARAB

FELINE

M 17 FRAG GRENADE

LOCATE AND PROTECT NATHAN GOULD

Alcatraz arrives at an abandoned warehouse near Battery Park, on the southern tip of Manhattan Island. Something is different. His clothing. The visor. Alcatraz picks up the handgun near the body of his savior and is consumed by a flashback. The deceased went by the name Prophet. The mighty Nanosuit he wore could stop bullets, but it couldn't fully protect him from the infection sweeping the city. Prophet needed Team Omega's assistance in completing his mission, but Alcatraz was the only survivor. So he passed his suit on to Alcatraz in hopes that he'd finish what Prophet started. Alcatraz—you—must find Nathan Gould.

BREAK THE PADLOCK

DOG TAG

Don't miss the first collectible in your rush to break the padlock and exit the warehouse. The Dog Tag is on the end of the table beside Prophet's corpse.

Approach the locked door and strike the padlock with a melee attack when prompted to break it off. This is but a small taste of the Nanosuit's power; Alcatraz is no mere marine any more. Proceed down the hall and through the storage room to the partially-opened door in the distance. Crouch under the door and make your way through the makeshift medical examination room to the stairs. Ascend the steps, then sprint and jump across the gap in the balcony. Hold the Jump button to perform a Power Jump. Push through the wooden doors, leap through the hole in the ceiling, and grab the ledge on the right before exiting through the blue door.

LAPTOPS ADD BACKSTORY

Interact with the laptop on the lower floor of this room to listen to an audio recording from two of the doctors working to treat the infected civilians. Laptops such as this one can be found all over the city. Access the messages left on these devices to gain insight into the events leading up to August 23rd.

MAKE YOUR WAY THROUGH THE CAMP

SYSTEM OVERRIDE

USING THE VISOR

The blinding sun isn't the only thing to greet Alcatraz as he exits the warehouse. A system override stops him in his tracks and demonstrates the power of the visor. Scan the environment for hostiles, ammunition supplies, and tactical opportunities. Use the visor's zoom function to investigate various tactical options (the yellow, numbered hexagons) that appear on the visor's display. Highlight enemies or tactical options to show them as waypoints on the HUD even when the visor is turned off. Additional visor abilities can be unlocked as Alcatraz and the Nanosuit continue to symbiotically evolve.

The tactical visor provides increased battlefield awareness.

Alcatraz exits the warehouse just in time to watch two CELL Operators mercilessly gun down a civilian near the fountain. Zoom in on the hostiles with the visor to discover their weak spot, then pan the area for tactical options. Use this concealed vantage point to study the lay of the land, the available cover, and the enemy's patrol pattern. The opportunity to get your first taste of combat has arrived.

ENCOUNTER A

BATTERY PARK FOUNTAIN

1. **RESUPPLY:** Use the ammunition crates directly below the vantage point to load your M 12 Nova pistol.

2. **TAKE:** Equip the Scarab assault rifle located by the weapon crates on the west side of the fountain.

Drop from the upper, blown-out floor of the building onto the balcony below and, from there, onto the street near the truck. Use the available cover to avoid detection and resupply at the ammo crates (1) near the yellow storage container. The hostiles are slowly making their way to the far side of the fountain. Stay crouched to avoid detection and circle around the left side of the bushes and trees to the fountain and take the Scarab (2). Gather up the ammunition from the adjacent crates and take aim on the two CELL Operators in the distance. Aim the Scarab's site just above the far hedgerow and wait for the enemies to pop their heads up.

Restock your ammo supplies via the corpses and continue on an easterly heading to the castle steps. The blue indicator on the HUD and mini-map serves as a guide to aid in completing the primary objective.

SYSTEM OVERRIDE

STEALTH INDICATOR & CLOAK

Alcatraz isn't alone inside the narrow hall within the park's castle and the CELL Operators think they may have heard something. The Stealth Indicator in the lower left-hand corner displays the level of enemy awareness. The meter is currently yellow because nearby hostiles have become suspicious. Activate the suit's Cloaking ability to become virtually invisible. Remain stationary until the enemy turns and walks away. Activating Cloak gradually consumes energy over time, but consumes progressively more energy the faster you move while Cloaked.

Sneak up behind the enemy while Cloaked and perform a stealth kill by pressing the Melee button once the reticle turns red and the on-screen prompt appears. Alcatraz grabs the enemy from behind and thrust his knife through the enemy's throat. Quickly back away, deactivate Cloak to allow the Energy Meter to refill, then reactive Cloak and use it to kill the enemy approaching from the other side of the room. Stand off to the side to approach him from behind; he opens fire if he notices you approaching. Enemies can detect Alcatraz even when he's Cloaked if he approaches too closely from the front. Eliminate the final enemy in the center of the courtyard.

THE ORIGINAL BFG

Want to put a scare into the enemy in the center of the castle interior? Use Cloak mode to sweep around the perimeter in a counter-clockwise direction towards the cannons. Approach the cannon facing the center of the castle and light the fuse to fire it.

EXIT THE CASTLE VIA THE ROOF

E-MAIL

This mission's E-Mail message is located on the table in the center of the castle courtyard, where the third CELL Operator was standing. Collectible E-Mails all appear on an upright tablet-style device, making them easier to spot. Don't confuse these collectibles with the laptops you see scattered throughout the city.

Cross the courtyard heading due north toward the large yellow container and climb onto it. Leap onto the castle roof and approach the edge overlooking the medical camp. Three CELL Operators exit an APC and take up position on the north side of the castle, just yards from your position. Stay crouched and survey the scene.

HEAD NORTH THROUGH THE CAMP

ENCOUNTER B

QUARANTINE CAMP

1. **INFILTRATE:** Use the narrow gap in the barricades on the eastern edge of the fence line to continue north.
2. **EXIT:** Exit the camp via the decontamination station on the north side of the park.
3. **COVER:** Use the metal barriers for cover against the CELL Operators nearest the castle.
4. **USE:** Use the decontamination showers to satisfy the monitoring station's requirements for exit.
5. **OBSERVE:** Eliminate the enemy in the watchtower and use Cloak to scout your next move.

The first step is to deal with the CELL Operators let out of the APC nearest your position. One option is to use Cloak to get in close, use the cover ③ and target the enemies from the ground. Another option is to open fire from the roof. The choice is yours. Either way, proceed northeast toward the statue of the mounted soldier and infiltrate ① the main perimeter via the gap in the fence.

The evacuation camp is crawling with CELL Operators and the most direct way to the exit isn't the easiest. Use Cloak to sweep along the inside of the camp in a counter-clockwise direction, staying behind the EMAT tents, and execute a stealth kill on the guard near the main entrance. Angle towards the café and parked vehicle to the west and eliminate any resistance with targeted headshots. Continue around the perimeter to the tent west of the guard tower ⑤. Eliminate the CELL Operator in the tower and use Cloak to steal a view of the camp. Target any remaining hostiles and either walk or drive the APC towards the double doors to the north. Try the keypad to the right of the doors (they won't open) to update the primary objective waypoint.

Proceed east through the checkpoint beneath the scrolling message sign towards quarantine station. This area has numerous enemies so either use Cloak to slip past undetected, or make use of the available cover and fight your way through. Be mindful of the flammable barrels and try to detonate them when CELL Operators are close by. Continue northeast to the camp's exit ② and proceed through the decontamination tents. Use the keypad ④ to access the decontamination shower.

Activate Cloak and stealthily kill the two enemies in the tunnel beyond the shower. Allow the second one to get a few steps away before making the first kill, or else he might hear the attack. Use the laptop in the office on the right to activate the vehicle cleansing station.

FORCE OPEN THE SECURITY DOORS

The magnetic locks were disengaged, but the system failed to open the doors due to foreign contaminants. Approach the doors on the north side of the bay and pry them open. It takes all the strength of the Nanosuit to open the doors, but doing so allows Alcatraz to step out of Battery Park and onto the streets of the Financial District.

ACHIEVEMENT

Foreign Contaminant

Fight your way through the evacuation center at Battery Park. Use the Nanosuit's Cloaking ability and the technology of the suit's visor to recon the situation and cross the camp to the northern exit.

LOCATE AND PROTECT NATHAN GOULD

The main avenue leading north from Battery Park is strewn with the garbage and detritus of a major evacuation center. Adding to the mess is more than a few burned-out vehicles, both military and civilian issue. Resupply at the ammo stash on the corner near the armored vehicle and continue north towards the roadblock in the distance.

FIND THE SUBWAY ENTRANCE

Turn onto the side street on the left and approach the roadblock. The gift shop on the right side of the road extends past the impassable barricade in the street. Exit the shop through the smashed window to continue west into the alley. Leap onto the garbage dumpster and climb onto the ledge above it.

NY SOUVENIR

The first mission's NY Souvenir is located on the counter in the gift shop near the barricade. It's a miniature model of the Statue of Liberty. Pick it up to unlock bonus art for this mission.

SYSTEM OVERRIDE

ARMOR MODE

The Nanosuit's other primary feature is Armor Mode. Activating the suit's enhanced armor provides added protection from bullets and exploding munitions and increases the chance of survival dramatically. Armor Mode consumes energy and slows movement speed, but absorbs incoming projectiles, thereby increasing stability while returning fire.

ENCOUNTER C

ALLEY AMBUSH

1. **DESTROY:** Target the explosive canister on the ground to kill the enemy hiding behind cover.
2. **COLLECT:** Locate the NY Souvenir on the counter inside the gift shop.
3. **LEDGE GRAB:** Climb onto the upper roof via the ledge to equip the enemy's dropped Feline assault rifle.

Activate Armor Mode to absorb the blast from the detonating fuel tanks on the roof then quickly take cover behind the ductwork to the right. Hold the Lean button while in cover carefully aim up and over the obstacle. Use the Look controls to adjust Alcatraz's position laterally or vertically. Shoot the CELL Operator on the upper roof to the right, then the two in the distance. Step out of cover and target the flammable canister ① on the ground near the fourth enemy in the alley below. Collect the NY Souvenir ② if you haven't already and swap the Scarab for the Feline. Gather up all of the available Feline ammo, including from the enemy on the upper ledge ③.

ATOP THE DONUT SHOP

1 **FLANK:** Bypass the enemy's defenses and drop below ground via the ruptured sewer grate to the east.

2 **INFILTRATE:** Take a westerly route through the sewers to slip past the enemy.

3 **EXIT:** Continue north to the subway exit and descend below surface.

4 **GRENADE:** Secure the M17 Frag Grenade from the ammo crate and throw them at the nearby enemies.

Crouch to avoid detection and quietly drop onto the lower rooftop near the massive fake donut. Acquire the grenades from the ammo crate ④ and use Cloak to stealthily throw one at the CELL Operators on the street near the ruptured gas line. Drop through the small hole in the ceiling to enter the donut shop and use counter for cover while you kill any surviving enemies in the street. Activate Cloak and angle to the northeast, around the right of the bus to flank the park ① and enter the alley beneath the scaffolding. Eliminate the enemies stationed there and drop into the sewer to avoid additional confrontations.

Crouch beneath the sparking wires and proceed north through the sewer to the junction room. Pull the lever on the control panel on the left to disable the current in the flooded section up ahead. Dive into the water and swim in a northwesterly direction back to solid ground. There's a hole in the wall on the left. Jump through this hole to slip inside the subway entrance undetected. The stairs on the left exit onto William Street, an area likely still crawling with CELL Operators. Grab hold of the gate and hoist it open to enter the William Street Station.

ACHIEVEMENT

Food for Thought

Unlock this bonus by using the giant donut atop the diner to kill one of the patrolling CELL Operators down below. Use Cloak to avoid detection and punch the donut off its stand at one of the enemies in the street.

STEALTH KILLS FOR THE TAKING

Want an extra two stealth kills to pad your stats? Activate Cloak and sneak up the stairs to the street. There are two CELL Operators just steps from the subway entrance, and both have their backs turned to Alcatraz's approach.

The subway has become a home for the few remaining infected who haven't yet been eliminated, but they pose no threat to Alcatraz. Unfortunately, they're not alone. Activate Nanovision (which is available at the end of this mission) to better spot the alien insects attacking the hapless infected civilians and proceed northwest through the station to a second gate.

FIND AN ALTERNATE GATE

Gould has detected a hive of sorts up ahead. Sprint past the body of the CELL Operator attacked by the alien insects, turn the corner to the right, and quickly leap and climb up through the hole in the ceiling. Ascend the stairs around the corner to complete this mission.

SUDDEN IMPACT

WILLIAM STREET | FINANCIAL DISTRICT, NY | AUGUST 23RD, 08:14 A.M.

COLLECTIBLES

NY SOUVENIRS	1
DOG TAGS	1
NY CAR KEYS	1
E-MAILS	0

HOSTILES ENCOUNTERED

CELL OPERATOR

CEPH ASSAULT UNIT

SUGGESTED WEAPONRY

MARSHALL

STEALTH NOVA

STEALTH SCARAB

JAW

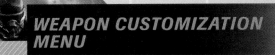

LOCATE AND PROTECT NATHAN GOULD

FIND A ROUTE TO NATHAN GOULD

Alcatraz escapes the alien insects in the subway by hoisting himself up through the hole in the floor of an office. Power Kick the toppled table blocking the entrance to the smaller room straight ahead and swap out the currently equipped assault rifle (probably the Feline) for the Marshall shotgun lying on the desk in the corner. This comes in handy much later, but for now swap to the sidearm.

Proceed through the spacious adjacent office, while trying not to be too distracted by the window-shattering explosions shaking the building's exterior. The source of these blasts is revealed as soon as Alcatraz starts across the skyway to the left. Watch as an alien ship much like the one Prophet destroyed on the docks of Hudson River crashes through the bridge and drops Alcatraz to the street below. Two CELL helicopters successfully manage to shoot the alien craft down, much to Gould's delight.

REACH THE CRASH SITE & OBTAIN XENO-TISSUE EXTRACT FOR GOULD

Enter the looted convenience mart on the right to pick up some additional ammo for the Marshall then enter the parking garage on the north side of the street. Swap out the secondary weapon for the Stealth Nova lying beside the ammo crate on the left.

WEAPON CUSTOMIZATION MENU

Access the Weapon Customization Menu and use the appropriate buttons to toggle between options for the Nova's barrel and scope accessories (some weapons have a third accessory category). The Stealth Nova comes equipped with a pistol silencer and laser sight. Experiment with toggling these on and off, but leave both accessories active. The Stealth Nova is an excellent short- to medium-range firearm for those who wish to remain undetected.

Lift the gate to the garage and slowly ascend the ramp to the upper floor. Activate Cloak Mode, round the corner, and take fix the laser sight on the head of the right-hand CELL Operator. Pause to let the other one walk away then open fire. Rush forward to eliminate the one that walked away.
A third CELL Operator may be near the vending machine in the bay to the right.

The parking garage contains many more CELL Operators, stationed in the corners of each floor in pairs. Continue the slow spiraling ascent up through the garage while using Cloak and the Stealth Nova to eliminate the enemies with single headshots. The Stealth Nova can drop a CELL Operator with a single bullet to the head from up to a distance of roughly 25 meters. Several of the enemies will likely take up position near a fuel barrel; only opt for the explosive kill if you don't mind drawing the attention of other CELL Operators. Exit the parking garage in the northwest corner of the second level and enter the stairwell on the right.

Exchange the Stealth Nova for the Stealth Scarab lying near the stairs—it's time for something with a bit more range—and head up a half flight of stairs to stock up on ammo. Crouch down here out of sight and use the visor to scan the area ahead.

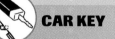

CAR KEY

Continue all the way up the stairs to the pile of rubble near the top. The first collectible Car Key is lying on the step next to the corpse on the final landing.

ENCOUNTER A

EXITING THE PARKING GARAGE

1. **FLANK:** Descend the stairs to the side-street and use the sewer across the street to flank the enemy.
2. **EXPLORE:** Enter the lower levels of the parking garage via the street entrance to the south.
3. **ASCEND:** Climb the scaffolding to the rooftop of the blue building diagonally opposite the parking garage.

The streets outside the parking garage are crawling with over a dozen CELL Operators. There are multiple ways to reach the crash site, but both require getting past the armed defenses. Though it's possible to snake through the below-ground parking garage (2), it's often risky to forfeit higher ground when other options are available. Toggle the Stealth Scarab's firing mode to single shot (better for sniping) and stealthily eliminate the CELL Operator manning the turret gun on the back of the APC in the intersection below. Stay Cloaked and eliminate any other enemies visible from this vantage point then de-Cloak and sprint down the stairs to street level. Reactivate Cloak, swap to the Marshall, and run across the street to the open sewer grate (1).

Proceed southeast through the sewer, past each of the open grates, to the terminus at the far end. Grab the grenades from the box and leap out of the hole while Cloaked. The orange scaffolding ③ leading up to the roof is just steps away. Eliminate any CELL Operators patrolling this side street then quickly climb the scaffolding to the roof and angle to the left, up the stairs and past the ventilation system to the area overlooking the crash site. Don't leap over the ductwork onto the beams though, as this position is far too exposed.

INVESTIGATE THE CRASH SITE

EXAMINE THE ALIEN PODS

Gould believes the aliens onboard the craft ejected before the ship went down and may still be in the escape pods down below. The first two alien pods are marked in blue, but another dozen or more CELL Operators have already moved in to secure the area. Getting to those pods without going down in a blaze of gunfire is going to be tricky. But it's certainly possible, as long as you focus on the nearest enemies first and make patient use of Cloak and the Stealth Scarab.

Activate Cloak and slip into the stairwell on the left. Descend the steps quietly and perform a stealth kill on the enemy occupying the landing. Slip out onto the collapsed floor of the building down the stairs another flight and snipe the two CELL Operators guarding the nearest alien pod. Pan to the left and eliminate the two across the crater, behind the concrete barriers. Descend to the ground level, switch to the Marshall and use the planters and plywood walls for cover en route to the alien pod. Blast a hole in any stragglers that appear at close range.

Approach the alien pod and examine it per Gould's instructions. Now it's time to check the other one. Head north around the left-hand side of the flaming alien craft. Take cover behind the corner of the building on the left and snipe the remaining CELL Operators in the distance to the south, particularly the one manning the turret atop the APC. Examine the second alien pod to find that it is also empty. Alcatraz is going to have to examine the actual wreckage for the sample Gould wants.

NY SOUVENIR

Descend into the crater of the crash site and approach the underground parking garage entrance. Duck under the partially-raised door and approach the attendant's booth on the right. The NY Souvenir is atop the filing cabinets inside this office. Power Kick the door around back to break into the booth.

Load up on ammo and descend into the crater beneath the flaming wreckage of the alien ship. The glass windows have miraculously not shattered; Alcatraz is going to have to find another way inside.

FIND A WAY INTO THE WRECKAGE

Before Alcatraz can further explore the crash site, he must first deal with the CELL helicopter that has flown into position overhead. The chopper is armed with two mounted machine guns, one on each side. Dealing with such a threat would be really difficult, if not for the JAW missile launcher lying on the floor inside the crater. Locate the JAW near the corner of the office and use it to fire a guided missile at the helicopter. The helicopter will likely remain stationary, but it is possible to guide the projectile post-launch by continuing to hold the Weapon Fire button and using the Look controls to steer the missile.

THE BACKPACK LAUNCHER

Alcatraz can carry a heavy weapon (such as the JAW or a detached turret gun) without having to discard either of his two primary weapons. Use the Weapon Select button to switch back to either of his other equipped weapons. Explosive devices such as the JAW and C4 can be selected using the D-Pad on console controllers and number keys on the PC.

Ascend out of the crater to the tower of rubble in the center of the area, where all that remains is a crumbling stairwell and elevator shaft. Climb the stairs to the upper floor, activate Cloak, and take out any CELL Operators that have moved in on the street to the northeast. Pry open the left-hand elevator doors, activate Armor to protect Alcatraz from the ensuing impact, and leap into the elevator shaft. The sudden jolt to the elevator causes it to plummet to the maintenance tunnels far underground. Exit the elevator and wade through the water to the crash site.

ANALYZE THE BIOLOGICAL MATERIAL

Climb up out of the tunnel to the office interior where the biological matter is spread thickly over much of the surface. Activate the visor and follow the on-screen prompt to scan the matter for Gould. Leap through the now-broken window to exit the crater just as Alcatraz had done moments earlier. An alien creature known as a Ceph Assault Unit leaps down and attacks at close range. Wait for the Nanosuit to reboot and switch to the Marshall; it's time to put the shotgun to work!

STALKER

ACQUIRE AN ALIEN TISSUE SAMPLE

The Ceph flees just as quickly as it attacks, but it hasn't gone far. Activate Nanovision to spot the creature on the thermal imagery. Slowly advance out of the crater to draw the creature out of hiding then blast its soft jelly torso with the Marshall. Put a second shell into it to ensure it's dead then approach and collect the 100 Nano Catalyst—the tissue Gould needed.

CLOSE ENCOUNTER

DELIVER XENO-TISSUE SAMPLE TO GOULD

NANOSUIT CUSTOMIZATION

Each and every Ceph you kill, regardless of type, yields some amount of Nano Catalyst. Access the Nanosuit Customization menu and press the button corresponding with the category you wish to upgrade. There are a total of 12 Nanosuit upgrades grouped essentially into the following four categories: Enemy Awareness, Armor, Movement, and Stealth. Each upgrade requires a set amount of Nano Catalyst, ranging from 100 to 16,000. Only one per grouping can be active at a given time. We recommend investing this first 100 Nano Catalyst on the Armor Enhance upgrade. Also, we strongly recommend replaying missions that contain numerous Ceph before advancing too far in the story in order to build up your collection of Nano Catalysts. This makes it possible to sooner afford the more expensive ones.

More than Human

Unlock this bonus by killing your first Ceph Assault Unit and spending the 100 Nano Catalyst it yields on an upgrade in the Nanosuit Customization menu. We recommend opting for the Armor Enhance upgrade first, as it reduces the drain rate of the Energy Meter during Armor mode.

REACH GOULD'S LAB VIA FDR DRIVE

Exit the crash site area and parking garage and head south past the checkpoints to where the road dives below ground as part of the Battery Park Underpass. Bypass the smoldering busses and burned-out taxicabs and continue through the opened doors of the stray cargo containers to where the road bends to the east.

Use the Stealth Scarab to snipe the two CELL Operators beyond the fence in the distance and watch for a Ceph Assault Unit to appear. Switch to the Marshall and move in for the kill. The underpass is crawling with Ceph Assault Units, and a few CELL Operators too. Use Cloak and the Marshall shotgun to slip into blasting range undetected. Quickly activate Armor mode if the Ceph opens fire, as its guns are quite deadly. Use the range of the Stealth Scarab and proximity of explosive barrels to eliminate the CELL Operators while they're distracted by the Ceph.

AMMO CONSERVATION

Running low on ammo? If so, hang back and allow the CELL Operators and Ceph Assault Units to fight it out. This allows you to conserve ammo by only having to kill the victor. Just remember to collect the Nano Catalyst from the Ceph Assault Unit's corpse should the CELL Operators prove triumphant.

The road exits into a trench deep below the primary road surface. Continue south through this stretch, up and over the piles of rubble and debris. Numerous Ceph are lurking in the area where the trench gives way to the next section of underpass. Eliminate the two in the open daylight then slip through the container on the left of the roadblock and take on another two within the fenced area. Continue to the pile of debris and exit the underpass via the hallway beyond the final door on the right.

DOG TAG

Kill the last of the Ceph Assault Units in the second underpass segment and proceed to the large bus with the red, white, and blue paint job. This mission's lone Dog Tag is just inside the doorway on the right-hand side of the tunnel, near the dumpster. This doorway is just before the stairs leading out of the underpass.

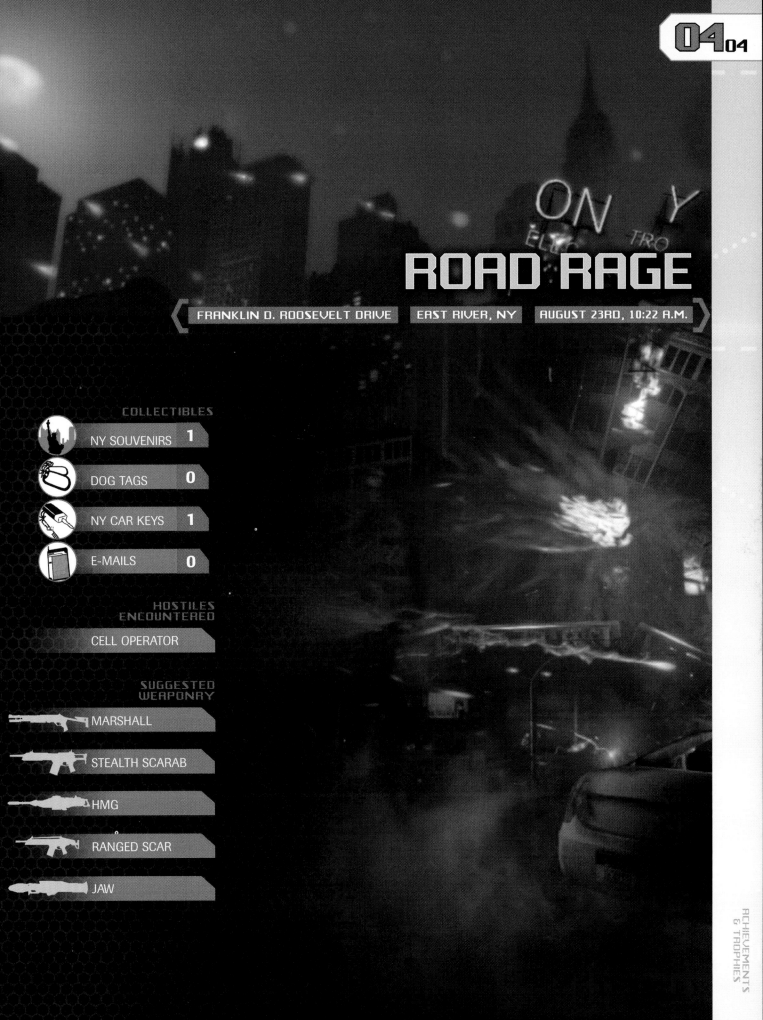

ROAD RAGE

FRANKLIN D. ROOSEVELT DRIVE | EAST RIVER, NY | AUGUST 23RD, 10:22 A.M.

COLLECTIBLES

NY SOUVENIRS 1

DOG TAGS 0

NY CAR KEYS 1

E-MAILS 0

HOSTILES ENCOUNTERED

CELL OPERATOR

SUGGESTED WEAPONRY

MARSHALL

STEALTH SCARAB

HMG

RANGED SCAR

JAW

DELIVER XENO-TISSUE SAMPLE TO GOULD

FIND A WAY ONTO THE FDR FREEWAY

NY SOUVENIR

Back away from the fence gate just atop the stairs and enter the small room to the north. It's hard to spot, but there's a model of a NYPD Cruiser in the far right-hand corner, beside the "God Help Us" graffiti.

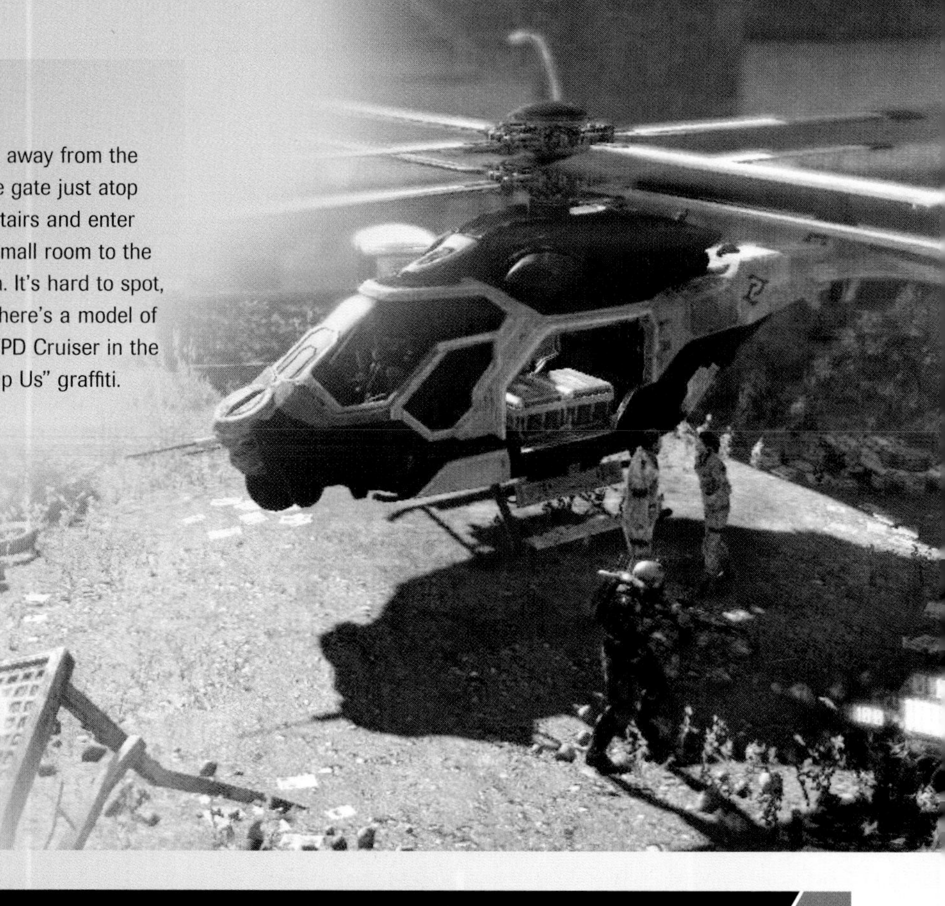

Alcatraz exits the underpass in a maintenance area below the city streets. Ascend the stairs on the right and Power Kick open the gate to continue. There's only one way out; follow the corridor around the bend and up the stairs to the hole in the ceiling. Leap through the holes in the collapsed walls and proceed toward the window to the southeast, overlooking a small courtyard. Eavesdrop on the conversation between Lockhart and Tara.

ENCOUNTER A

APPROACHING FDR DRIVE

1. **LEDGE GRAB:** Climb up onto the elevated train tracks and stealthily kill the CELL Operator overlooking the street.
2. **MOUNT:** Eliminate the gunner atop the APC and open fire with the mounted machine gun.
3. **OBSERVE:** Use the window to study the situation along the street leading south to FDR Drive.
4. **STEALTH:** Use the subway station on the corner to sneak past the enemies and resurface behind them.

Activate Cloak and use the visor near the window (3) to study the lay of the land and enemy positions then draw the Stealth Scarab (or Stealth Nova) to quickly snipe the two enemies on the grass directly below the window. If using the rifle, turn and snipe the CELL Operator on the train tracks too. Allow the Energy Meter to recharge, move to the exit, and use Cloak to slip around the collapsed portion of the elevated tracks and climb up onto makeshift walkway over the sidewalk (1).

Proceed south atop the walkway in a crouched position to remain undetected. Activate Cloak, drop off the walkway, and dash down the stairs into the safety of the subway station ④. Proceed through the corridor underground and partially ascend the stairs leading up to the other side of the intersection. Snipe the CELL Operator manning the turret atop the APC and any other visible enemies. Rather than mount the gun atop the APC ③, slip around south side of the kiosks and eliminate the enemy at the machine gun nest farther to the west.

BRING THE NOISE!

Not worried about the sound of your rifle going off? Want a little extra oomph behind each bullet fired? Remember that you can always take the silencer attachment off the Scarab to give the rifle a bit more lethality for long-range shots.

Detach the HMG from the concrete Jersey barrier and proceed west to the collapsed portion of the freeway. Ascend the rubble pile near the flames and step out onto the elevated highway.

HEAD NORTH ALONG THE FDR

Lug the HMG towards the eighteen-wheeler parked sideways across the freeway and set it down. Listen for the approaching vehicles and activate Cloak. Crouch beneath the truck trailer and snipe the two enemies manning the rooftop machine guns. Back away, pick up the HMG and take out the CELL Operators on foot. Climb up onto the toppled trailer to continue north onto the freeway on foot.

Hop the right-hand guardrail and use the bushes and support columns for cover as you close the distance on the enemies ahead. Use Cloak to move undetected and cast aside the cumbersome HMG and shoulder the rifle. Four additional CELL Operators rappel down onto the street near the tunnel entrance. Fire a couple rounds into the fuel drum near the median to detonate it as they land, then finish off the others en route to the tunnel. Alcatraz exits the tunnel just in time to watch the next segment of elevated highway collapse during an earthquake.

TECTONIC SHIFT

Leap down into the rubble of the collapsed freeway and activate Nanovision to better spot the CELL Operators moving about in the smoke and dust caused by the earthquake. There are two or three enemies on the freeway itself directly north of the collapse and several more patrolling the park on the left. Use the Stealth Scarab, the suit's Cloaking ability, and Nanovision to pick these enemies off one by one.

Move freely in and out of cover, using the power of Cloak and the vision-reducing blanket of dust to remain concealed. Consider eliminating the nearest two enemies on the freeway first, then doubling back to the where Alcatraz first leapt down onto the rubble, then sweep through the park on the left. There is additional ammunition amongst the electrical boxes on the left—the ammo crate gives off a faint blue signal when Nanovision is on.

ALL THE BETTER TO SEE YOU WITH

Activate the Visor and Nanovision simultaneously to toggle on the highlighting of individual enemies. This makes the enemies glow under normal viewing conditions, thereby making them much easier to spot through the dust without having to move about with Nanovision active.

BREACH CHECKPOINT AND ACQUIRE VEHICLE

Continue north past the vending machines and circular benches around the trees in the park, then return to the collapsed elevated freeway. Just watch for other CELL Operators amidst the rubble. Don't hesitate to switch to the Marshall and blast away at close range (with Armor mode active) should reinforcements swarm Alcatraz's position. Advance northward on the freeway, going up and over the pancaked portions of the road and around the abandoned vehicles, until reaching the portion of the FDR that remained intact.

INCOMING ROCKETS

The armored vehicle to the north doesn't just have a machine gun turret! It's also equipped with side-mounted rocket launchers. The driver within the vehicle will fire these rockets at first sight of Alcatraz so stay concealed!

ENCOUNTER B

FDR CHECKPOINT

1. **GRENADE:** Gather up the grenades near the support column and lob one into the elevated machine gun nest.
2. **AVOID:** Stay clear of the USMC Bravo ICV assault vehicle located farther up the street at all costs.
3. **OBSERVE:** Scan the checkpoint for enemy positions from the patio near the edge of the shops.
4. **STEALTH:** Use the sewer tunnels to advance through the checkpoint without being detected.

The dust finally clears as Alcatraz makes his way north past the freeway collapse. Stay to the right, collect the grenades from the ammo crate, and use Cloak to move close enough to the watchtower to throw one up through the opening ①. Quickly back away, snipe any enemies in the immediate vicinity, and pick up the Ranged Scar to the left of the watchtower. Drop into the sewer tunnel ④ to the left and follow it past the first opening, around the turns, to the northwest.

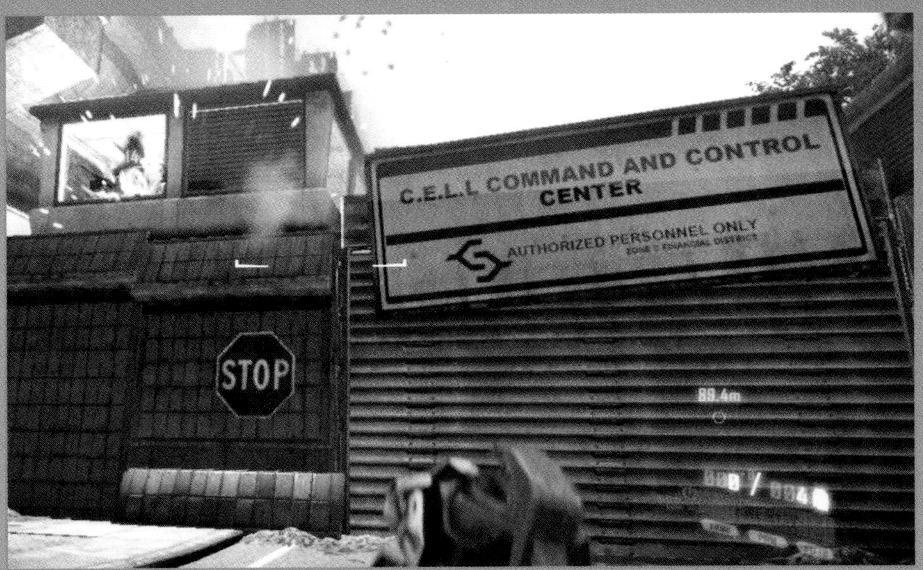

Exit the sewer and eliminate the enemies on the plaza. Climb the stairs towards the vantage point near the shops ③. Collect the ammo and turn and snipe the enemy manning the turret atop the vehicle. Return to the east side of the street, remain behind cover, and advance northward through the checkpoint. Activate Cloak and round the corner towards the mobile offices to the right ② to avoid the vehicular threat to the north. Use the Ranged Scar to snipe any enemies in the area south of the trailers. Gather up grenades and ammo from the office to the east.

Alcatraz must reach the armored vehicle beyond the large concrete wall, but barbed wire prevents him from climbing over; he'll have to go under it instead! Turn to the north and slowly advance towards the sewer grate on the right side of the road while Cloaked. It's just left of the entrance ramp. Lift the grate and drop into the sewers before being spotted. Swim through the water in an easterly direction, activate Cloak, and leap out onto dry ground.

Kill the two CELL Operators guarding the armored vehicle and take a look around. The storage container with the open doors can be exited on the far end to reach a secluded area beyond the mobile offices on the far side of the office. Slip through to sneak up behind a machine gun nest and other enemies guarding an ammo dump.

CAR KEY

Continue south past the machine gun turret (beyond the container) alongside the lengthy wall with the barbed wire on top and round the corner to the right. The Car Key is located inside the shipping container, along with a number of weapons and ammo crates.

EXIT THE COMPOUND

Climb aboard the ICV and practice using both its primary weapon (high caliber machine gun) and secondary weapon (rockets) while taking aim on the cracked wall directly in front of it. Blast the wall with rockets to destroy it and slowly drive the vehicle onto the fallen wall.

Two enemy vehicles approach as soon as the wall falls. Ignore the smaller vehicle on the left and take aim on the rocket-firing ICV across the street. Use rockets to destroy the vehicle then turn and blast the vehicle on the left with the heavy guns; the lesser vehicle is neutralized as soon as its rooftop gunner has been eliminated.

CONTINUE NORTH ALONG THE FDR

Ascend the on-ramp (or collapsed freeway) to join the main FDR road surface and continue north towards the tunnel. Blast the vehicle that exits the tunnel ahead and snake around the barriers and abandoned cars (there's another available armored vehicle behind the first barrier should you need it). Ignore the chopper to the right and continue to the next small checkpoint. Eliminate the enemy vehicles and CELL Operator manning the HMG atop the barricade.

Fire a rocket at the upper edge of the second checkpoint directly ahead and destroy the APC to the right of it. Hop out of the ICV and search the upper level of the checkpoint to find a discarded JAW. This comes in handy soon enough. Climb aboard the undamaged ICV parked below the mounted HMG and continue north to the edge of the tunnel and third checkpoint.

ENCOUNTER C

EXITING THE FDR

1. **DRIVE:** There is another Bravo ICV parked to the right of the tunnel. Use as necessary.
2. **COLLECT:** The storage container behind the building contains C4 explosives for use against enemy ICVs.

Two enemy ICVs are parked uphill beyond the third checkpoint near the end of FDR Drive. It is extremely difficult for Alcatraz to survive a direct assault on them, either on foot or in the ICV. Exit the ICV before reaching the end of the tunnel and move into cover near the checkpoint. Wait for the Energy Meter to recharge, activate Cloak, and slowly ascend the ramp to the checkpoint's upper level and collect the C4 located there. Take cover behind the large concrete pillar. Reactivate Cloak, step out from cover and use the JAW to destroy either of the ICVs. Alcatraz should have at least one rocket left from the crash site; otherwise, he'll need to employ the C4.

Sneak over to the building near the parked ICV and gather up C4 (2) if needed. Be patient, use cover and Cloak, and circle around behind the ICV—do not approach from the front! Place at least two blocks of C4 directly on the ICV's rear, activate Armor mode, and dash away to safety while detonating it remotely. Press the Fire Weapon button to place the C4 and the Aim button to detonate it. This is very risky, but can be done. A third option is to destroy one of the two vehicles with the JAW collected earlier, then attack the other with the ICV Alcatraz parked to the right (1).

Alcatraz is getting closer! Use the Ranged Scar to snipe the distant CELL Operators that come to inspect the second explosion. Fall back and climb aboard the ICV parked beside the checkpoint and drive to the loading dock around the corner to the right. Use the high-caliber guns and rockets on the ICV to eliminate the remaining enemies. Approach the door leading inside on foot, with the Marshall in hand; there's one final enemy to blast before heading inside.

TAKE A DEEP BREATH

Click the Movement controls to have Alcatraz hold his breath while aiming through the Assault Scope of the Ranged Scarab. This steadies the rifle and greatly reduces the natural bob and sway of the rifle while aiming. This technique does consume energy.

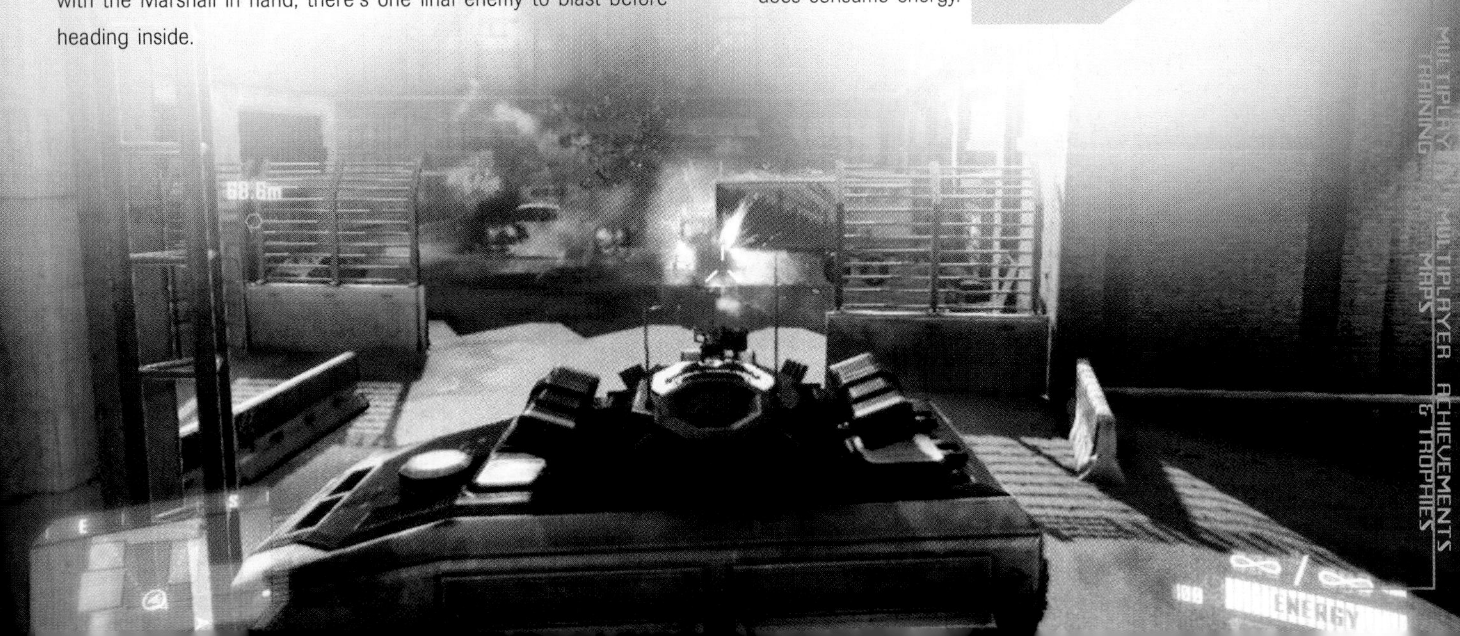

LAB RAT

HARBOR LIGHTS PIER | EAST RIVER, NY | AUGUST 23RD, 11:02 A.M.

COLLECTIBLES

NY SOUVENIRS 1

DOG TAGS 1

NY CAR KEYS 1

E-MAILS 1

HOSTILES ENCOUNTERED

CELL OPERATOR

SUGGESTED WEAPONRY

RANGED SCAR

DSG-1

HMG

MARSHALL

INFILTRATE THE WAREHOUSE

DESTROY EVIDENCE OF GOULD'S WHEREABOUTS

The FDR led Alcatraz to a small building overlooking the Harbor Lights Pier Gould's lab is at the far end of the pier, on an upper floor of a warehouse currently under tight surveillance. Alcatraz must plan his moves carefully if he's to cross the pier in one piece.

ENCOUNTER A

CROSSING THE PIER

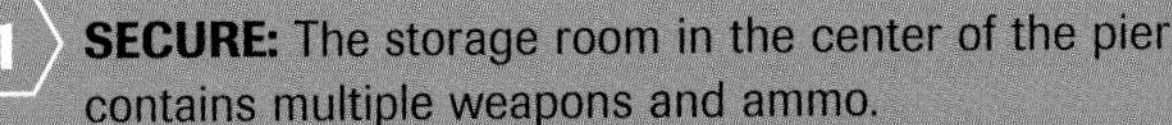

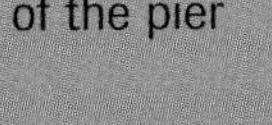

1. **SECURE:** The storage room in the center of the pier contains multiple weapons and ammo.

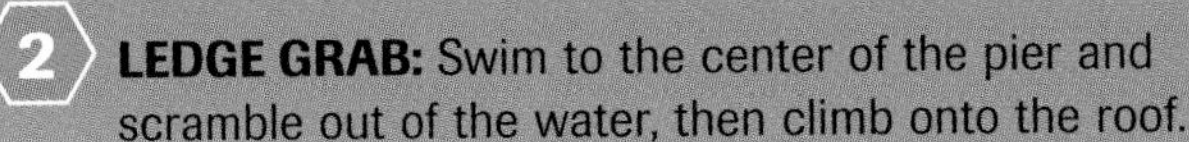

2. **LEDGE GRAB:** Swim to the center of the pier and scramble out of the water, then climb onto the roof.
3. **STEALTH KILL:** Carefully assassinate the sniper just outside the window to gain his rifle.
4. **TARGET:** Shoot the red barrels atop the platform to cause the concrete pipe to break free and crush the nearby enemy.

Activate Cloak, crouch down, and slip out the window while the sniper is facing away. Execute a stealth kill on this nearest of enemies ③ and equip the DSG-1 he drops. Remain on this upper ledge, take cover to the left, and attach the silencer to the DSG-1. Snipe the enemies patrolling the pier to the northwest, including those on the road and below it. Continue sniping as many enemies in the central pier area (particularly on the center dock) as possible, until the DSG-1 is out of ammo. Consider sniping the red drums near the distant concrete pipe to crush the distant enemy and create a diversion ④. There are other explosive barrels in the area that can also be utilized to reduce enemy numbers.

Move to the east side of the upper ledge once done sniping and jump into the river. Swim northward to the floating dock, climb over the wall on the left, then quickly ascend to the upper level of the building on the center dock via the scaffolding ②. Quickly eliminate any remaining enemies then detach either of the HMGs from the roof ①. Carefully cross the dock back to the southwest corner near the APC, gain the road surface via the stairs, and use the HMG to cut a path through all remaining CELL Operators en route to the north. Move slowly, utilize cover, and watch the radar screen for enemy movement. CELL Operators appear both on the road and on the pier directly below. Advance along the road until reaching the toppled big rig, then drop to the pier and continue via the walkway.

SLOW AND STEADY

The section of pier running west to east alongside the warehouse isn't initially free of enemies, but Alcatraz can draw them all out of hiding by taking his time advancing north alongside the freeway. Snipe everyone possible early on, and then methodically sweep the area from south to north with the HMG. It's much easier to deal with all these enemies along the walkway where Alcatraz can avoid being surrounded, and can see them coming.

Ascend the metal stairs at the north end of the pier, then turn and leap over the wall into the weeds to the northwest. Eliminate the lone CELL Operator near the smoldering 18-wheeler to ensure he doesn't open fire from behind. Return to the top of the metal steps and continue eastward towards the crane in the distance.

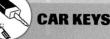

CAR KEYS

This pair of Car Keys is on the ground near the abandoned blue car at the north end of the freeway. They are beside the body beneath the two stop signs.

There are two ways inside the warehouse where Gould's computers are located. Alcatraz can slip under the partially opened bay door on the south side of the building or enter through the door on the east end. The first entrance allows Alcatraz to sneak up behind an enemy for a stealth kill, but this isn't necessary if he's still carrying an HMG. If so, opt for the second entrance (the one nearest the crane) and use Cloak and the HMG to gun down enemies in each hallway. Carefully sweep the building's lower level in a zigzag pattern, moving from room to room.

E-MAIL

The next E-Mail is located in the downstairs office inside the warehouse. This room is between the two entrances on the south side of the warehouse. Download this E-Mail before riding the elevator.

Ride the lift up to the third floor, activate Cloak, and swap out a ranged weapon or pistol in favor of the Marshall near the ammo crates. Enable Cloak and stealthily move to the doorway near the windows; listen and watch carefully. When ready, eliminate the three CELL Operators patrolling the lab to the right. Follow the blue indicator to Gould's primary server and open fire on it.

DEFEAT THE CELL GUNSHIP

A CELL gunship is en route to the warehouse laboratory, along with a large number of CELL Operators. Sprint to the southwest corner of the lab and equip the DSG-1 sniper rifle. The helicopter is going to fly back and forth outside the lab, firing a mounted HMG at Alcatraz through the windows. There are two gunners, one on each side of the chopper. Use Cloak and the DSG-1 to snipe the enemy manning the near-side turret. It may take a couple shots to get the clean kill, but keep at it.

Immediately equip a M17 Frag Grenade as soon as the first gunner has been defeated and rush to the elevator. Toss the grenade through the opening in the doors as the two CELL Operators ascending in the lift come into view. Gather up additional ammo, shoulder the DSG-1 and head back into the lab to take on the enemy manning the chopper's other mounted HMG. The chopper turns around and flies back and forth while facing the other direction, providing Alcatraz with a clean shot of the second gunner. Watch the radar map for additional enemies.

Quickly swap the DSG-1 for a Ranged Scar or Feline and retreat to the room near the elevator. Numerous CELL Operators are about to deploy to the roof of the lab and open fire through the skylights. Use an assault rifle to pick them off while they're on the roof. Play the angles and stay out of the main laboratory area. Some of the CELL Operators eventually rappel down into the lab. Several of those rappelling down have JAW rocket launchers on their backs. Use the assault rifle and Marshall to clear the room—Armor mode certainly comes in handy—then quickly gather up the JAWs.

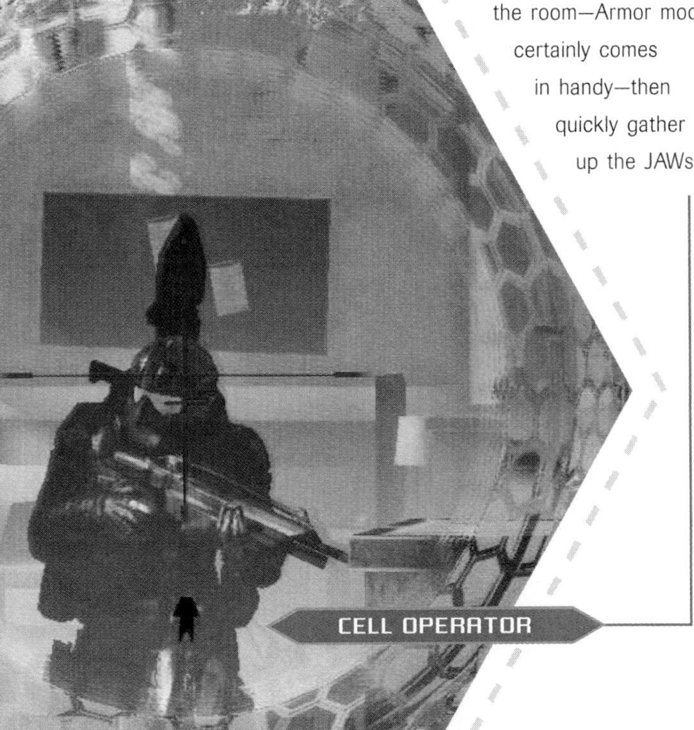

CELL OPERATOR

The gunship makes a third and final appearance after the footsoldiers have been dealt with, and this time it launches rockets! Use Cloak and move into cover near front right-hand corner of the room. Shoulder the JAW, aim, and carefully fire through a window at the chopper. Use Nanovision to see through the smoke and haze if necessary. Nanovision also helps reveal the JAW rocket locations. Quickly back away and activate Armor to avoid any splash-damage from the ensuing crash.

NY SOUVENIR

Drop through the hole left by the fallen helicopter and move about the perimeter of the second-floor room. This NY Souvenir is a model of the NYC skyline within a glass case. It's atop a wooden crate in the southeast corner of the room.

The helicopter's weight collapses the floor in the lab, thereby giving Alcatraz access to the second floor. Drop through the hole in the floor and descend the stairs to the ground floor. Shoot the padlock off the grate under the stairs and drop onto the rocky riverbank beneath the pier. Climb the stairs outside and continue up another flight to the topped crane. Walk along the fallen crane to cross over the gap in the flood gate and continue north along the river.

Activate Cloak and put the Ranged Scar to use in sniping the CELL Operators on the stairs and throughout the plaza in front of the apartment building. Additional foes may approach from the south so keep a low profile and check in all directions before advancing. Power Kick the front doors to the apartment building and head inside. Wait for Gould to send the elevator down, then ride it up to meet him. Follow Gould to his office in room 704 and take a seat in the cradle. From there, walk with him to the larger room next door.

ACHIEVEMENT

False Prophet

Meet up with Gould and allow him to scan the Nanosuit's data, along with Alcatraz's DNA. He quickly discovers the man in the suit is not who he expected and that Prophet is no more.

DOG TAG

Follow Gould to the larger room next door. The Dog Tag is on the bookshelf closest to the window, to the right of the two terrariums and near the telescope.

PROTECT GOULD AND ESCAPE

DEFEAT THE CELL SQUAD

A squad of CELL Operators has tracked Alcatraz to Gould's hideout and has launched an assault. Gould flees via the fire escape; it's up to Alcatraz to eliminate the attackers and escape.

ENCOUNTER B

APARTMENT HALLWAY

1. **STEALTH KILL:** Clear the apartment at the end of the hall once the nearest enemy opens the door.

2. **STEALTH:** Hide out inside the disabled elevator to surprise the CELL Operators approaching.

Either hide in the elevator (2) or advance down the hall towards the door to apartment 701 and stand flat against the wall on the left. The door swings open. Wait behind the door for the enemy to turn around and go back inside (1). Slip out of hiding while Cloaked and stealth kill him. Use the Marshall and clear the apartment of enemies and proceed northward across the apartment to the window near the fire escape. Alcatraz finds his own faster way down to the alley below.

GATE KEEPERS

FINANCIAL DISTRICT, NY
AUGUST 23RD, 12:48 P.M.

COLLECTIBLES

 NY SOUVENIRS **1**

 DOG TAGS **0**

 NY CAR KEYS **1**

 E-MAILS **1**

HOSTILES ENCOUNTERED

CEPH ASSAULT UNIT

CELL OPERATOR

SUGGESTED WEAPONRY

 REFLEX SCARAB

 MARSHALL

 RANGED SCAR

 DSG-1

INFILTRATE THE CELL NANOTECH FACILITY

BREACH THE CELL COMMAND POST

Alcatraz heeds Gould's advice and makes his way onto the rooftops leading across the apartment buildings towards Wall Street. Proceed west across the rooftops, paying no mind to the infected civilians left to eke out an existence while fruitlessly praying for a rescue. Sprint and jump from building to building to avoid falling into the alleys. There are no collectibles in this area, nor are there any threats of which to speak, other than a deadly fall off the side of one of the buildings. Bypass the medical waste and abandoned patio furniture and other detritus and slowly descend from roof to roof along a westerly heading.

RANGED OR REFLEX?

Alcatraz all but trips over the Reflex Scarab and ammo crates near the barbecue area and leaking water tower on one of the early rooftops. Consider swapping the ranged assault rifle for this Reflex Scarab. Alcatraz will face numerous enemies at close to medium range during this mission and the reflex attachment makes aiming much easier, as it enables the weapon to track moving targets.

The path across the buildings curves to the south. Continue until reaching a collapsed brick ledge. Drop to the roof below and continue this series of step-downs from roof to roof until reaching a window washing scaffold. The platform breaks free under Alcatraz's weight and freefalls to the roof above the building's entrance. Don't worry; the Nanosuit will protect him; it helps even more if Armor mode is activated.

CAR KEYS

Descend via the window washing scaffold and immediately turn left and head to the far northern end of the adjacent alley. There is a set of Car Keys on the metal stairs near the door in the far right-hand corner.

There are three Ceph Assault Units on the cross street up ahead. Advance slowly to the south and circle around the left-hand side of the large Echelon Cargo truck. Dive over the dumpster and take aim on the nearest Ceph with the Scarab. Use the cover of the construction scaffolding above the left-hand sidewalk and proceed up Broadway to the west. Switch to the Marshall and finish off the Cephs up close. Chase them inside the shattered storefronts if necessary, but don't let them escape. Collect the Nano Catalyst from each Ceph and consider upgrading the Nanosuit with the Mobility Enhance upgrade.

The CELL that were firing on the Ceph have established a sizable roadblock at the intersection up ahead. Duck into the loading bay on the left side of the street to replenish ammunition and to scope out the enemy position.

A SOUTHERLY DIVERSION

Slip through the narrow hallway leading from the loading dock to the side-street farther west and pinpoint the lone CELL Operator to the left. Use Cloak and shoot or stealth kill this enemy here then toss a grenade at the others to the right before slipping back the way you came.

CIRCUMVENT THE PERIMETER BARRICADE

All roads leading to the CELL facility have been blocked; Alcatraz must make his way through one of the nearby buildings. He must first eliminate the threat at the checkpoint. Activate Cloak and sprint across the street to the convenience mart and enter through the doors on the right. Take cover behind the shelves at the rear of the store, ready a grenade, and watch the radar screen to see if any CELL Operators are in pursuit. If so, draw them into the narrow aisles of the shop and lob a grenade at them; opportunities like this are ideal for unlocking the "Blast Radius" Achievement/Trophy.

Advance to the store's counter, activate Cloak, and equip the laser sight to the Scarab. Take aim on the gunner manning the turret atop the APC in the center of the intersection. The laser sight makes pinpoint aiming at long range much easier than with the reflex sight. Exit the shop to the south and flank the CELL Operators near the mounted HMG at the roadblock, then open fire.

Cross the street and enter the building on the southwest corner. Head up the stairs to the second floor hallway and leap out of the bombed-out room to the rubble-filled plaza below. Ascend the stairs, pass the park benches, and angle for the stairs in the far left corner.

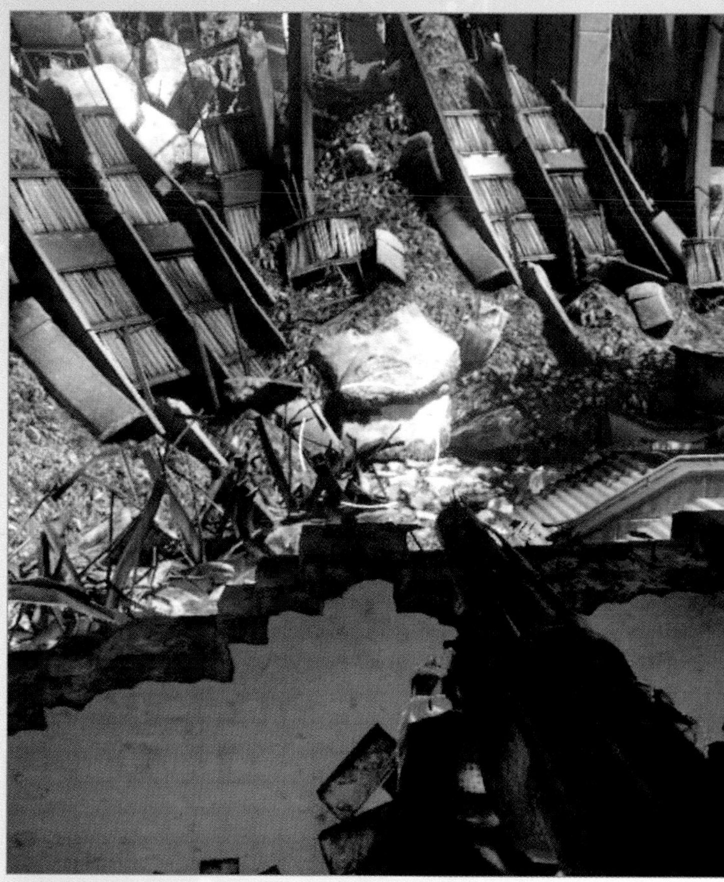

EASTER EGG!

There are three Easter eggs in the grass atop the stairs—literally. Just thought you might want to know. Carry on...

CREATE A DIVERSION FOR GOULD

DETONATE THE AMMO DUMP

Proceed northward slowly while Cloaked, as there may be a CELL Operator on this rooftop plaza. If so, kill him and take his JAW. Crouch down to avoid detection and use the visor to survey the situation in and around the churchyard across the street. Alcatraz must light fuses within two separate ammo dumps to successfully generate the diversion Gould seeks. One ammo dump is straight ahead, in the Command and Control Center to the east of the church while the other is to the west, in the churchyard.

ENCOUNTER A

COMMAND AND CONTROL CENTER

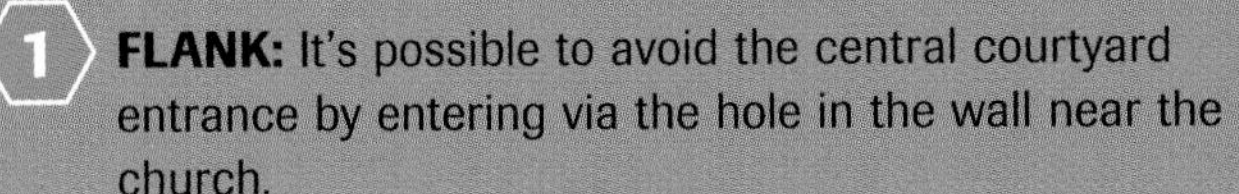

1 **FLANK:** It's possible to avoid the central courtyard entrance by entering via the hole in the wall near the church.

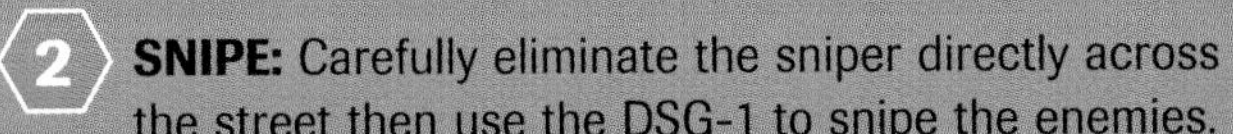

2 **SNIPE:** Carefully eliminate the sniper directly across the street then use the DSG-1 to snipe the enemies.

Equip the Scarab with the laser sight and silencer, activate Cloak, and take out the sniper across the street ②. Alcatraz has multiple options at this time. One option is to cross to the sniper's position via the awning and ramps, lay claim to the fallen DSG-1, and set about sniping as many CELL Operators as possible from the relative safety of the dilapidated office overlooking the command center. This can be an effective—and fun—way to handle the crowd of enemies, but it certainly draws attention to Alcatraz's position.

Another option is to drop to the street, use Cloak, and stealthily pick off the enemies at close range with the help of a silencer-equipped Scarab and stealth kills. Clear the street of enemies by moving between the trailers then infiltrate the main control area, beyond the black tractor trailer. Flank around the main entrance via the hole in the wall where the CELL truck had crashed ①. Either way, make your way inside the green fenced area where the ammo dump is and light the fuse on the explosive canister. Activate Armor mode, and dash back towards the cover of the trailers and mobile offices for cover. Methodically sweep across the compound towards the church, blasting away any CELL Operators with the Marshall. Use the JAW to destroy the vehicle that enters the area.

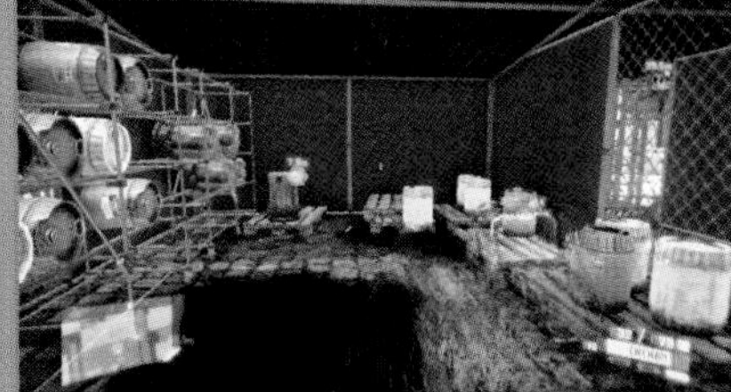

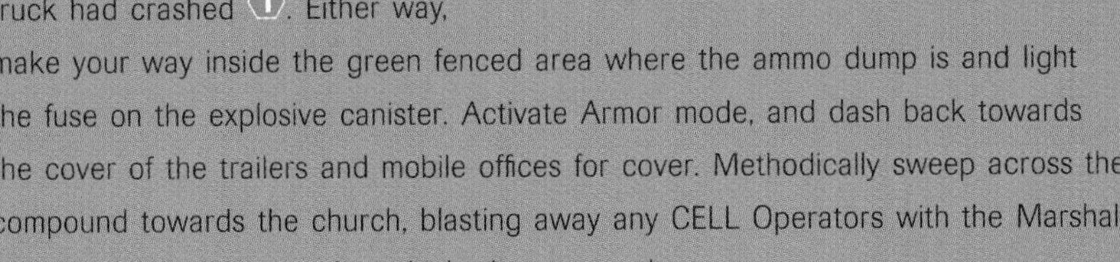

Head west towards the main church archway leading from the initial grave area to the other. Take cover amongst the cardboard boxes and missing people posters and snipe any CELL Operators in the vicinity. Shoot the gunman in the top of the central tomb and collect the ammo and JAW in the base of that structure. Light the fuse of the canister in the second fuel dump and make a run for it.

ALTERNATE TACTIC

THE REAR ASSAULT

The tactics outlined previously for Encounter A describe a relatively head-on approach to this situation. Another option is to eliminate the sniper then stealthily run past the churchyard to the west; turn right at the corner, and circle around the entire city block to the north. Leap from the bus stop onto the CELL perimeter wall, gun down the enemies in the street, and infiltrate the Command and Control Center from the less-guarded north side. Note the electrified gate near the rear of the church. This is the gate that must be powered down to gain access to the secret passage of which Gould spoke.

NY SOUVENIR

There is a small model statue of the cathedral sitting atop the cardboard boxes of medical supplies piled in front of the main church entrance. The NY Souvenir is on the right, as viewed while facing the front doors of the church.

E-MAIL

The final collectible on this mission is located inside the orange command and control trailer on the northeast side of the churchyard. Collect this E-mail when cutting the power to the electrified gate leading to the secret tunnel.

INFILTRATE THE CELL FACILITY AT WALL STREET

UNLOCK THE ESCAPE TUNNEL

Activate Cloak and make your way northward around the church to the top of the large barricade blocking the street. Drop into the street behind the church and head east down the road, past the electrified gate on the right, and up the stairs to where the first ammo dump was located. Have the Marshall ready and blast a path through any CELL Operator that get between Alcatraz and the orange trailer housing the control panel for the electrified gate.

ENTER EVAC TUNNEL UNDER CHURCH

Exit the trailer and descend the stairs leading back to the street behind the church. Expect to encounter moderate to heavy resistance depending on how many CELL Operators were previously dealt with. Sprint westward along the sidewalk to the gated area beneath the very rear of the church. Push the gate open and enter the secret tunnel.

HEAD TO THE WALL STREET FACILITY

Descend into the catacombs and proceed past the graves of the cathedral's famous priests and cardinals. Alcatraz may see or hear a Ceph Assault Unit, but it's uncatchable—at least for now. Continue farther into the darkness.

DEAD MAN WALKING

WALL STREET | FINANCIAL DISTRICT, NY | AUGUST 23RD, 2:32 P.M.

COLLECTIBLES

NY SOUVENIRS 1

DOG TAGS 1

NY CAR KEYS 1

E-MAILS 1

HOSTILES ENCOUNTERED

CELL OPERATOR

CEPH COMBAT UNIT

SUGGESTED WEAPONRY

STEALTH SCARAB

DSG-1

SPEC OPS SCARAB

JAW

LOCATE THE NANOSUIT DEEP SCAN CRADLE

▶ FIND A WAY INTO THE CELL FACILITY

Gould believes that Alcatraz can enter the CELL facility via a locked entrance on the roof across the street to the southwest. The Financial District is crawling with all manner of CELL Operators, both on the street and along the rooftops. The only way to access the roof (and the entrance) is to stay high and use the skybridge.

ENCOUNTER A

WALL STREET INTERSECTION

1. **RESUPPLY:** The rooftop café contains numerous ammo crates and a sizeable weapons stash.
2. **INFILTRATE:** Use the skybridge to cross the street to the café where the CELL entrance is.
3. **ENTER:** Alcatraz can reenter the building with the skybridge from a door on the street to the south.
4. **SNIPE:** Eliminate the sniper on the nearby building; use his DSG-1 to pick off the CELL defense force.

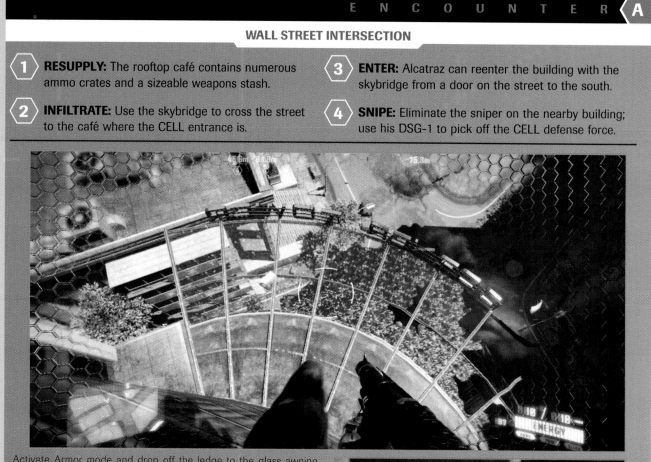

Activate Armor mode and drop off the ledge to the glass awning below; Armor mode is necessary to survive the impact. Aim to stay close to the building and land on the portion overlapping the concrete ledge below the glass, otherwise Alcatraz may fall through the glass to the street. Use the Scarab to pick off any CELL Operators on the adjacent building, then take a running leap from the balcony to the roof where the sniper surveys the area (4).

Clear the roof of enemies and put the DSG-1 to use against the enemies on the street below and near the rooftop café to the west. Most importantly, eliminate any and all CELL Operators manning mounted HMGs, both on the rooftops and atop the APC in the street. There is plenty of available DSG-1 ammo in the crates near the breach in the wall overlooking the intersection. Fire a shot and quickly duck behind the wall to the right to allow the Energy Meter to replenish. Activate Cloak and take another shot. Scan for the telltale laser sights that betray the enemies' positions.

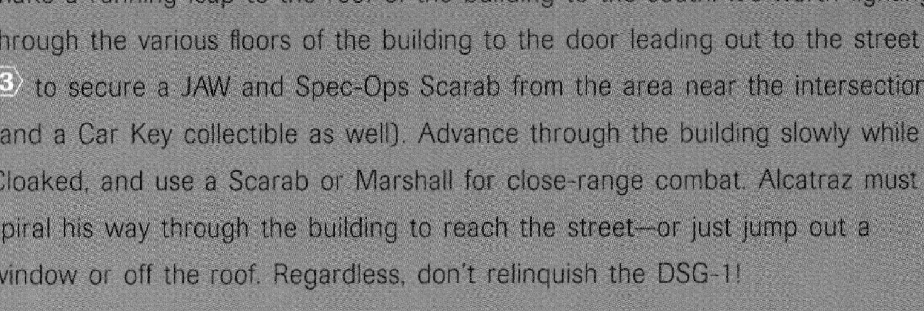

Make a running leap to the roof of the building to the south. It's worth fighting through the various floors of the building to the door leading out to the street ③ to secure a JAW and Spec-Ops Scarab from the area near the intersection (and a Car Key collectible as well). Advance through the building slowly while Cloaked, and use a Scarab or Marshall for close-range combat. Alcatraz must spiral his way through the building to reach the street—or just jump out a window or off the roof. Regardless, don't relinquish the DSG-1!

Return to the rooftop near the skybridge entrance, shoulder the sniper rifle, and slowly approach the bridge ②. Use Cloak to avoid detection and eliminate the two CELL Operators in the enclosed bridge then turn and fire on the reinforcements that have taken up position on the rooftop café to the west ①. Quickly eliminate the enemies using the mounted HMG, and beware the occasional enemy with the JAW. Listen for the radio communications signaling the arrival of a CELL Gunship. Switch to the JAW, activate Cloak, and blast the whirlybird out of the air.

JAWS OF DEATH

Check your supply of ammo for the JAW at the start of the mission. It's worth descending to the street after clearing the area of CELL Operators from long range. This presents the opportunity to locate the JAW behind the jersey barriers in the northeast corner, near the ammo crates.

CAR KEYS

This mission contains one of each type of collectible and the Car Keys are by far the easiest to miss. Descend to the street surface and head west past the intersection to the end of the road opposite the starting point. The Car Keys are on a planter beside a small stuffed bear.

SPEC OPS SCARAB

The Spec Ops Scarab contains an under-barrel attachment that allows Alcatraz to fire light shotgun shells. This ammo is rare, so don't waste it. The ability to toggle between full-auto machinegun fire and shotgun blasts makes the Spec Ops Scarab the equivalent of having two weapons in one. It can be found near the ammo crates on the street below the building where Alcatraz began this mission.

BLAST OPEN THE SECURITY DOORS

The doors leading into the facility are locked tight, but Alcatraz can blast them open with the JAW or, preferably, with C4. There is C4 available at the ammo dump at the southern end of the cross street (beneath the skybridge), but Alcatraz should have some remaining from the Road Rage mission. Otherwise, just stand back and use the JAW to blast the doors open.

ACCESS THE SECURITY TERMINAL

Descend the steps into the bank, activate Cloak, and eliminate the three CELL Operators patrolling the lobby around the corner. Use the Spec Ops Scarab's machinegun mode to eliminate the first two, then switch to shotgun mode and take out the third in the office up ahead.

Locate the control panel behind the desk in the security office and press the button to call the elevator. The elevator door opens across the hall.

NY SOUVENIR

The next NY Souvenir is a model of the city's iconic hot dog carts. It's on the end of the counter in the security office. Collect it before boarding the elevator.

E-MAIL

The E-Mail tablet is on the security counter, next to the computer monitor. Download the E-Mail before boarding the elevator—it's right near the button that controls the elevator.

LOCATE GOULD

DOG TAG

The Dog Tag is on the floor just outside the elevator on the floor with the vaults. Leap over the red velvet ropes to the left to pick it up out of the open deposit box.

Ride the elevator down to the vault and head down the hall and around the corner to meet up with Gould. Follow him to the Deep Scan Cradle and heed his instructions.

ACHIEVEMENT

Internal Affairs

This bonus unlocks upon reaching the vaults deep within the bank. Blast the doors on the roof open, access the security terminal to call for the elevator, and ride it down to meet up with Gould and unlock this Achievement/Trophy.

FATAL: 0XA0907000DF

Alcatraz suffered a near-catastrophic system failure, but using his on-suit defibrillator, he was able to escape death. The Nanosuit, however, is still in need of a successful system reboot. Multiple Ceph Combat Units have just wiped out a squad of CELL Operators and now they're coming for Alcatraz—as is the spreading disease emanating the alien ark that sprang from underground. Use whatever weaponry Alcatraz was able to get his hands on and take on the nearest Ceph. Use Armor mode and available cover to blast them with a shotgun if possible. Otherwise, hang back and target their gelatinous tissue with an assault rifle. Collect the Nano Catalysts they drop quickly, there isn't much time.

ESCAPE THE ALIEN SPORE

The disease is spreading quickly. Watch the incoming pod crash land in the middle of the street and rush to it. A never-before-seen variety of Ceph approaches quickly. It's too much for Alcatraz to deal with in his current state. Fortunately, the Ceph aren't interested in the suit, or so it seems. They simply want to exterminate life. Alcatraz's failure to continue fighting may be what saves his own life.

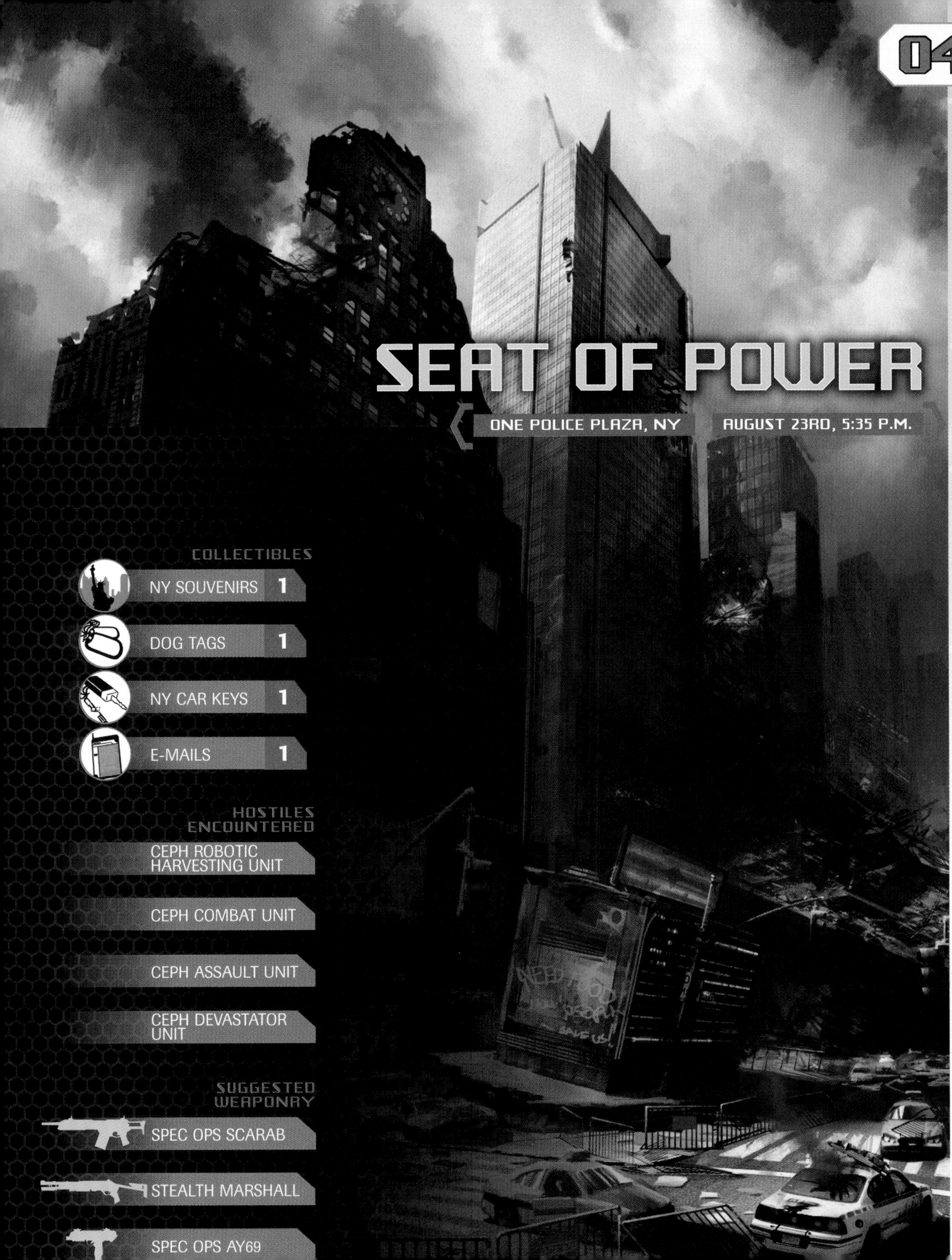

SEAT OF POWER

ONE POLICE PLAZA, NY | AUGUST 23RD, 5:35 P.M.

COLLECTIBLES

 NY SOUVENIRS 1

 DOG TAGS 1

 NY CAR KEYS 1

 E-MAILS 1

HOSTILES ENCOUNTERED

- CEPH ROBOTIC HARVESTING UNIT
- CEPH COMBAT UNIT
- CEPH ASSAULT UNIT
- CEPH DEVASTATOR UNIT

SUGGESTED WEAPONRY

 SPEC OPS SCARAB

 STEALTH MARSHALL

 SPEC OPS AY69

Left for dead by the Ceph, Alcatraz eventually awakens in a forsaken portion of the city. Hargreave has assumed the supporting role formerly held by Gould and is bent on earning Alcatraz's trust, regardless of what Gould may have said about him. Alcatraz isn't alone, however. The Ceph deploy an army of tiny Robotic Harvesting Units to clean up after the disease. These tiny alien insects essentially suck the decaying human corpses dry, leaving nothing to waste, and scamper about the area in droves.

Kill as many of the Robotic Harvesting Units as deemed satisfactory, either by shooting them or by squashing them underfoot. Each one yields 20 Nano Catalyst. Continue east through the trench of collapsed street and ruptured utility pipes. There aren't any enemies to worry about, nor are there any collectibles in this area so feel free to double-time it. The road bends back and forth, but there's only one way to go. Follow it off the ledge just before the sealed-off tunnel entrance.

LOCATE HIVE ENTRANCE

MAKE YOUR WAY THROUGH THE PLAZA

Turn to the right and head north along the street and the small park-like courtyard beside it. There are multiple Robotic Harvesting Units near the small fountain from which to collect more Nano Catalyst. Enter the pedestrian tunnel under the "Evacuation Post C1" sign to continue west.

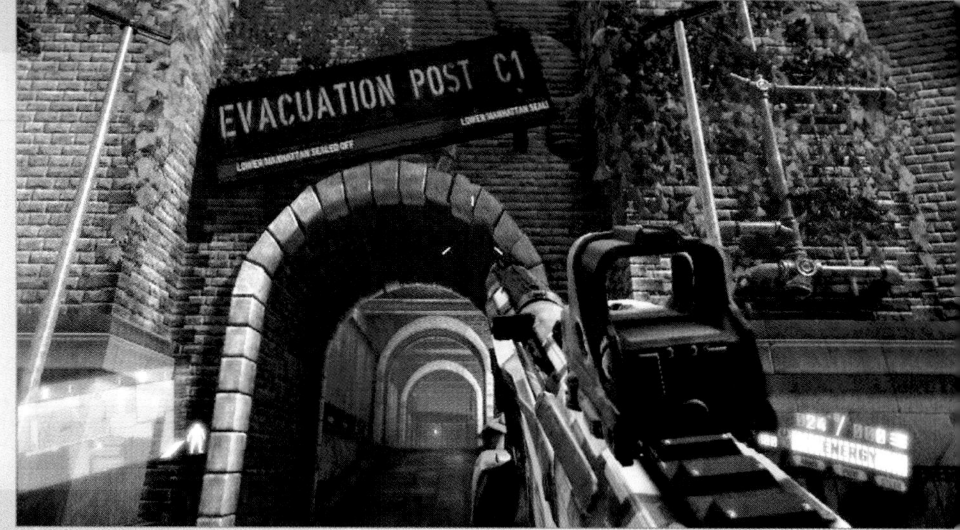

It's extremely dark inside the evacuation post and the majority of the inhabitants are piled up within body bags. Activate Nanovision to increase visibility and leap onto the platform above the gated entryway. Ignore the suffering infected civilians and meander through the evacuation post in a southerly direction. The route is limited to a single path that winds through temporary emergency response structures. It's a wretched sight and Alcatraz lowers his weapon in reverence to those still struggling to survive this calamity.

DOG TAG

Follow the path through the showers to where the main walkway turns hard to the right, at the southeastern corner of the evacuation post. Enter the structure straight ahead at the turn—the one with the hundreds of body bags and twin fluorescent lights. There is a Dog Tag on the table to the right. Use Nanovision to spot it.

Continue through the camp to the stairs in the far corner of the area and drop off the western end of the catwalk. Cross the empty plaza towards the police headquarters building in the distance and head inside. If still carrying a DSG-1 from the previous mission (or other atypical weapon), swap it for the Marshall lying on the counter. Ascend the stairs, turn left at the top, and proceed through the offices and down the hall to the northwest. Take some time to squash as many Robotic Harvesting Units as possible to collect more Nano Particles.

EMAIL

The E-Mail tablet is sitting on the reception desk just inside the main entrance to the building beyond the evacuation post. Alcatraz won't be coming through here again, so download it now.

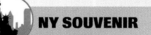

NY SOUVENIR

Look for the souvenir model of the NYC City Hall on the table to the left. It's in the middle office along the western side of the building (where many of the Ceph Robotic Harvesting Units are located).

Load up on grenades and ammo at the end of the hall and ascend the stairs to the third floor. Alcatraz must now reach the fifth floor. There is a small atrium-like area in the center of the building with wraparound balconies on the fourth and fifth floors. Head west past the statue in the center on the third floor and climb the stairs all the way to the fifth floor (there is nothing of note on the fourth floor). Power Kick the door near the ammo crates and swap the Marshall for the Stealth Marshall just on the other side of the doorway.

SPEC OPS AY69

Alcatraz can pick up this fully-automatic pistol atop the ammo crate beneath the stairs on the third floor. This weapon comes attached with an extended clip and reflex sight. It can be tough to aim as the recoil is significant, but its rate of fire and mobility are exceptional.

FASTER. HIGHER. STRONGER.

Looking for a place to check out just how far and high Alcatraz can jump? If so, exit the stairwell on the fourth floor and take a sprinting run towards the gap in the railing in the center of the atrium. Leap high and aim for the break in the railing on the fifth floor. Alcatraz

can soar across the gap, grab hold of the fifth floor ledge, and hoist himself up all in one swift motion. Impressive!

BREAK THROUGH INTO CITY HALL

ENCOUNTER A

CROSSING THE PLAZA

1 **LEDGE GRAB:** Leap up to the walkway above the graffiti to gain some additional ammo and flank the enemy.

2 **OBSERVE:** Crouch on the skybridge to survey the situation. Cephs are directly below and to the south.

The area leading to City Hall is crawling with Ceph Assault and Combat Units. Activate Cloak and move onto the skybridge to scan the area (2). Both varieties of Ceph in this area can be dropped with a single well-placed shotgun blast—two at the most. Use Cloak and the Stealth Marshall to avoid detection and begin a sweep of the area from the northern end of the plaza. Drop off the left side of the skybridge (or use the stairs before the bridge) and blast the two nearest Ceph. These enemies are aware of Alcatraz's presence and they pack a punch; don't hesitate to activate Armor mode if they start firing!

Duck into corners and behind planters to allow the Energy Meter to replenish before reactivating Cloak to advance. Don't fire on the Robotic Harvesting Units—squash them if the opportunity presents itself—and focus on the main threats. Collect the additional shotgun shells from the ammo crates scattered throughout the area surrounding the Ceph pods and statues.

Clamber up to the elevated walkway via the ledge near the coffee billboard ⟨1⟩. Use cover and clear out the Cephs on the arched bridge spanning the plaza. Look for opportunities to execute a stealth kill on a Ceph by keeping a low profile and circling around to its blindside at a wide radius. Descend the stairs in the corner and continue south through the evacuation checkpoint. Eliminate the other Cephs in this area and angle to the left to cut through the openings in the earthquake-ravaged City Hall.

LOOKING FOR AN HMG?

There's a mounted HMG atop the checkpoint just north of the main fountain. The raps leading up to it are pretty steep, but Alcatraz can make the climb without trouble. Rip the HMG free if you'd like to try it out on some Cephs. We prefer the Marshall, but feel free to experiment!

Take a moment to purchase a new Nanosuit Module—Covert Ops for example—once inside the building. Equip the Spec Ops Scarab near the ammo crates to complement the Stealth Marshall and load up on grenades and ammo before continuing.

HARGREAVE

The Ceph have inflicted considerable damage to the area around City Hall. Hargreave directs Alcatraz to advance on anything resembling a silo or tower, of alien construction obviously. Arcing tentacles of alien origin spread throughout the area. Alcatraz can run atop these lengthy structures, but will likely fall off at an inopportune time. Best to stick to the ground.

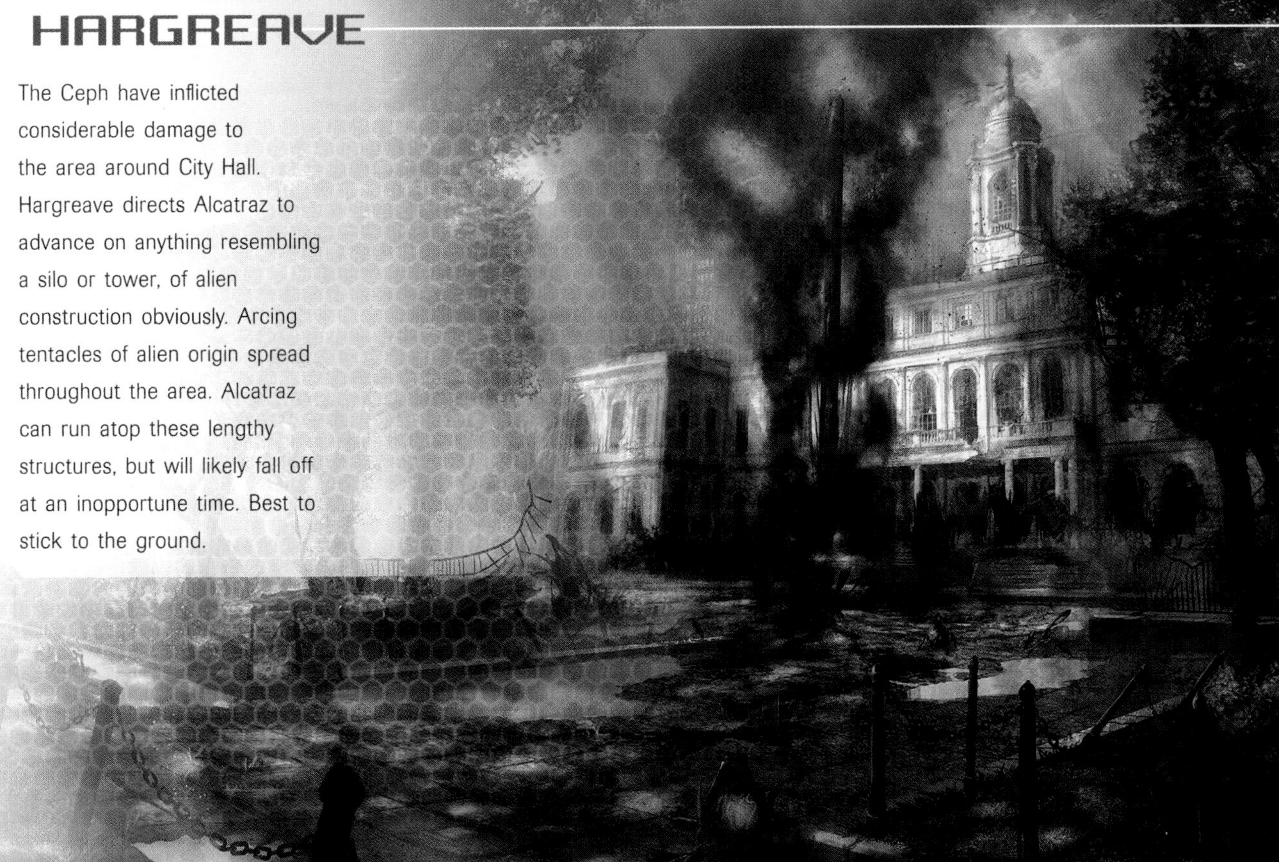

ACCESS HIVE CORE ENTRANCE

INFILTRATE THE ALIEN STRUCTURE

ENCOUNTER B

FIGHTING CITY HALL

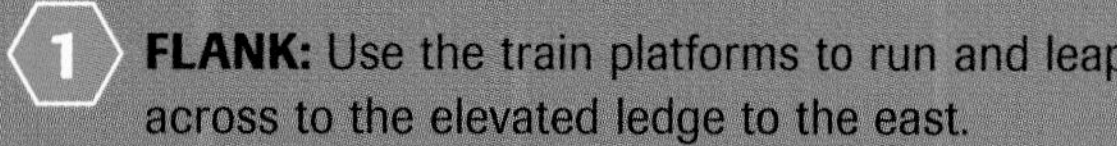

1 **FLANK:** Use the train platforms to run and leap across to the elevated ledge to the east.

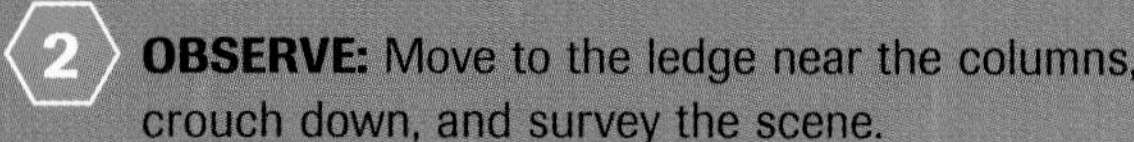

2 **OBSERVE:** Move to the ledge near the columns, crouch down, and survey the scene.

Crouch near the ledge overlooking the area (2) and scout an approach to the near-side train platform. The majority of the visible Ceph are far off in the distance, but they will attack quickly if they detect an intruder this close to the hive. Stealth is a must! Drop off the ledge and ascend the stairs to the near-side train platform. From there, Alcatraz can run and leap across to the second platform. Move quietly to the edge of the tracks and use the Spec Ops Scarab to silently gun down one or two Cephs on the ground below. Run and leap to the rocky ledge to the southeast to continue a perimeter flanking of the enemy (1).

Advance through the park slowly, using the Stealth Marshall and the large alien blast shields to minimize exposure. It's going to be extremely hard to avoid detection as Alcatraz advances southward so be ready to activate Armor mode when necessary. Don't hesitate to fall back to the north side of a sandwich shop or other cover and allow the Energy Meter to recharge. Wait for the Cephs to approach then lob a grenade or two at them when they do.

The Cephs primarily fire machinegun rounds at Alcatraz, but some charge energy blasts. Look for the glowing projectile being readied and quickly dash out of the way either by leaping for cover or by running and sliding out of the shot's path. Collect the Nano Catalysts from each victim and continue past the circular fountain in the center of the park. The area should be relatively free and clear of Cephs by that point.

CAR KEY

Climb the stairs to the train platform nearest the entry point to this area. Run and leap across the gap in the tracks to the other platform and approach the corpse on the bench. The Car Key is on the seat to the left of the corpse.

Angle to the west from the fountain and ascend the steeply slanted road surface. Enter the trailer at the top of the hill and stock up on munitions and, most importantly, C4. Having C4 on hand will greatly simplify what would otherwise be an awfully tough battle against a Ceph Devastator Unit.

Round the corner to the main drive paralleling the front of the mansion and crouch down, activate Cloak, and stealthily head for the ammo crates near the barriers to the east. The area contains several Ceph Combat Units as well as the aforementioned Ceph Devastator Unit. This massive alien has extremely thick armor and very potent weaponry (heavy machine guns and rocketry), befitting its size. Work quickly to eliminate the nearest Ceph Combat Units then lay down some C4 on the floor near the ammo crates. Use the Spec Ops Scarab to get the Devastator Units attention and lure it down the road towards Alcatraz's position. Round the corner and advance partially up the narrow path between the edge and the barrier. Detonate the C4 as soon as the Devastator Unit gets near it. A dead Devastator Unit yields 500 Nano Catalyst!

CEPH DEVASTATOR UNIT

Proceed to the far end of the road, near the burning car and ruptured gas lines, and cross over the exposed pipes to the tunnel in the rock. The pipe leads Alcatraz into the subway system and, from there, to the hive.

DARK HEART

COLLECTIBLES

Collectible	Count
 NY SOUVENIRS	1
 DOG TAGS	 2
 NY CAR KEYS	 0
 E-MAILS	0

HOSTILES ENCOUNTERED

- CEPH ROBOTIC HARVESTING UNIT
- CEPH COMBAT UNIT
- CEPH ASSAULT UNIT
- CEPH DEVASTATOR UNIT
- CEPH COMBAT COMMAND UNIT

SUGGESTED WEAPONRY

- STEALTH MARSHALL
- MK.60 MOD 0
-  DSG-1
-  X-43 MIKE

ASSAULT THE HIVE CORE

LOCATE REEVES AND HIS TEAM

Alcatraz exits the pipe in the heavily compromised subway tunnel, along the City Hall branch. This portion of the tunnel is devoid of Cephs, save for a few scavenging Robotic Harvester Units. Follow the tracks north around the abandoned train cars and through the partially-flooded craters. A small tremor causes some damage beyond the merger; avoid open flames or electrified water. Enable Nanovision when Alcatraz approaches the track merge, as visibility diminishes substantially after the explosions.

One of Reeves's men is not far ahead, and he's about to be attacked by a Ceph. Have the Marshall on hand and finish what the marine started. Additional Ceph Assault Units approach from the north. Draw them toward the columns near where the marine had fallen and fight them there; don't let the fight against them bleed into the following encounter.

ENCOUNTER A

SUBWAY TUNNELS

1. **EXPLORE:** Sneak into the maintenance corridor on the west side of the tunnel to secure the MK.60 machinegun.
2. **LEDGE GRAB:** Leap and grab the catwalk above the red lights to get up above the Cephs.
3. **OBSERVE:** Acquire the JAW on the elevated catwalk and scan the area for fuel drums and enemies.

Eliminate the Ceph Combat Unit approaching alongside the train car then head to the left and enter the maintenance tunnel (1). Head to the far end of the tunnel and swap the current assault rifle for the MK.60 Mod 0 leaning against the wall. This weapon has an extremely large-capacity magazine (100 rounds), but takes longer to reload. Return to the main subway tunnel while Cloaked and stealth kill the two Cephs that have approached. Save the MK.60 for later.

Jump onto the subway car in the center of the tunnel and, from there, leap up to the catwalk above the tracks (2). Collect the JAW from this location and advance to the far end of the catwalk. Use the visor to study the enemy positions below (3). There are several Cephs milling around, many of which happen to be precariously close to highly explosive fuel barrels. Target them with the visor to avoid losing track as they flee, then activate Cloak and leap into action. Switch to the MK.60 and put a round or two into each of the fuel drums to damage or kill the nearby Cephs. Round the corner to the right and proceed to the door at the end of the tunnel.

DOG TAG

Enter the maintenance corridor on the east side of the subway tunnel, opposite from where the MK.60 was. Proceed north, to the end of the hallway, and locate the Dog Tag on the ground near the dead marine.

Open the door at the northern end of the tunnel, beyond the Cephs and continue past the struggling civilians and the room with the radio to the upper landing. Crouch beneath the pipes (there is a DSG-1 on the right) and round the corner towards the magnified shadow of the Robotic Harvesting Unit. Collect the C4 on the floor to the left and exit via the green door. Follow the tunnel branching eastward to the station ahead.

NY SOUVENIR

Don't exit through that green door just yet! Turn around to find ammo crates, C4, and a model of a subway train car. It's lying near some corpses in the back corner of a forgotten maintenance room. It has a bright pinkish glow to it and is directly opposite the green door leading out of this area.

DESTROY THE SPORE CONDUIT

ACCESS THE SPORE SILO

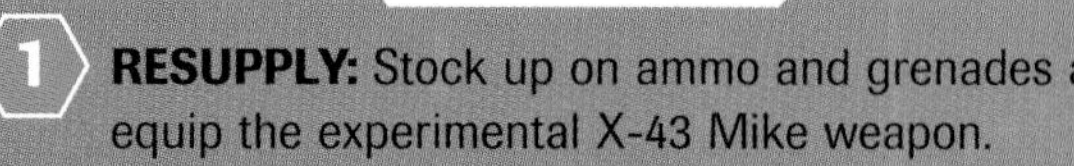

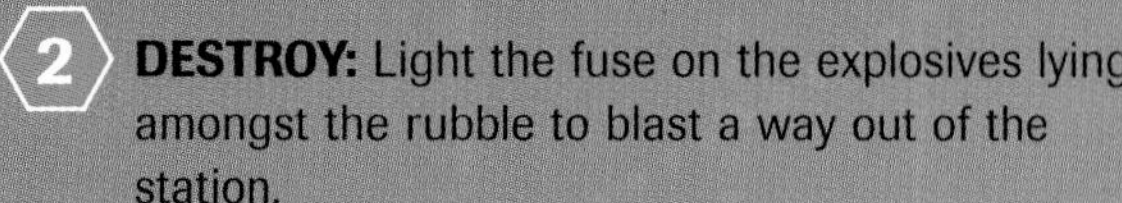

1. **RESUPPLY:** Stock up on ammo and grenades and equip the experimental X-43 Mike weapon.
2. **DESTROY:** Light the fuse on the explosives lying amongst the rubble to blast a way out of the station.
3. **LEDGE GRAB:** Climb onto the red scaffolding at the start of the subway platform to find a Dog Tag.

Step off the tracks onto the station platform and leap up to the red scaffolding to find this mission's final collectible and a DSG-1 (3). Equip the Marshall and advance across the station to the ammo dump where Alcatraz can load up on grenades and all manner of ammunition (1). Swap the Marshall for the X-43 Mike lying on the ground near the ammo crates. This high-tech weapon emits a beam of weaponized microwaves that cause the jelly-filled Cephs to explode (the X-43 Mike is most effective at short-range).

Try out the X-43 Mike on one of the Robotic Harvesting Units ahead, but don't waste too much ammo on them; battery units for the X-43 Mike are in short supply! Squash those buggers instead!

Approach the end of the subway station where wreckage and debris have blocked access to the rest of the tunnel. Light the fuse on the explosive canister and quickly run for cover. Use the Nanosuit's Armor mode for additional protection and watch as the obstruction is vaporized. Take a moment to collect the C4 from the ammo crates near the aging corpse of the Ceph Devastator Unit.

DOG TAG

This second Dog Tag is atop the red scaffolding, near the body of a fallen marine. Leap and grab onto the scaffolding at the west end of the subway station to find it.

Proceed to the end of the train tunnel, then slip through the red-lit utility pipe angling northward to another section of track. Descend the sloping surface past the rubble to the beginning of a large crater. Alcatraz is nearing the hive; he must now identify and exploit the spore conduit's weakness.

INTERFACE WITH THE SPORE VEINS

ENCOUNTER C

FIRST VEIN

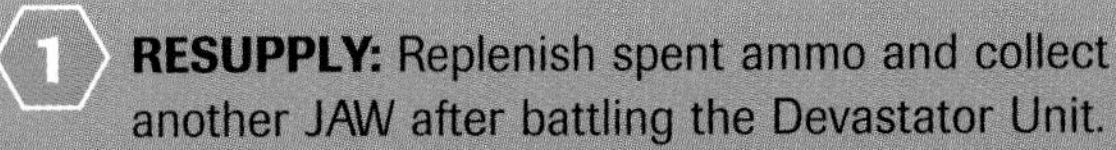

1 **RESUPPLY:** Replenish spent ammo and collect another JAW after battling the Devastator Unit.

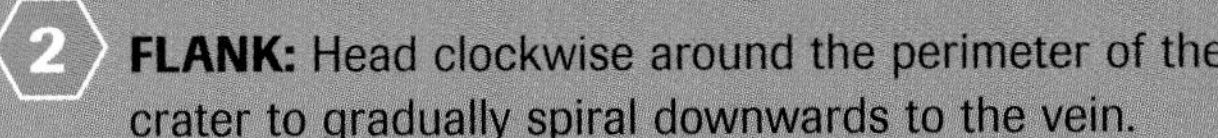

2 **FLANK:** Head clockwise around the perimeter of the crater to gradually spiral downwards to the vein.

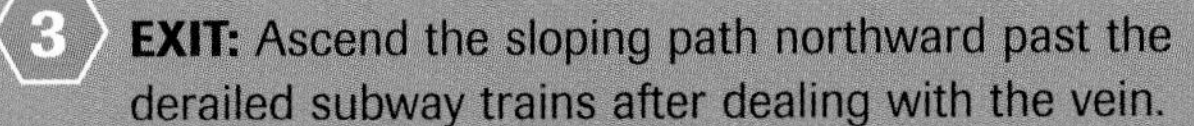

3 **EXIT:** Ascend the sloping path northward past the derailed subway trains after dealing with the vein.

Survey the situation from the ledge near the burned-out vehicle then begin a gradual descent along the perimeter in a clockwise direction ②. Move while Cloaked and keep an eye out for the lone Ceph Combat Unit in the area. Alcatraz may have an opportunity to stealthily kill it inside the sewer pipe; otherwise, try to slip past it while Cloaked. Continue past the storage container and off the ledge above the vein.

The vein is guarded by a Ceph Devastator Unit and though the MK.60 might seem like a good weapon to use against it, it's not nearly as effective as two sticks of C4. Stealth kill any lesser Cephs in the immediate area then activate Cloak and sneak into the watery area near the Devastator Unit. Place the C4 down then de-Cloak to get its attention. Lead it to the C4 and detonate it. Equip the X-43 Mike and deal with the other Cephs that come to investigate the explosion.

Take a brief detour to the east to resupply and gain another rocket for the JAW ①. Alcatraz can find the munitions inside the breached storage container at the bottom of the crater. Return to the spore vein and follow the on-screen prompts to have Alcatraz punch through its casing and damage it. Vacate the area via the sloping path to the north ③. Continue through the abandoned train cars, duck under the wreckage, and push on to the area containing the second vein.

SAVING THAT NANO

Alcatraz is going to earn plenty of Nano Catalyst during this mission, more than enough to buy some of the second- or even third-tier Nanosuit upgrades. We recommend continuing to save the Nano Catalyst for the Nano Recharge upgrade (8000). It's expensive, but it's extremely helpful for those who find themselves using Cloak and Armor nearly every step of the way.

ENCOUNTER D

SECOND VEIN

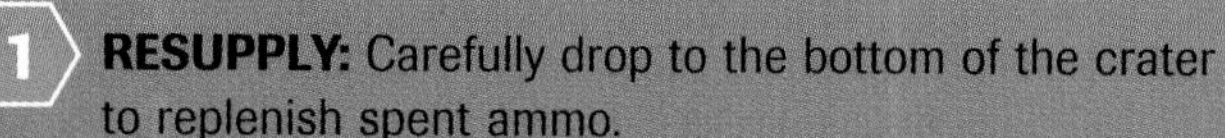

1 **RESUPPLY:** Carefully drop to the bottom of the crater to replenish spent ammo.

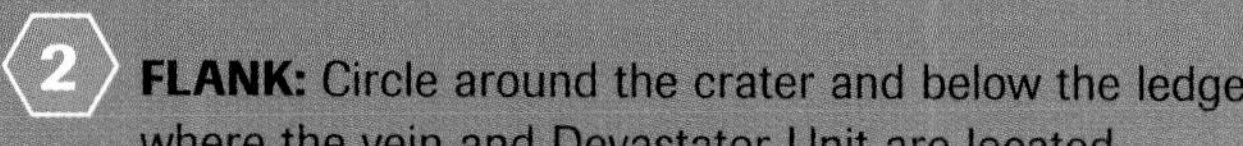

2 **FLANK:** Circle around the crater and below the ledge where the vein and Devastator Unit are located.

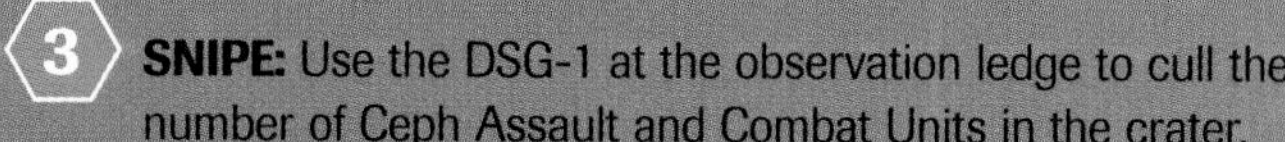

3 **SNIPE:** Use the DSG-1 at the observation ledge to cull the number of Ceph Assault and Combat Units in the crater.

4 **ASCEND:** Run along the vein's metal-plated exterior to reach the upper ledge and escape the crater.

5 **NEUTRALIZE:** Use the JAW rockets found earlier to destroy the Devastator Unit guarding the vein.

Temporarily swap out one of Alcatraz's weapons for the DSG-1 lying near the ammo crate and use the sniper to begin clearing the area of Ceph Assault and Combat Units (3). Use the visor to pinpoint their locations and highlight them to make it easier to spot them in the distance. There are Cephs directly below this vantage point, along the path leading around the tentacle-like structures, and on the distant upper ledge to the west. Line up the shot, stabilize the weapon, and blast their heads off. Alcatraz can decapitate each Ceph with a single sniper round, provided the silencer is not equipped.

Discard the DSG-1 and drop off the ledge to the road below and head northwest around the washout (2). Crawl through the angled train car to regain the road and carefully drop into the crater to resupply and eliminate any stray Cephs that are still patrolling the area. The ammo dump (1) also contains two JAW rockets; don't bypass this supply point if Alcatraz isn't already carrying at least three. Climb the rocks to return to the road.

Shoulder the JAW, activate Cloak and line up a shot on the Devastator Unit near the vein (5). It's going to take three hits with the JAW to defeat it. Activate Armor mode as soon as the Devastator returns fire and take cover behind the car while Alcatraz reloads the JAW. Repeat this tactic until the Devastator Unit has been defeated. Punch through the chamber of the vein to rupture it just as Alcatraz did with the first one. Climb up the ledge to the north and continue along the highway to the tentacle above the collapsing road surface. Run along the tentacle to reach the upper ledge and continue (4).

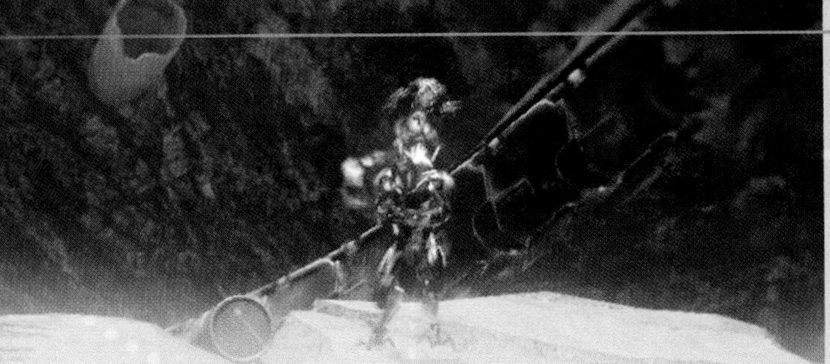

The third vein is not far ahead. Round the corner on the road and activate Cloak to avoid detection by the Ceph Combat Command Unit. Use the MK.60 to detonate the fuel drum as the enemy walks past it. The Combat Command Unit is twice as durable as the standard Combat Unit, so prepare to unload on it with the Marshall once it gets close, or Power Kick the car into the alien.. (Alcatraz can gain 300 Nano Catalyst from it.)

Descend the stepped remains of the highway to the shipping container near the ammo crate and assault rifle. The third vein isn't far ahead, but the area is crawling with Ceph Assault Units, joined by a Ceph Combat Command Unit. Use the MK.60 and either the Marshall shotgun or the Ranged Scar to get their attention. Draw them back behind the container to retain cover from those bringing up the rear.

ACHIEVEMENT

Hole in One

Locate the circular sinkhole within the crater near the vein and throw one of the Cephs down the hole to unlock this bonus. Grab hold of a Ceph, line it up with the hole, and throw it out of sight!

PREPARE A TRAP

If you have any C4 left, lay some down just to the left of the shipping container. Bait the Combat Command Unit to chase toward it, then detonate it when it gets close. It might not kill it, but a single blast from the Marshall should finish it off.

The third vein is guarded by a Devastator Unit just like the previous two. Sneak up behind it and lay down some C4 while Cloaked. Allow the Energy Meter to recharge, then strafe around it to get its attention, activate Armor, and lure it into the explosive trap. Finish it off with the MK.60—or fire a remaining JAW rocket.

SABOTAGE THE CENTRAL ALIEN STRUCTURE

Round the corner to the east and approach the primary Ceph structure. The doors open automatically as Alcatraz gets close, a result of the increased pressure caused by the three ruptured veins. The force of the venting is strong, but so is Alcatraz. Fight against the spore trying to expel Alcatraz from the interior and push inside.

ACHIEVEMENT

Into the Abyss

Sabotage the three veins to increase the pressure on the spore silo and force Alcatraz's way into the central alien structure. Watch as Alcatraz goes for a swim in the alien murk. How will the Nanosuit react to the infection?

The silo soon expels Alcatraz with so much force that he lands on a steeply slanted road. Follow the on-screen button prompts to prevent him from plummeting to his death. Crawl back up the grade in time to hear Hargreave's dire announcement: the Department of Defense has launched their bombers! Lower Manhattan is about to be flooded.

ESCAPE THE FLOOD

REACH THE HELICOPTER FOR EXTRACTION

Hargreave has dispatched a rescue helicopter to extract Alcatraz, but there isn't much time. Sprint as quickly as possible through the subway tunnel and back out onto the street surface. Continue running towards the pink smoke signal as fast as Alcatraz can go in effort to escape the floodwaters. A valiant effort, but one that ultimately proves futile.

SEMPER FI OR DIE

MADISON SQUARE PARK, NY | AUGUST 24TH, 11:52 A.M.

COLLECTIBLES

NY SOUVENIRS 1

DOG TAGS 1

NY CAR KEYS 0

E-MAILS 0

HOSTILES ENCOUNTERED

- CEPH COMBAT UNIT
- CEPH ASSAULT UNIT
- CEPH COMBAT COMMAND UNIT
- CEPH ASSAULT COMMAND UNIT
- CEPH DEVASTATOR UNIT

SUGGESTED WEAPONRY

MAJESTIC

DEMOLITION SCAR

DSG-1

L-TAG

SWARMER

JAW

ASSIST DELTA COMPANY

REACH THE EXTRACTION POINT

Alcatraz was washed a considerable distance by the floodwaters and was unconscious for over 12 hours. Luckily for him, Delta Company managed to locate him before the Ceph did. Take the pistol from Chino and collect the Nano Catalyst from the two Ceph corpses nearby. The flood has scoured the landscape, throwing cars and trains askew, ripping through bridges, and leaving waterfalls and canyons where city streets once stood. This makes getting around much tougher for the marines, but the varied terrain gives Alcatraz and the Nanosuit a tremendous advantage. Alcatraz lost all of his weapons in the flood, so the first priority is to get him outfitted for combat.

ACHIEVEMENT

Band of Brothers

Keep the Marines alive throughout this mission to unlock this bonus. Keep close to them to attract enemy gunfire and to provide a morale boost that increases their fighting ability.

ENCOUNTER A

WEAPON PROCUREMENT

1. **RESUPPLY:** Collect ammo and a Ranged Majestic near the crates atop the ledge on the east side of the ravine.
2. **SUPPORT:** Head up the hillside to the west to find a JAW that fell out of a supply truck.
3. **EXPLORE:** The upper ledge on the west side of the valley provides an elevated path from which to scout ahead.
4. **GRENADE:** Alcatraz can find grenades and C4 on the rocky island between the yellow container and statue's arm.

Drop off the ledge amongst the spontaneously made waterfalls and head north with Delta Company toward the severed arm of the Statue of Liberty rising from the rubble. Clamber up the ledge on the right to gain some additional ammo for the Majestic ①. Cross the water to the grassy slope on the west and equip one of the Demolition Scars near the yellow container; this assault rifle has a grenade launcher attachment under the barrel. Continue up the hill to acquire a JAW near an abandoned supply truck ②.

Take a moment to leap from the roof of the bus in the ditch to the rocky island where the grenades and C4 are located ④. Continue after the guys from Delta Company.

FIRST CONTACT

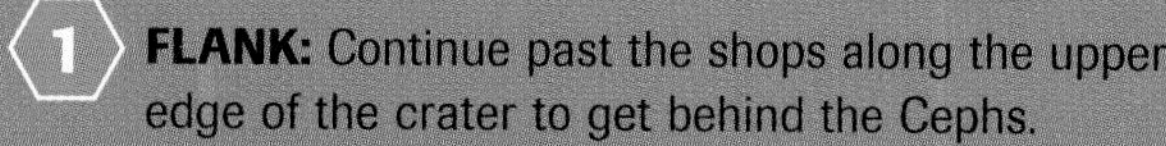
FLANK: Continue past the shops along the upper edge of the crater to get behind the Cephs.

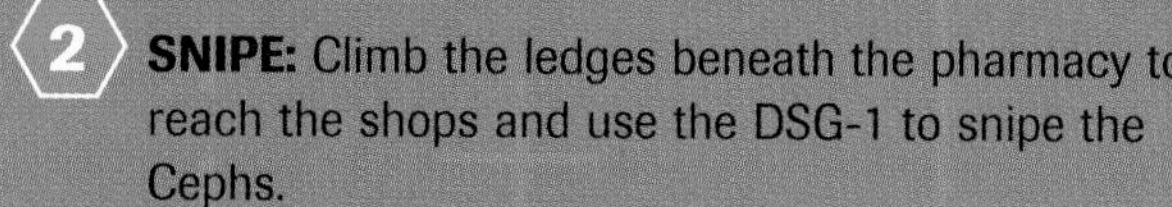
SNIPE: Climb the ledges beneath the pharmacy to reach the shops and use the DSG-1 to snipe the Cephs.

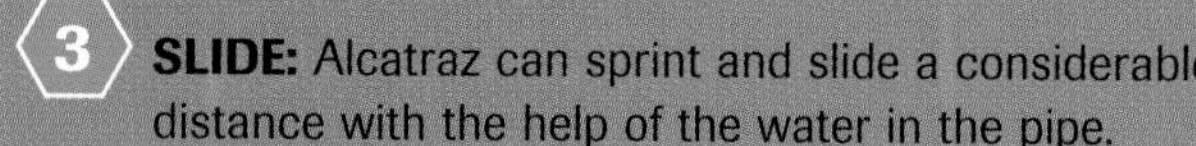
SLIDE: Alcatraz can sprint and slide a considerable distance with the help of the water in the pipe.

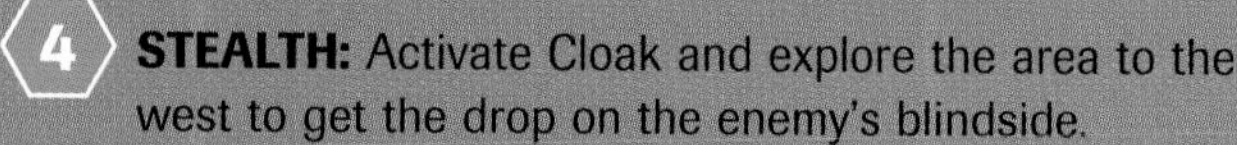
STEALTH: Activate Cloak and explore the area to the west to get the drop on the enemy's blindside.

A number of Ceph Assault and Combat units have infiltrated the area. Use the Demolition Scar to lend some support and take aim on whichever Cephs the marines are firing on. Run and slide through the severed water pipe ③ and open fire as Alcatraz comes out of the slide to suppress the nearby Cephs. Fire in short bursts to control the recoil and advance alongside the marines to the edge of the building on the left, where the area begins to spread out. Stay Cloaked and wait for Cephs to march past, then sneak up from behind and stealth kill them.

Follow Delta Company to the watery depression beneath the shops to the east. Run and leap from the yellow container to the ledges above and climb up to the pharmacy. Put the HMG to use if any Cephs are dangerously close; otherwise, grab the DSG-1 from the window of the discount store and set to sniping the Cephs located across the clearing to the east ②. There are two DSG-1 sniper rifles by this store. Load up on ammo and take the rifle in lieu of the Majestic pistol Chino had given Alcatraz earlier.

Exit the shop and continue north along the series of ledges ①. Use the upended buses and train cars as platforms to leap across the wider gaps. This position grants a wider view of the area and can be used as a secondary sniping position. Regroup with the rest of Delta Company to the west, near the graffiti-covered wall and follow them through the breach. Enemy Dropships continue to deliver Cephs to the area, so don't take too long to finish your business.

NY SOUVENIR

Enter the Super Savin' discount store on the rim of the crater and head to the checkout counter to find a harbor ship in a bottle. The other collectible in this area isn't found until the end of the mission.

Wade through the water to the ammo dump and exchange the DSG-1 for the Stealth DSG-1, and collect the JAW rocket and C4. There are many other weapons across the room, on the bench. Continue through the water-logged lower floor of the building down the hall to where a fuel drum rests near the door to a much larger area.

DE-SCOPE THE SCAR

There's no reason to have scoped weapons equipped. The Stealth DSG-1 is all the sniping power you'll ever need, so swap out the assault scope on the Demolition Scar for the reflex sight or ironsight.

ENCOUNTER C

FLOODED BUILDING

1. **RESUPPLY:** There are a large number of ammo crates and available weapons near each of the yellow containers.
2. **SLIDE:** Alcatraz can run and slide beneath 18-wheelers, especially when they're parked in water.
3. **USE:** Open fire with the mounted HMG to eliminate the Cephs beneath the overpass.

Equip the Stealth DSG-1 and slowly approach the door near the fuel drum; open fire on the Ceph Assault Units near the containers. Several may charge Alcatraz's position. Lay some C4 down near the fuel drum and quickly back away; trigger the explosion as soon as they come through the door! A second wave, including a red-headed Ceph Assault Command Unit, follows quickly behind the first. Equip the Demolition Scar, toggle it to grenade mode, and fire away.

Utilize the abundance of ammo crates and available weaponry in the area east of the yellow container (1). There are two JAW rockets available; Alcatraz should be carrying the maximum allowance at this point.

Leap onto the second yellow container and grab the handles of the mounted HMG (3). Activate Armor mode and take aim on the Cephs under the bridge to the west. Leave the heavy HMG behind and continue on foot. Put Alcatraz's enhanced mobility to the test by running and leaping across the gorge via the rocks on the right. Gather up the Nano Catalyst and keep moving. This latest batch of Nano Catalyst should be enough to purchase the "Nano Recharge" upgrade for the Nanosuit.

Clamber up the stack of shipping containers to the road surface and take cover behind the car, near the corpse (and another JAW). A Ceph Devastator Unit is leading a small group of lesser Cephs straight for Alcatraz's position. Ready the JAW and put two rockets into it as soon as it is within range. Decimate any Assault Units that get too close with melee strikes. Don't hesitate to Power Kick some cars down the road at the Cephs; this can also be an effective tactic for creating a little breathing room. Continue west along the roadway. Climb the contorted mountain of road and leap off.

ENCOUNTER D  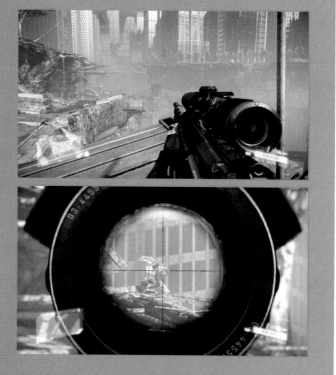

HIGHWAY RAMPAGE

 **DRIVE:** Climb behind the wheel of the Bulldog HMLTV and drive the length of the crumbling highway.

The abandoned vehicle ahead presents a welcome respite for Alcatraz's weary feet, but don't slip behind the wheel just yet! First, run up the tilted cargo trailer to the ledge then leap from the protruding pipe to the other raised platform across the street. Gather the DSG-1 ammo inside the container then climb on top and start sniping the Cephs in the distance (detach the silencer for added power and range). There are a number of Ceph Combat Units along the highway as it winds its way to the northwest. Many of them remain stationary while Alcatraz picks them off, making the sniping as simple as it is effective. Locate the two Cephs on the street surface to the south, one or two on the rise above them, then several more far in the distance to the northwest to the right of the large tree. Pick up the JAW leaning against the container and return to the vehicle.

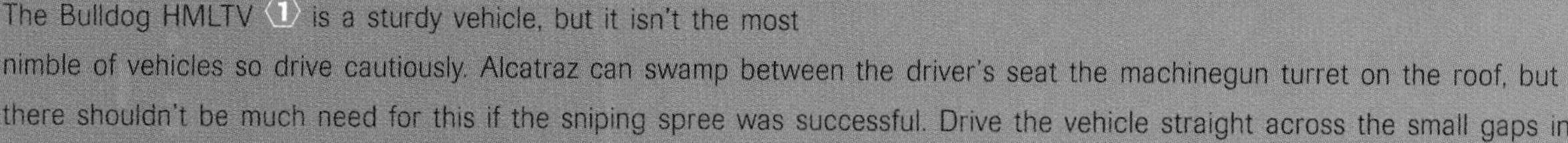

The Bulldog HMLTV ① is a sturdy vehicle, but it isn't the most nimble of vehicles so drive cautiously. Alcatraz can swamp between the driver's seat the machinegun turret on the roof, but there shouldn't be much need for this if the sniping spree was successful. Drive the vehicle straight across the small gaps in the bridge surface then around the sharp turn to the right to double-back on the other side of the valley. Continue driving northward, even as the ground starts to shake, and steer the Bulldog right off the cliff to where the road abruptly ends.

Exit the vehicle and proceed on foot past the piles of twisted metal and crumbling rock to the severed train tunnel. Leap down into the watery clearing and reunite with Delta Company; they've already laid down a smoke signal for the incoming helicopter.

ENCOUNTER E

SHIP'S AHOY!

1 **SUPPORT:** Board the stranded ship and use the L-TAG to defend Delta Company during the attack.

The Cephs have spotted the pink smoke and are launching an attack. Delta Company needs someone to board the ship beached in this crater by the flood, and lend some additional firepower. Climb aboard via the rocks on the right and locate the L-TAG in the container ①. The L-TAG fires smart grenades and can launch projectiles that either ricochet off objects or behave as mines. Leave the L-TAG in ricochet mode, head over to the port railing, and launch a few grenades at the Assault Command Unit and Devastator Unit moving in on Delta Company. There isn't much ammo for the L-TAG and it takes three direct hits to bring down a Devastator Unit—make each shot count!

Switch back to the DSG-1 once the L-TAG runs dry and set to sniping the lesser Cephs on the ground below. Alcatraz should remain safe from enemy fire on the ship, except for when a gunship flies overhead. Watch the radar map and activate Armor mode as soon as a larger red blip appears moving in Alcatraz's direction. The tilted deck of the ship makes it possible to escape incoming gunship attacks with a lengthy slide to safety.

Hop off the ship and follow behind Delta Company while using the DSG-1 and Cloak mode to provide some much-needed support fire. Swap out the L-TAG for the Demolition Scar or other assault rifle and continue on to the train bridge in the distance. Or what's left of it...

DEFEAT ALIEN RESISTANCE AND SECURE EVAC ZONE

THE SWARMER

The Swarmer is a heavy weapon, much like the HMG in that it can be carried or discarded without replacing one of Alcatraz's two primary weapons. The Swarmer fires a barrage of energy-based explosives that can be guided by the weapon's laser sight. It's particularly effective against groups of enemies and Commander-class Cephs.

ENCOUNTER F

GUNSHIP BATTLE

1 **DESTROY:** Use the Swarmer and JAW to take out the Ceph Gunship patrolling the skies overhead.

The rescue choppers can't land to evacuate Delta Company as long as that Ceph Gunship is circling overhead. Alcatraz must take it down! Regroup around Chino, load up on ammo (there's another L-TAG in the container near the subway tracks) and take up position atop the containers near the cliff. The first wave of inbound Cephs approaches on foot from the south. Use the DSG-1 to snipe as many as possible then switch to the L-TAG to frag the ones that get too close to Delta Company.

A dropship deploys a second wave of Cephs to the west. Allow Delta Company to take them head-on while Alcatraz moves to the eastern edge of the area and snipes across the map from their flank. Pick up the Swarmer inside the middle shipping container and fire on the Ceph Assault Command Units that force their way up off the grass toward Delta Company. A Devastator Unit won't be far behind. Empty the Swarmer on the Devastator then finish it off with the L-TAG's or Demolition Scar's grenades. If all else fails, activate Cloak mode and lay down some C4 in front of the Devastator's path.

Now it's time to take on the Ceph Gunship ⟨1⟩. Shoulder the JAW, activate Armor mode, and watch the skies. The Gunship doesn't appear to move quickly, but neither do the JAW rockets. Wait to fire until the Gunship approaches Alcatraz head-on, rather than attempting a shot at its side. Keep the JAW's laser pointed at the Gunship to guide the rocket to its mark. It's going to take at least three direct hits with the JAW to bring it down. There are a large number of JAW rockets scattered throughout the area—particularly on the flatbed trailer near the cliff—so finding enough to use against the Gunship shouldn't be challenging. Stay in the center of the defense area and duck into the container where the Swarmer and JAW rockets were to escape return fire while reloading.

Throw down the heavy weapon and leave the defense post behind. Continue up the piles of rubble and onto the higher ledge where Chino and the others are waiting. With the rescue chopper shot down, Delta Company has no choice but to continue along the path of destruction to the exposed pipe in the distance. Hargreave radios Alcatraz, providing him and Delta Company with their new objective.

ACHIEVEMENT

Once a Marine, Always a Marine

Assist the marines of Delta Company in securing an evacuation zone by defeating the alien resistance and destroying the Ceph Gunship. Rejoin Chino and his men atop the slabs of rubble to the northwest to unlock this bonus.

DOG TAG

The Dog Tag is on the ground next to a deceased marine, just meters before the area's conclusion. Don't follow the others into the pipe until first picking up this collectible.

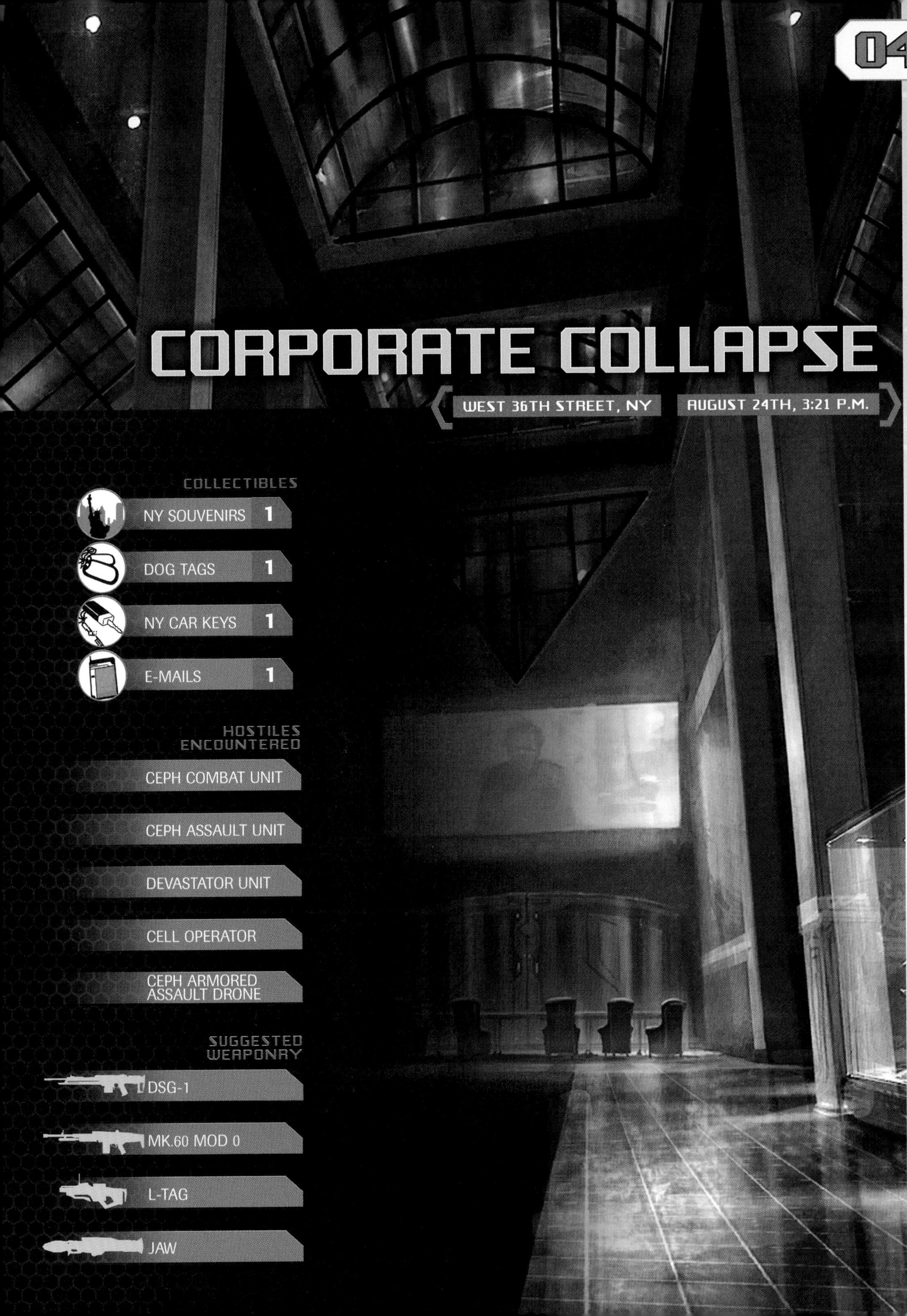

CORPORATE COLLAPSE

WEST 36TH STREET, NY | AUGUST 24TH, 3:21 P.M.

COLLECTIBLES

NY SOUVENIRS 1

DOG TAGS 1

NY CAR KEYS 1

E-MAILS 1

HOSTILES ENCOUNTERED

- CEPH COMBAT UNIT
- CEPH ASSAULT UNIT
- DEVASTATOR UNIT
- CELL OPERATOR
- CEPH ARMORED ASSAULT DRONE

SUGGESTED WEAPONRY

DSG-1

MK.60 MOD 0

L-TAG

JAW

INFILTRATE THE HARGREAVE-RASCH BUILDING

FOLLOW CHINO

Alcatraz and Delta Company exit the pipe not far from the Hargreave-Rasch building that they're trying to reach to obtain the bio-sample. Follow the squad through the narrow river valley. Stick to the left-hand side to flank the two Cephs that attack one of the other marines ahead. The marine can't be saved, but he can be avenged. Kill the Cephs and take the soldier's MK.60 so his death isn't in vain. Stay high on the left-hand ledges where the path narrows; this provides an excellent position from which to snipe during the ensuing battle.

USE ICV TURRET TO BLAST OPEN SECURITY DOORS

CAR KEY

The Car Key for this level is close to the starting point, inside the toppled train car within the valley. It's lying next to a dead body on the floor.

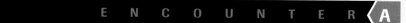

ENCOUNTER A

OUTSIDE THE HARGREAVE-RASCH BUILDING

1. **USE:** The mounted HMG in front of the Hargreave-Rasch building is effective against the Cephs.
2. **STEALTH:** Alcatraz can sneak onto the front of the Hargreave-Rasch building along the southeast trail.
3. **USE TURRET:** Board the vehicle parked to the west and fire at the doors to the lower parking garage.
4. **TAKE:** Scour the parking garage on the north side of the crater for a JAW and L-TAG, along with other weaponry.

Equip the DSG-1 leaning against the ammo crates at the edge of the waterfall and take a moment to look over the area. The Hargreave-Rasch building is to the left (south) but the entrance to the underground parking garage is located clear across the area to the west. The best way to reach the vehicle with the turret is to circle around to the north, eliminating any enemies as you progress. Snipe the Cephs approaching from the right, between Delta Company's position and the yellow containers to the north. Kill each of the Cephs on the damaged parking garage to the north and use the MK.60 to take out the two or three that try to charge Alcatraz's position. Avoid descending beyond the containers until you're relatively certain that there aren't any Cephs left near the structure.

Climb the stairwell inside the parking garage on the north to find the bodies of several dead marines, along with their weaponry. Collect the JAW from the upper landing and any needed ammo along the way. Return to the ground floor and swap the DSG-1 for the L-TAG and ammo from the garage ④. Load up on C4 as well.

There are two ways to go about blasting open the security doors to the Hargreave-Rasch building. Option 1 is to use the powerful cannon on the camouflaged armored vehicle parked uphill from the garage ③. This can work, but is not only a tough shot because of the angle, but it also attracts a dropship full of Cephs to the area, including a Devastator Unit. Use the turret to take out the Devastator Unit quickly, then exit the vehicle before the other Cephs blow it to pieces. Option 2 is much easier. Simply use the JAW recovered from the stairwell to blast open the doors and walk right in.

NY SOUVENIR

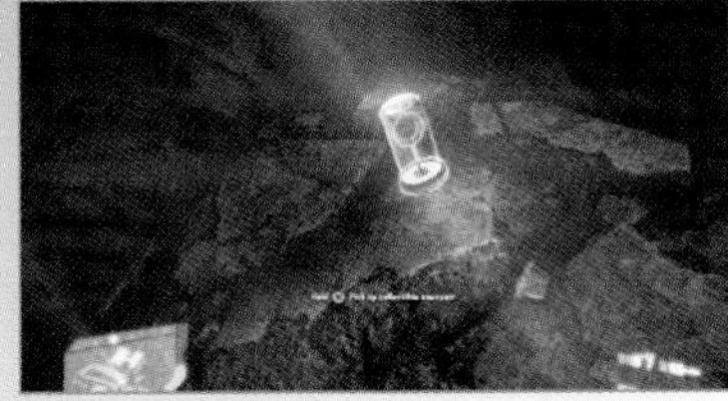

Dive into the water-filled crater near the Statue of Liberty's head and swim to the west to find a fractured opening with an ammo crate. This crevice also contains this level's NY Souvenir.

ACHIEVEMENT

Hung Out to Dry

Successfully blast open the doors to the parking garage beneath the Hargreave-Rasch building and swim through the flooded entrance to emerge on dry land inside the parking structure.

UPGRADE NANOSUIT WITH BIO-FIXING PROTOCOL

TAKE THE ELEVATOR TO THE LOBBY

The elevator entrance is on this floor of the parking garage, but that Lockhart's men from CELL have gone rogue and are stationed throughout the area, bent on stopping Alcatraz in his tracks. Approach the fenced area on the left, activate Cloak, and ready an M17 Frag Grenade to toss at the first two CELL Operators who attack. There are many more around the corner to the left, assisted by an APC with a mounted HMG on the roof. Use Cloak to study their position safely then either lob a grenade at them or use the L-TAG to launch one their way.

MAGNIFIED EXPLOSION

An excellent way to take out multiple CELL Operators and destroy the turret gun is to throw a grenade under the vehicle. The grenade detonates the vehicle's fuel tank, thereby doubling the explosion radius and killing many of the others in the area.

Gather up more grenades from near the vending machine inside the security office and stealthily advance through the parking garage. Use the L-TAG to defeat grouped enemies with a single shot. One of the CELL Operators is carrying an L-TAG so tread carefully; attempt to stealth kill him and collect his weapon for extra ammo. Hang back near the burned-out APC and wait for reinforcements to attack in small batches. Perform stealth kills when possible, and use the MK.60 to detonate fuel drums as enemies wander past them.

Switch to the L-TAG as Alcatraz rounds the corner beyond the APC and launch a couple of grenades quickly, then turn and take out the APC with the machine gun turret to the left. The fenced-off supply area in the back corner behind the second APC contains numerous grenades and L-Tag ammo.

SHORT-CIRCUITED BY THE K-VOLT

The Nanosuit's Cloak and Armor abilities can be negated when hit by the electrically-charged K-Volt's projectiles. Take cover immediately if static charges begin appearing on-screen, signaling the temporarily deactivation of the Nanosuit's abilities.

Leap the barrier near the vending machines, crouch down, and activate Cloak to avoid premature detection. Collect the E-Mail from the office on the left and step through the metal detector on the right. This naturally sets off the alarm. Stand in the corner—Cloaked—and open fire as the CELL Operators come to investigate. Use the L-Tag and MK.60 to clear the lobby of the other enemies and advance down the hall to the mounted HMG. Dislodge the enemy manning the HMG with a grenade then rip it off its mount and carry it to the elevator. Alcatraz needs to set the HMG down in order to operate the elevator buttons—bring it up to the main lobby.

E-MAIL

Enter the office to the left of the metal detectors and head to the window looking out to the lobby. The E-Mail tablet is on the left end of the ledge, near the vending machines.

ACCESS SECURITY TERMINAL

The lobby is currently devoid of enemies. Don't expect that to last, however! Carry the HGM around the information desk and down the hall on either side to the grand lobby ahead. The glass windows and doors, looking out to the flooded street, give the impression the building is confined with a surreal aquarium. Locate the computer terminal on the reception desk and interact with it.

ELIMINATE LOCKHART'S ROGUE CELL SQUAD

Quickly pick up the HMG and take cover behind the desk. Lockhart's men are swarming the area from both sides and are equipped with heavy weaponry, including an L-TAG of their own. Use the HMG to quickly cut down any enemies foolish enough to not take cover, then switch to the L-TAG and launch grenades at the others. Slip out from behind the desk and take cover behind the planters. Activate Cloak and hunt down the remaining CELL Operators with the MK.60.

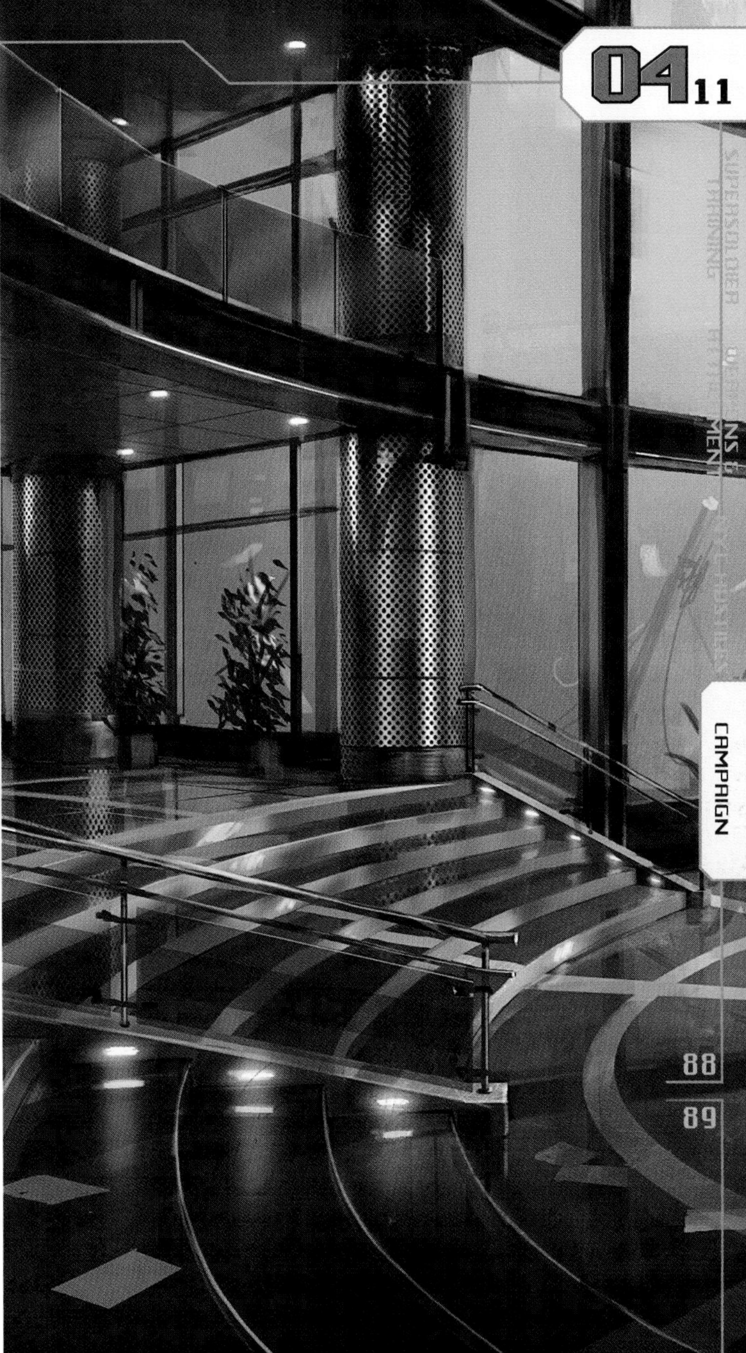

Hargreave will instruct Alcatraz to reboot the security system via the computer terminal at the front desk. Do as he asks, then watch as the glass walls of the lobby fracture and Alcatraz is quickly swept up in another flood.

CALL TO ARMS

Alcatraz was able to escape the Hargreave-Rasch building before debris (and a rather large ship) blocked the exit. He won't be able to get the bio-fixing protocols Hargreave requested—at least not at the moment. He'll have to regroup with Chino and the others while Hargreave develops a course of action.

DOG TAG

Turn back toward the water after escaping the flood and swim down into the murky depths, but not too far. There is a hard-to-spot Dog Tag underwater near the car directly south of where Alcatraz washes ashore.

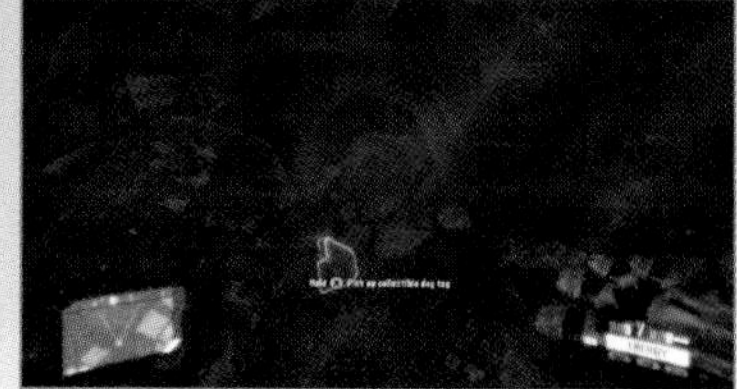

REJOIN CHINO AT CENTRAL STATION

REGROUP WITH THE MARINES

Enter the pipe near the corpses on the shore and follow it northward to where it ends in a trench. Up above, the chaotic sounds of an intense firefight can be heard. Alcatraz must hurry to their aid! Proceed along the scoured trench, past the mangled vehicles and police barricades, to where the trench eventually dead-ends. Climb into the sewer pipe sticking out the north end of the trench. This leads Alcatraz back to the street where several marines are located.

Follow after the marines, pausing just for a moment to collect the C4 in the mobile office on the left. Chino is in the diner straight ahead, and he and his men have their hands full.

ELIMINATE THE PINGER

Chino and the others are doing their best to fend off a massive Armored Assault Drone known as a Pinger. This gigantic Ceph walks on three legs, is heavily armored, and attacks with deadly energy weapons. It also releases a powerful electromagnetic pulse capable of draining the Nanosuit of energy. The marines distract and chip away at the Pinger to the best of their abilities, but they lack the firepower to bring this beast down. Victory is up to Alcatraz.

ENCOUNTER B

PINGER BATTLE

1 RESUPPLY: The building due north of the diner contains extra ammo and a JAW on the second floor.

2 EXPLORE: Run along the elevated train tracks to procure extra C4 and other weaponry.

3 ACQUIRE: Duck through the hole in the foundation of the building to the northwest to find another JAW.

The Pinger's lone weak point is the red energy cell mounted on its back. Bullets and explosive projectiles simply bounce right off its metal armored head and legs. If Alcatraz is to defeat the Pinger, he must get a clean line of sight on the red energy cell and hit it hard. The best way to do this is with the JAW and C4. They inflict the same level of damage to the Pinger regardless of where they hit, unlike bullets which must hit its weak point. But hitting it once or twice won't be enough; Alcatraz must load up on rockets and hit it multiple times to inflict any significant damage.

First, load up on JAW rockets and C4. Avoid straying too close to the Pinger, as its EMP blast renders Alcatraz's Cloak and Armor ineffective and leaves him dangerously susceptible to retaliatory attacks. Locate the JAW on the roof of the diner (there are stairs in the alley behind the shop), then sprint across the street and up the angled container to the second floor of the building to the north ①. There is another JAW located here, as well as one beneath the nearby Super Savin' store ③. There is also another two blocks of C4 inside the store.

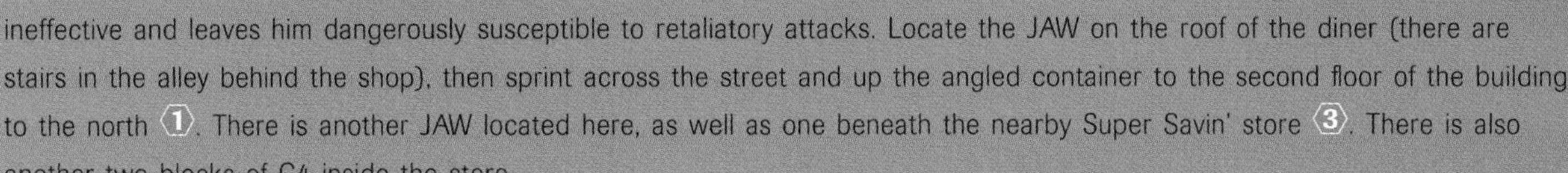

Now that Alcatraz is loaded up with high explosives, step out onto the street and use Cloak to flank the Pinger. Stay far enough away from it to avoid its EMP attack and open fire with the JAW. Immediately sprint for cover behind solid obstacles capable of offering protection, then activate Cloak and flank it again. A large red cylinder emerges from the Pinger's back right before it unleashes its EMP blast, thus providing just enough warning to dash away.

Continue flanking and firing on the Pinger with the JAW until out of rockets. If the Pinger is still not dead, climb up onto the train tracks via the train that had slid off (near the hole in the base of the Super Savin' store) and equip the C4 ② . This elevated perch gives Alcatraz an excellent vantage point from which to lob C4 onto the back of the Pinger. Detonate the explosives then run and slide down the tracks and take cover under the discount store. Detonating C4 on the ground beneath the Pinger is also effective. If all else fails, the MK.60 and the Demolition Scar's grenades can also do the trick.

REGROUP AT THE VEHICLES

The Pinger yields 2000 Nano Catalyst. Rush over to the site where it stood when it was destroyed to get it. As for Chino, he won't be making the trip to meet Alcatraz personally, but his men arrive in vehicles and they're all too willing to get Alcatraz to Central Station, where Chino needs his help.

TRAIN TO CATCH

BRYANT PARK | NEW YORK PUBLIC LIBRARY, NY | AUGUST 24TH, 7:31 P.M.

COLLECTIBLES

NY SOUVENIRS	1
DOG TAGS	0
NY CAR KEYS	1
E-MAILS	0

HOSTILES ENCOUNTERED

- CEPH COMBAT UNIT
- CEPH ASSAULT UNIT
- DEVASTATOR UNIT
- CEPH COMBAT COMMAND UNIT

SUGGESTED WEAPONRY

- MK.60 MOD 0
- L-TAG
- JAW
- RANGED SCAR

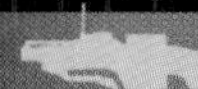

EVACUATE CIVILIANS FROM BRYANT PARK

JOIN THE RETREAT AT THE LIBRARY

The marines are pushing through a heavily damaged portion of the city to meet up with the civilians believed to be waiting evacuation at the library. Drop off the ledge where Alcatraz begins the level and cut through the crumbling building to the west to join the marines. Open fire on the Cephs flanking the doorway across the street with the MK.60 then leap over the sandbags and continue toward the library. Take the MK.60 inside the next building for additional ammo.

Crawl through the hole in the wall in time to see the Ceph Gunship fly past. The library is just down the road from here and the marines are doing all they can to hold off the Cephs; they need Alcatraz's help on the double!

BRING THE MISSILE BATTERIES ONLINE

ENCOUNTER A

LIBRARY EXTERIOR

1. **USE:** There is a mounted HMG on the roof of the café that could prove useful once the batteries are online.
2. **STEALTH:** Access the missile battery to the north by sneaking around the back of the café.
3. **TAKE:** Slip through the hole in the fence to load up on C4, a JAW rocket, and extra ammo.

Grab the JAW and ammo and drop off the roof to the street below. EMAT has erected a massive fence around the perimeter of the library, but there's a hole in the left-hand side. Crawl through the hole to reach the C4 and JAW located in this area (3). Alcatraz may not need during this fight, but it comes in handy soon enough. Slip back through the hole, cross go through the checkpoint, and sneak down the alley behind the shop to flank the enemy while remaining undetected by the gunship (2).

Don't waste what limited JAW rockets Alcatraz has on the gunship; let the missile batteries take care of them! use Cloak to avoid being spotted and head west down the street to the fenced missile battery. Grab the other JAW rockets in the area (for later...) and start toward the southeast end of the avenue to activate the other missile battery. Use the MK.60 and L-TAG to sweep along the avenue and clear it of Ceph Combat and Assault Units. Move along the front stairs to flank the enemies at the far end of the road while ensuring Alcatraz has plenty of available cover.

FALL BACK THROUGH THE PUBLIC LIBRARY

Finish off any remaining Cephs in the street on the way to the library's front doors. Break open the doors and head into the flaming interior. It's too late to save those in the lobby, but there are more beyond the library that need Alcatraz's help.

NY SOUVENIR

This level's NY Souvenir is on the reception desk in the library's front lobby. It's on the right-hand end of the desk, next to the postcard racks.

Climb the stairs on either side of the lobby and follow the walkway to the central door leading deeper into the library. The flames are quite severe here so activate Armor mode before approaching the opening. Sprint through the flames to the space inside the next room where there aren't any flames.

ACHIEVEMENT

Literary Agent

Enable the visor to view the recommended tactical assessment. Note the HUD icon on the bookshelf to the north. Enable Nanovision and zoom in on that marker to scan the books and unlock this secret bonus.

ENCOUNTER B

PUBLIC BOOK BURNING

1. **RESUPPLY:** Gather up the available ammunition and consider equipping the Ranged Scar if out of L-TAG ammo.
2. **SCAN:** Activate Nanovision and use the visor to scan the books on the north bookcase.

Use Nanovision and scan the books on the north side of the room (2) to unlock the Literary Agent bonus then circle around to the southwest to continue. Activate Armor mode whenever the flames get close and continue through the burning library to the ammo crate in the next room (1). Continue along the walkway past the flames to the hole in the wall and drop through to a portion of the building not yet on fire. Exit the library through the door in the southwest corner.

ASSIST MARINE FALLBACK THROUGH THE PARK

ENCOUNTER C

BEYOND THE LIBRARY

1. **RESUPPLY:** Head down the hall before leaping off the ledge to collect the available munitions.
2. **STEALTH:** Use Cloak to approach the Cephs near the containers from the west.
3. **TAKE:** Follow the indicator to the L-TAG on the stairs behind one of the upper columns.

Proceed down the hallway on the left to the top of the stairs outside the library. Gather up the weapons ③ and ammo ① near the columns and lion statues and open fire on the Cephs in the street. Circle around to the right, activate Armor mode, and leap off the ledge to the far western end of the area. Use Cloak to sneak up behind the Cephs near the yellow containers ② and take them out. Move from container to container to flank the Cephs while they focus on the marines near the concrete barriers. Advance down the road to the south, along the serpentine path near the rubble.

ENCOUNTER D

WEST 40TH STREET

1. **THROW GRENADE:** Lob a grenade or use the L-TAG to detonate the in the center of the intersection.

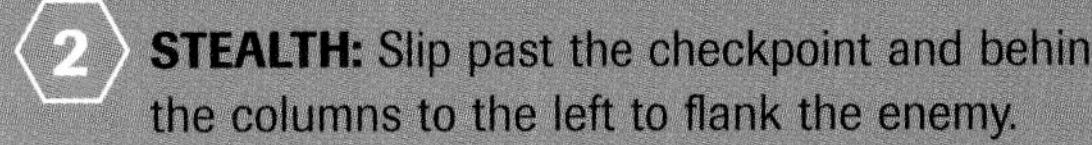

2. **STEALTH:** Slip past the checkpoint and behind the columns to the left to flank the enemy.
3. **USE TURRET:** The turret draws enemy attention away from the marines.

Draw the MK.60 and start down the left-hand side of the street toward the subway stairs and pedestrian checkpoint. The marines are doing a good job of repelling the Ceph attack, but they need Alcatraz's help. Use the MK.60—or even the JAW or C4 if available—to destroy the Ceph Combat Command Unit. Head up the ramp to the walkway above the checkpoint if carrying a weapon with sniping ability, otherwise flank the enemy to the left ② while the marines hold them off in the center. Cross the street to the north to enter Bryant Park.

ENCOUNTER E

BRYANT PARK

1. **RESUPPLY:** The ammo crate on the walkway also contains multiples packs of C4.
2. **USE TURRET:** Detach the mounted HMG next to the ammo crate and carry it down the road to the civilians.

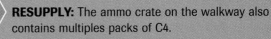

Another wave of Cephs is attacking in Bryant Park, near the fountain. Let loose with the MK.60 on any Cephs to the right of the fountain as Alcatraz enters the area, then dash to the corner in time to watch a Devastator Unit arrive. Activate Cloak, shoulder the JAW, and pull the trigger. Quickly switch to C4 and lob a packet of explosives at it and squeeze the detonation device; it's quicker than reloading the JAW. Regroup with the marines inside the decontamination center to the right.

PROTECT THE CIVILIAN EVACUATION

CAR KEY

The Car Key is inside the office of the vehicle decontamination bay. Grab it before proceeding through the orange plastic tunnel.

Load up on ammo and weapons in the supply room before exiting the decontamination area. The MK.60 and L-TAG are a fine combination and perfect for the job at hand. Escort the civilians out of the compound and into the street.

ENCOUNTER F

EVACUATION SITE

1. **SLIDE:** Run and slide beneath the trailer if in need of cover.
2. **STEALTH:** Sneak around the perimeter of the intersection to flank the Cephs.
3. **USE TURRET:** Resist using the mounted HMG, as it traps Alcatraz in a very exposed position.

Run straight across the street to the bookstore (1) and circle around the perimeter of the intersection in a counter-clockwise direction with the HMG from earlier, or with the MK.60 on hand. Use Armor mode for protection and eliminate any Cephs en route to the containers. Take cover behind the yellow container to the north, lob grenades into the fray, and watch for the Devastator Unit to emerge. Equip the JAW and take aim on the Devastator Unit from the relative safety of the northern side-street.

GET IN THE ARMORED CAR

ACHIEVEMENT

Fire Walker

Survive the journey to Bryant Park and assist the marines in evacuating the civilians. Alcatraz needs all the power of the Nanosuit's Armor mode to withstand the inferno enveloping the library en route to the park.

Open the gate for the convoy via the security terminal on the south side of the compound. Wait for the APC to drive forward then man the turret. The marine behind the wheel drives Alcatraz to where he's needed next.

UNSAFE HAVEN

CENTRAL STATION, NY | AUGUST 24TH, 9:02 P.M.

COLLECTIBLES

NY SOUVENIRS	1
DOG TAGS	1
NY CAR KEYS	0
E-MAILS	0

HOSTILES ENCOUNTERED

- CEPH COMBAT UNIT
- CEPH ASSAULT UNIT
- DEVASTATOR UNIT
- CEPH COMBAT COMMAND UNIT

SUGGESTED WEAPONRY

- MK.60 MOD 0
- DSG-1
- JAW
- RANGED GRENDEL

JOIN PERIMETER DEFENSE AT CENTRAL STATION

REACH THE STATION EXTERIOR

Gather up ammo for the MK.60 and step into the utility closet on the left to collect some C4 before following the marines to the parking area out back. Duck under the yellow caution tape to reach the loading area. Grab hold of the gate on the right and lift it so Alcatraz and the others can exit.

Angle to the right and use the MK.60 and look for a Ceph Combat Command Unit. Activate Armor and take it down, leaving the marines to handle the weaker Cephs for the time being. Back into the garage for extra cover and don't stop firing until all four Cephs in the area have been defeated. Continue down the street to the left to join the perimeter defense.

LOCATE STAFF SERGEANT RAINER

Scale the perimeter wall on either side of the road by leaping off the pile of rubble and grabbing the ledge. Proceed through the security fence on the right and up the ramp to the left-hand side of the security station. Climb the wall beneath the missile battery and continue through the gate to meet Staff Sergeant Rainer.

DEFEND CENTRAL STATION

Staff Sergeant Rainer tells Alcatraz about their plan. They are going to topple the Onyx building to block the Ceph's mortar fire, but they need someone to re-prime the fuses on the explosives inside the building. That's where Alcatraz comes in. He must make it on foot to the parking garage beneath the Onyx building; prime the detonators, then high-tail it out of there before the building is blown up!

FIND AND PRIME THE DETONATORS

DOG TAG

Continue east along the upper defense station, past the soldiers near the ammo crates by the bridge, all the way to the pallets of supplies in the distance. The Dog Tag is on the stack of boxes in the center.

Join the marines near the start of the bridge and equip the DSG-1 (keep the MK.60 as a primary weapon). Take cover behind the metal blast shields and set to sniping the numerous Ceph Combat and Assault Units marching across the bridge. A single headshot can decapitate and kill these Cephs, but two quick shots to the body will also suffice, unless the bullet enters through their gelatinous backs. Resist the urge to rush forward to collect the Nano Catalyst until at least ten Cephs have been destroyed. One of the marines yells that it's time to move forward if Alcatraz delays too long.

Advance to a shield stationed in the middle of the bridge and resume sniping. The goal is to gradually push across the bridge until Alcatraz reaches the collapsed portion that angles down to the street below, but to not do so too hastily. It's also possible to use the Visor and highlight enemies for the missile launchers to take care of—this is a fun way to save some ammo. Continue to the end of the bridge then leap down on the left-hand side (the diner beneath the bridge contains a Grendel, which may come in handy.

STEALTH ENHANCE

Saving for another expensive Nanosuit upgrade? If so, Alcatraz should have more than enough Nano Catalyst to purchase the Stealth Enhance module. This upgrade quickens the transition in and out of Cloaking and decreases the consumption of energy while Cloaked.

Activate Cloak and sneak along the street to the left to the ammo crates near the fencing. There are multiple Cephs in the area, in close proximity, so it's important to be careful here. Switch to the MK.60 and either use Cloak to sneak past them undetected or open fire and activate Armor mode for enhanced protection. Wait until they are bunched together before opening fire, else Alcatraz could be quickly surrounded and outmatched.

Head up the stairs toward the statue and immediately take cover. The entrance to the Onyx building is to the left, but the path is guarded by several more Cephs. Use Cloak to slip into sniping position without being spotted and take them out with a couple of well-placed headshots. Seek out the ammo crate by the building nearest the statue to find an L-TAG and MK.60. Hug the path to the left to circle around the plaza in front of the building in a clockwise direction around the fountain, toward the parking attendant office to the southeast. Enter the office and push the button to raise the gate to the garage.

C4 ON THE READY

There's a chance that a Ceph Combat Command Unit will follow Alcatraz into the office. Look around before entering the office, for risk of being cornered. If one is coming, drop some C4 near the entrance, run to the far corner inside the office, and detonate it as the enemy funnels through the doorway.

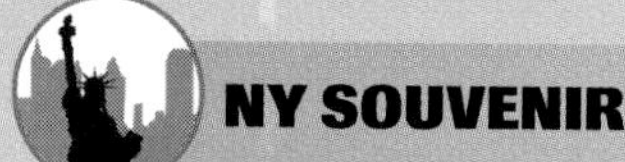

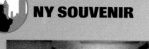

NY SOUVENIR

Grab the NY Souvenir in the glass case on the desk to the right of the button in the parking office. This NY Souvenir glows red and adjacent the fan on the desk.

FIND AND PRIME THE THREE DETONATORS

Two of the three detonators are on the first level of the parking garage while the third is located one level down. Slide down the slope to the first level of the garage and prime the detonator nearest the entrance first. Circle around the left-hand side of this level to find the second detonator in the southwest corner. Activate that one and swap the DSG-1 for the Ranged Grendel lying on the floor. Head down the ramp in the northwest corner and circle around the wall in the center of the floor to the third and final detonator to the north.

REACH A SAFE DISTANCE

The lights go dark as soon as the third detonator has been primed. Activate Nanovision, turn directly around, and sprint back up the ramp to the upper floor of the garage. Alcatraz isn't alone in the garage anymore, but there's no reason to fight. Just keep sprinting and loop back around the upper floor of the garage to the exit ramp in a counter-clockwise direction, past the second detonator and first.

The threat doesn't end outside the garage: a Devastator Unit is fast approaching from the left. Equip the C4 Alcatraz has acquired and throw two sticks at the Devastator Unit and detonate. Proceed down the road to the west to get away from the blast zone.

LOCATE SGT. TORRES

Sergeant Torres is on the second floor of the office building to the northwest. He's trying to move into range with the remote trigger so he can detonate the explosives Alcatraz just primed. The blue icon on the HUD marks Sergeant Torres's location. Watch as he runs through the building's second floor toward the southeast corner, where he can get a clear view of the Onyx building. Unfortunately for Torres, the Cephs get to him before he can squeeze the trigger. Now Alcatraz must find him in the office building and trigger the demolition himself.

PICK UP THE TRANSMITTER

Approach the corner of the building nearest where Sergeant Torres succumbed to the Ceph attacks. Sidestep the rubble to find a section of missing windows on the first floor. Alcatraz can leap and climb up through the missing window to enter the building directly below the transmitter's location.

Cut through the nearby hallway with the elevators and loop around to the northwest. The building is C-shaped and the only way to reach the second floor is via the elevator shaft in the northern wing. Stay Cloaked while navigating the building and keep the MK.60 on hand to deal with the stray Ceph encountered along the way.

Two additional Cephs are located near the elevator shafts. Activate Armor and dispatch each of them with a pair of rapid melee attacks. Enter the right-hand elevator shaft, leap onto the roof of the adjacent elevator then climb up through the open doors to the second floor. This floor's layout is identical to the one below. Retrace the path Alcatraz took below to reach the transmitter in the southeast corner.

RETURN TO THE TERMINAL

Activate Nanovision to deal with the reduced visibility due to the dust and smoke from the explosion. Return through the plaza to the bridge leading back to the defense terminal. Run up onto the bridge, activate Armor mode, and sprint and slide from cover to cover to outrun the Cephs in pursuit. The marines stationed on the far side of the bridge work to keep Alcatraz safe. There's enough light on the bridge to turn the Nanovision off.

SECURE THE ENTRANCE

There's one final Ceph with which to deal! A Devastator Unit has appeared beneath the bridge, near the entrance to the train station's primary terminal. Approach the railing looking down onto the Devastator Unit and blast it with a pair of JAW rockets or C4, depending on whichever Alcatraz has the most of. Leap down to collect the 500 Nano Catalyst once it's been defeated and enter the terminal through the door to the west.

TERMINUS

CENTRAL STATION, NY | AUGUST 24TH, 9:49 P.M.

COLLECTIBLES

NY SOUVENIRS 1

DOG TAGS 1

NY CAR KEYS 0

E-MAILS 0

HOSTILES ENCOUNTERED

CEPH COMBAT UNIT

CEPH ASSAULT UNIT

CEPH DEVASTATOR UNIT

CEPH ARMORED ASSAULT DRONE

SUGGESTED WEAPONRY

MK.60 MOD 0

SWARMER

JAW

DEFEND CENTRAL STATION

LOCATE COLONEL BARCLAY

It's been a tough couple of days for Alcatraz, but an even harder time for the civilians forced to watch their homes crash down around them, their loved ones ripped away and placed in quarantine. Guide Alcatraz on a slow and somber walk through the evacuation camp, past the infected, the dying, and the marines forced to try and maintain order. At least there are a few of those CELL bastards locked in a tiny cage to bring a little joy to the place. Approach the marine in the yellow HAZMAT suit at the far end of the camp for inspection and continue through the decontamination tents to meet Colonel Barclay.

DOG TAG

The Dog Tag is on the table in the room where Alcatraz meets Colonel Barclay. It's on the left, between the two marines looking over the monitors.

Follow Colonel Barclay onto the elevator in the adjacent room and ride it up to Central Station. Approach the window and look out upon the civilians being ushered onto the trains—will the evacuation work? Enter the switching room next door with the Colonel and listen along until the building begins to shake—another Ceph assault!

NY SOUVENIR

Follow Barclay into the planning room and approach the table in the center of the room. This glass-encased model clock, similar to the kind that used to hang on the side of railroad stations, is on the corner of the table, next to the map.

HOLD BACK THE CEPH ASSAULT

Shoulder the MK.60 that has served Alcatraz so well these past few missions and journey through the maintenance corridors, past a pair of flimsy wooden doors, and up a spiraling staircase to the main station. The last flight of steps has collapsed. Run and jump the gap to the marine waving the way.

TAKE BACK THE TERMINAL

ENCOUNTER A

TRAIN TERMINAL

1. **COLLECT:** Gather the C4 located inside the ticket booth for use against the Pinger that attacks.
2. **ACQUIRE:** Pick up the JAWs and C4 on the upper walkway for the battle with the heavy units.

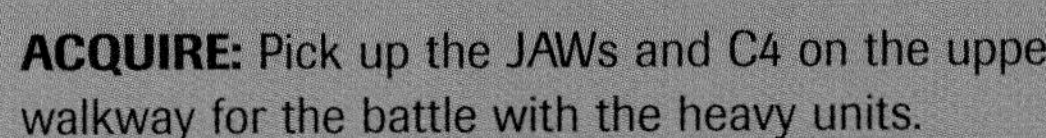

3. **USE:** Collect the JAWs, C4, and ammo located on the lower west walkway.
4. **TAKE:** Grab hold of the Swarmer and use it against the Devastator Unit that appears.

The battle in Central Station is underway by the time Alcatraz arrives on the scene and the Cephs aren't backing down a bit. Waste no time in getting to the Swarmer up the stairs to the left ④. Carry it to the top of the escalators leading down to the middle of the terminal and look for the Devastator Unit patrolling the lower level. Fix the Swarmer's laser on it and open fire. Release multiple volleys of rockets until the Devastator Unit is destroyed.

Load up on the C4 atop the crates near the top of the escalators, pick the Swarmer back up, and go hunting for any Cephs remaining from this initial wave. Stick to the perimeter of the area and load up on C4 and ammo for the JAW ③.

A Pinger bursts through the southern window not long after the Devastator Unit bursts to pieces. Toss the Swarmer aside, shoulder the JAW, and work around the perimeter while Cloaked to get a clean shot at the Pinger's weak point.

Ignore the other Cephs that may be in the area for now and focus on the Pinger. If one of the Ceph Combat Units does attack, simply beat it over the head with the JAW and keep moving. Maintain a safe distance from the Pinger to avoid its EMP blast. This enables Alcatraz to put the JAW's tremendous range to use.

If hitting it with the JAW proves too difficult, don't hesitate to switch to the C4. Unlike the JAW, the C4 can inflict heavy damage without having to directly hit the generator on the Ceph's back. Hang back until the Pinger emits its EMP blast then activate Armor mode, run in close enough to throw C4 onto it, then back away and squeeze the transmitter. Launch hit-and-run dashes in and out of the ticket booth until the Pinger's giant legs buckle and it comes crashing down. Grab the 2000 Nano Catalyst immediately!

ACHIEVEMENT

Dark Night of the Soul

Come to the marines' rescue at Central Station and fend off the Ceph assault. This is a heavy weapons battle against a Devastator Unit and a Pinger. Use the Swarmer against the Devastator, then switch to the JAW and C4 when the Pinger comes calling.

ESCAPE CENTRAL STATION COLLAPSE

BOARD THE VEHICLE TO TIMES SQUARE

The Cephs have unleashed another round of mortar attacks and Central Station is sure to collapse. Board the vehicle that drives to the center of the terminal so Alcatraz can escape with the rest of the convoy to Times Square.

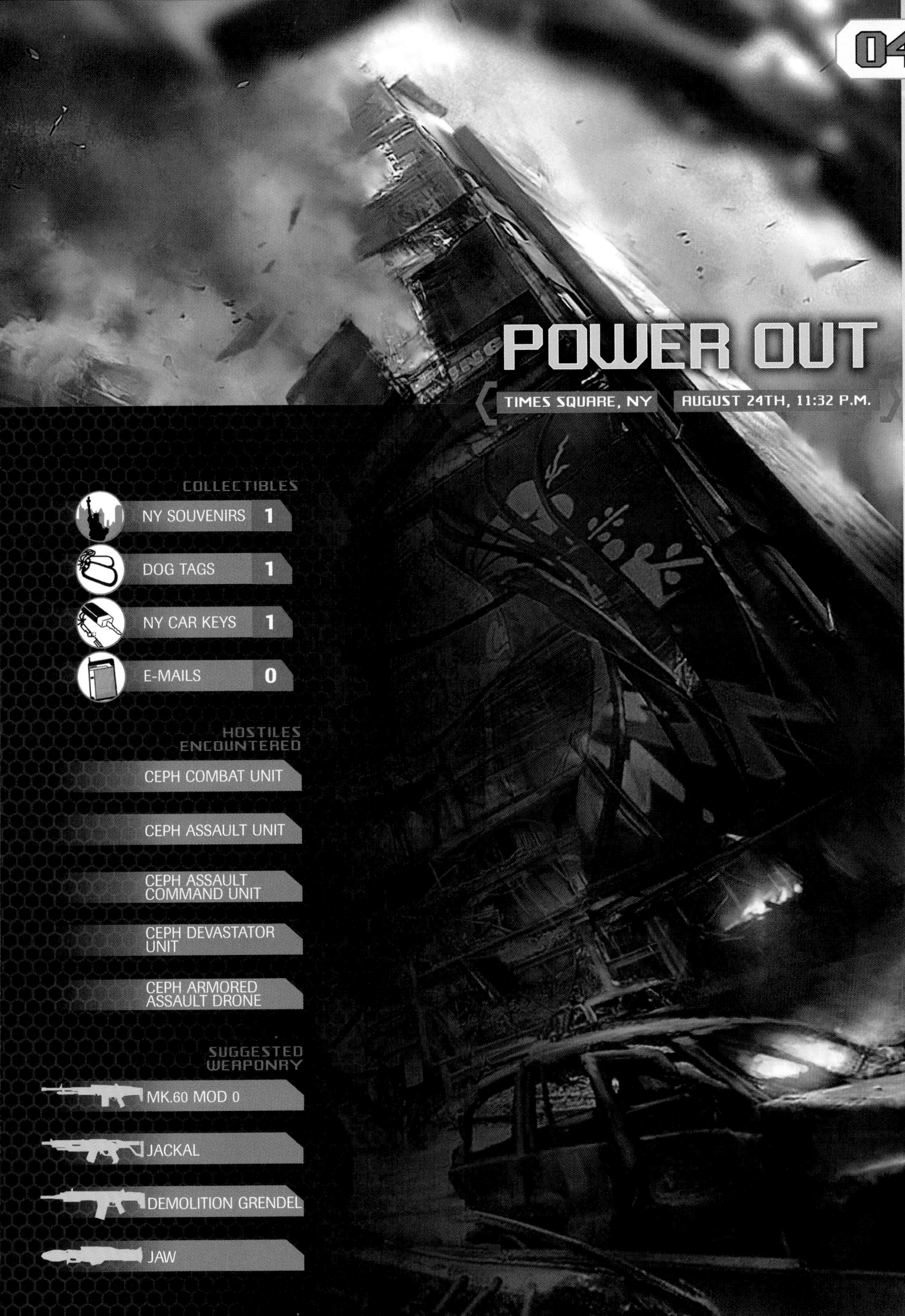

POWER OUT

TIMES SQUARE, NY | AUGUST 24TH, 11:32 P.M.

COLLECTIBLES

NY SOUVENIRS 1

DOG TAGS 1

NY CAR KEYS 1

E-MAILS 0

HOSTILES ENCOUNTERED

- CEPH COMBAT UNIT
- CEPH ASSAULT UNIT
- CEPH ASSAULT COMMAND UNIT
- CEPH DEVASTATOR UNIT
- CEPH ARMORED ASSAULT DRONE

SUGGESTED WEAPONRY

- MK.60 MOD 0
- JACKAL
- DEMOLITION GRENDEL
- JAW

DEFEND AIRLIFT EVAC SITE

REGROUP WITH MARINES AT TIMES SQUARE

Proceed down the road to the east and drop off the ledge to the road below. Times Square is just a short walk to the south. Continue through the checkpoint to a second ledge, providing Alcatraz with a view of the defense efforts.

HOLD BACK THE CEPH ATTACK

CAR KEY

Enter the security trailer to the right of the checkpoint en route to Times Square. The collectible Car Key is on the table, directly in front of the entrance.

ENCOUNTER A

TIMES SQUARE

SEARCH: Scour the police and fire department office near the intersection for weapons and explosives.

USE TURRET: Man the HMG above the digital news scroll in the southeast corner.

The Cephs are emerging in large numbers from the road leading to the west. Though the sushi shop on the corner to the right does provide some good coverage, it's too close to too many Cephs to be useful. Instead, circle around to the east and follow the perimeter in a clockwise direction to gather up the ammo and weapons behind the military trucks and blast shields. Consider swapping currently equipped weapons for the Demolition Grendel and Jackal. This pairing will serve Alcatraz well in this fight.

Continue around the edge of the area to the mounted HMG on the awning above the digital news scroll in the southeast corner ②. A Devastator Unit is among the early arrivers on the scene for the Ceph. Using the HMG against it allows Alcatraz to conserve JAW rockets and C4 for bigger foes yet to appear. Run the HMG until its dry then shoulder the Jackal or Demolition Grendel and angle toward the police department office to gather up the explosives inside and on the roof ①.

Use the police department office for cover and lure enemies through the narrow doorway and open fire with either weapon. Look for groups of enemies in close proximity to one another and switch the Demolition Grendel to grenade mode and let fly with the ranged explosive. Alcatraz has enough firepower and Nanosuit upgrades at this time to hunt the lesser Cephs with little concern. Go on the offensive, use the Jackal's automatic firing to blast through Ceph Combat and Assault Units. Keep an eye out for Assault Command Units and switch to the Grendel. Seek higher ground, use Cloak to avoid detection, and pelt the Assault Command Unit with several bursts straight to the head.

NY SOUVENIR

The NY Souvenir is on the counter inside Amim's Sandwich Bar at Times Square. Proceed through the evacuation center checkpoint near the starting point, turn left and move back along the wall to enter the sandwich shop.

The power goes out just as the last of the initial Ceph assault is repelled. Take advantage of the short lull in the action and resupply the Jackal and Demolition Grendel. This is a good time to also make sure that Alcatraz has a full supply of rockets for the JAW and C4. There is plenty of both scattered throughout the area, particularly near the military trucks and above and within the police department office.

A small cadre of Cephs is going to herald in the second assault. Target the Assault Command Unit and work quickly to eliminate it. Stay close the police department office and eliminate any other Cephs that stray too close for their own safety.

SEEING THROUGH THE DARK

Nanovision can help with the initial detection of the Cephs' arrival, but we recommend switching it off and simply allowing your eyes to focus on the reduced light. There's enough ambient light to see (depending on your brightness settings) without the need for Nanovision.

PINGER

A massive explosion from a car being thrown over the perimeter wall signals the arrival of a Pinger. It slowly makes its way up the street on the south side of the police department office. Shoulder the JAW, head to the north side of the office and activate Cloak. Ignore the other Cephs from this point forward unless they happen to attack at close range. Remain out of the Pinger's EMP range and circle back and forth around the police office to fire on it once it nears the main intersection at Times Square. It's possible to detect which way the Pinger is facing via its red arrow-shaped blip on the radar screen. Use this to knowledge to determine which side to approach from. Keep the police building between Alcatraz and the Pinger at all times and rest behind it long enough to fully recharge the Energy Meter before making another attack.

EVACUATE WITH COLONEL BARCLAY

Collect the 2000 Nano Catalyst dropped by the Pinger and cross the avenue to the military post on the north side of the intersection. Colonel Barclay throws open a door and welcomes Alcatraz inside. Proceed through the small building and out the other side to the air lift area and.

ACHIEVEMENT

Crossroads of the World

Defend the evacuation site at Times Square from the Ceph assault. Use the Jackal and Demolition Grendel to dispatch the Ceph footsoldiers and Devastator Unit then turn to the JAW and C4 once the lights go out to destroy the Pinger.

DOG TAG

Watch as the first VTOL aircraft takes off then quickly run to the right, leap over the small barricade and approach the table near the military truck. The Dog Tag is on this table.

SABOTAGE THE ALIEN SPEAR

An alien spear identical to the one that emerged as Alcatraz was being captured by Lockhart at the bank has burst through the road near the air lift site. Fortunately for those on board the aircraft, Hargreave is able to radio Colonel Barclay and explain what must be done. Alcatraz must approach the spear and step into the flow of spore just like before.

The attempted sabotage works like a charm, but not without a considerable amount of trauma dealt to Alcatraz. Follow the on-screen prompts to use the in-suit defibrillator, then crawl to the awaiting aircraft and leap to board it in order to escape the area. It's been a long couple of days, but Alcatraz's work isn't done yet. It's time to search for Hargreave.

EYE OF THE STORM

ROOSEVELT ISLAND | EAST RIVER, NY | AUGUST 25TH, 1:16 A.M.

COLLECTIBLES

NY SOUVENIRS 1

DOG TAGS 1

NY CAR KEYS 0

E-MAILS 3

HOSTILES ENCOUNTERED

CELL OPERATOR

SUGGESTED WEAPONRY

JACKAL

DSG-1

MK.60 MOD 0

STEALTH SCARAB

M20 14 GAUSS

INFILTRATE ROOSEVELT ISLAND

HEAD NORTH TOWARD THE PRISM

Alcatraz lands in the river a hundred yards south of the lighthouse on Roosevelt Island. Lockhart's men have the island covered from end to end. The best way to reach Hargreave is to be as stealthy as possible. Swim to the stairs leading up out of the water, activate Cloak, and stealth kill the CELL Operator to the left of the lighthouse. Enter the lighthouse while cloaked and climb the stairs.

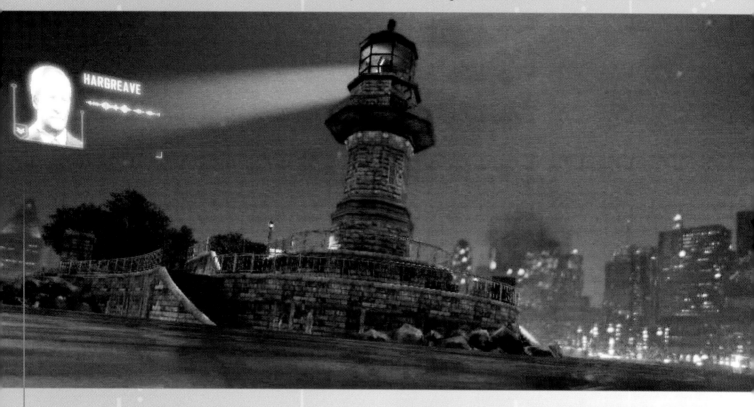

CLOAKED AND SILENCED

Success on Roosevelt Island only comes to those who master the art of stealth combat. Rely heavily on silenced weapons and stay Cloaked at all times. Move with a purpose, fall back to recharge the Energy Meter behind cover, and change positions frequently to keep the enemy guessing.

Listen for the enemy atop the lighthouse to radio his status back to the command post then sneak up behind him for the stealth kill. Equip his DSG-1, ensuring the silencer is attached, and load up on ammo inside the lighthouse landing. The enemy's failure to reply to the next status update will alert the others that something is afoot. Move around to the front and snipe the CELL Operators that drive up on the APC, starting with the one manning the turret gun. Clear the area near the lighthouse entrance of enemies then activate Cloak and descend the stairs to ensure none are scouting the area south of the lighthouse.

It's now time to begin the long, slow trek across the island to the north. Though it's possible to use Cloak and run past the enemies toward the prism, this could backfire with dire consequences. Uncloaking deep behind enemy lines is never a good idea! Instead, sweep back and forth across the island from east to west, using Cloak and the silenced DSG-1 to pick off the enemies as they appear. Keep all of the action in front of Alcatraz and fall back for cover to recharge the Energy Meter. If forced to make a run for it, run south; there is no safe haven to the north! Stealthily execute enemies or beat them with the butt of the rifle to avoid firing an un-silenced weapon while moving about the island exterior. Look for the laser sights betraying the positions of enemy patrols and move accordingly. Consider falling back to the lighthouse for additional ammo before advancing to the island's crumbling structures.

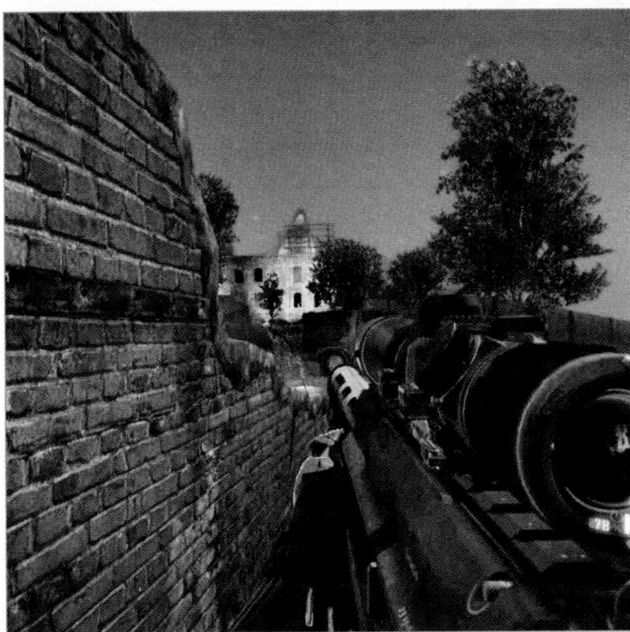

Scour the ruins near the center of the island for ammo and ensure that there aren't any CELL Operators in the area. Cautiously advance to the missile battery atop the hill in the center of the island to get a clear view of the defenses around the factory to the north.

ENCOUNTER A

ABANDONED FACTORY EXTERIOR

1. **FLANK:** Descend the hill to the west side of the island and sneak around the enemies to the left.
2. **LEDGE GRAB:** Run and leap from the container to the window ledge on the second floor to avoid the front door.
3. **STEALTH:** Bypass the CELL Operators outside the factory by using Cloak to reach the window ledge without them knowing.

Drop off the hill to the west side of the island and move alongside the rocks to flank the enemy's main defenses near the building's front entrance ①. Snipe the enemies nearest the front door then double back through the ruins to pick off the others in the area, starting with the CELL Operator manning the turret gun. Look for a dropped MK.60 and swap whatever Alcatraz's secondary weapon is for the powerful MK.60.

Snipe the enemy manning the HMG in the second floor window to eliminate the final threat in the area. The yellow tactical assessment options disappear once all of the enemies have been dealt with. Alcatraz can enter the building through a window or either of the two ground-floor doorways should this occur. Otherwise, either enter through the door on the west side of the building, or use Cloak to approach the containers ③ and run and leap to the window ledge ②.

E-MAIL

Download this E-Mail from the tablet on the desk inside the front entrance. Alcatraz can reach the main entryway from each of the three ways inside.

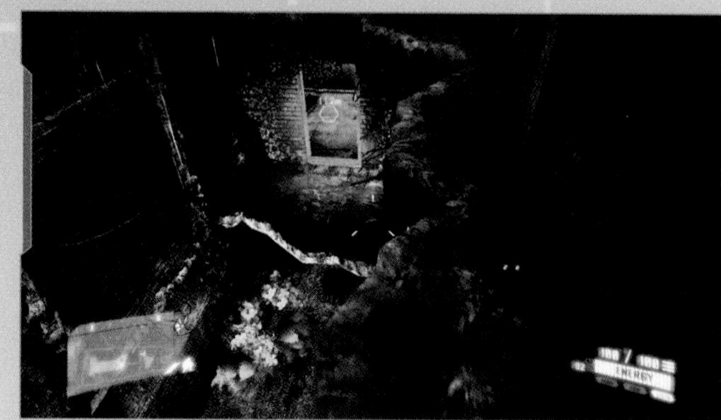

Resist the temptation to swap the DSG-1 for the Ranged Grendel in the weapon crate near the E-Mail, as it lacks the valuable silencer attachment. Head upstairs via the fallen floor and stealth kill the CELL Operator in the middle of the second floor. Leap and grab the ledge above to climb straight up to the third floor. Continue through the door to the north and drop to the water-filled ground floor room. Climb up to the second floor to continue on toward the north exit of the building as Hargreave provides Alcatraz with his next set of instructions. Run and leap from ledge to ledge while heading in a primarily northeasterly heading. It appears as if Alcatraz has come to a dead-end. Look up to the east and leap to the well-lit doorway on the third floor. Drop through the hole in the floor and continue on to the exit.

REACH THE ELECTRICITY SUBSTATION

ENCOUNTER B

APPROACHING THE SUBSTATION

1. **FLANK:** Alcatraz can work his way around the western edge of the substation and enter through the north gate.
2. **SNIPE:** Climb the stairs to the balcony on the powerhouse while Cloaked and snipe the guards.
3. **STEALTH:** Use Cloak to slip around the east side of the substation by swimming around the wall.

Snipe the two enemies standing behind the remains of the brick wall and lay claim to the Scarab rifle that one of them drops. Attach the silencer and laser sight and toggle the firing rate to semi-automatic. Move east to west along the southern edge of the substation to take out the CELL Operators patrolling the area. Use the Scarab, or DSG-1, to snipe the enemy in the watchtower and either enter through the break in the center of the wall or swim around the eastern edge (3).

Weave back and forth through the grid of generators while gradually progressing north. This is a safer tactic than simply heading due north and hoping to not run into too many CELL Operators. Pick them off from afar, circle around the south side of some of the generators, then snipe from the other side. Advance until the powerhouse comes into view. Eliminate the enemies near the APC out front and those manning the mounted HMGs on the balcony. Loop around to attack from the side.

Enter the powerhouse through the front door and board the elevator in the northeast corner. Press the button and descend to the basement.

NY SOUVENIR

A model lighthouse is on the table inside the watchtower in the corner of the substation area. Climb onto the transformer and run and leap to the tower. Beware the charged transformer spindles or return to do this after the power is off.

RE-ROUTE POWER AND DISABLE EMP TRAP

Exit the elevator, enable Cloak, and move west through the empty rooms to the CELL Operator in the distance. Snap his neck and crouch out of sight to allow the Energy Meter to recharge then inch out the doorway to the room with the catwalk and snipe the two enemies near the office across the room and those on the floor below.

E-MAIL

Stay on the catwalk in the generator room and cross to the office in the far corner. The E-Mail tablet is on the desk on the right.

Exit the room with the enemies via the door to the south. Advance slowly toward the high voltage room to inspect the area, then back up and sprint and slide past the arcing jolts of electricity. Pull the power switch to sink the entire powerhouse into pitch-black darkness.

LEAVE THE SUBSTATION

Activate Nanovision, grab the MK.60 or Jackal, and run north back the way Alcatraz just came. Several CELL Operators have opened a door inside the room with the catwalk. Gun them down and proceed through the door through which they exited. Enter the room with the numerous generators, activate Cloak, and work around the perimeter of the room, clearing it of enemies. Many attack from the catwalk directly overhead; open fire through the metal grating to shoot them from below. Exit through the door on the south side via the catwalk and ride the elevator back up.

NANOVISION COSTS ENERGY

The CELL Operators can see Alcatraz thanks to their night-vision goggles, so it pays to use the Nanosuit's Cloak ability even in the darkness. Keep in mind that Nanovision also consumes energy so the Energy Meter decreases faster than it normally would if Alcatraz were just using Cloak.

ENTER THE GATEHOUSE

A large number of reinforcements have amassed in front of the substation, including a second APC with another CELL Operator manning the HMG. Activate Cloak upon exiting the elevator and snipe those enemies nearest the door leading out of the substation; this is where Alcatraz entered minutes ago. Play it safe and loop around the north side of the powerhouse in a counter-clockwise direction to the gate on the west side, near the watchtower. Proceed north along the main path toward the next structure and crouch beneath the partially-closed garage door to head inside.

SHOWDOWN

DOG TAG

Enter the room to the left of the garage where Alcatraz is briefly trapped. The Dog Tag is beside the gun crate, on the cardboard boxes opposite the doorway.

ELIMINATE COMMANDER LOCKHART

Lockhart's trap didn't work, but it did cast Alcatraz in a tight situation. Enter the room to the left of the garage where he appeared to be stuck and quickly shoot off the padlocks on the sewer grates in the floor. Grab some ammo and the Dog Tag, and drop into the sewer to escape the approaching CELL Operators.

The sewer pipes split into two directions, one drains out into the water on the island and one leads to an open grate not far from Lockhart's compound. Make a left at the first intersection after entering the pipes and follow this lengthy section of pipe all the way to where it drains in the northwest corner of the island. Swim over to the docks and quickly take cover.

Lockhart has a seemingly never-ending supply of CELL Operators willing to defend him to the death. It's no longer advisable to try and kill each and every enemy, as more soon arrive to take their place. Many enter wielding L-TAGs and other powerful weapons. Alcatraz's best bet is to be as stealthy as possible while moving swiftly around the west side of the building where Lockhart is. Only engage those enemies who stand directly in Alcatraz's path.

WATCH THE COMPASS BEARINGS

Many of Lockhart's men have moved to the south, in anticipation of Alcatraz's exit from the rigged garage bay where the EMP was supposed to trap him. Regardless which sewer pipe you choose to exit, don't head south! There are too many enemies located in that direction to deal with economically.

Climb the stairs on the north side of the building and take cover near the base of a watchtower to avoid the searchlights. Snipe the few enemies near the green-lit door leading inside, and on the second floor balcony. Now make a run for it! Enter the green hallway on the right and dash straight away for the stairs leading up to the second floor. Lockhart is behind the locked door. Activate Armor mode then Power Kick the door off its hinges to get to him.

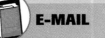

E-MAIL

The third and final E-Mail in this level is in the control room where Lockhart was holed up. It's on a computer terminal opposite the window through which Lockhart is given his flying lesson.

ACCESS PRISM FACILITY AND FIND HARGREAVE

Alcatraz made it through the compound and killed Lockhart, but now he has to make it out alive. Equip the M20 14 Gauss near the window and set to eliminating the CELL Operators on the ground below. The M20 only comes with eight rounds, but these Gauss solid slugs are capable of traveling straight through whatever they hit—metal or flesh, it doesn't matter. Detonate the fuel drums near the missile battery to the east where many of the enemies are located. Look for an opportunity to take out multiple CELLs with a single round. This unlocks the "Two Heads are Better than One" bonus. Discard the spent M20 before leaving and use the Stealth Scarab to snipe and enemies still standing, particularly those near the gate to the Prism facility far in the distance to the east.

Descend the stairs and cross past the missile battery toward the Prism facility in the distance. Move between cover and snipe each of the enemies spotted as they get within range. Sprint through the gate while Cloaked and take cover either behind the 18-wheeler trailers or the Crynet Systems sign in the corner of the yard. Snipe the final two enemies stationed near the door and head inside to meet Hargreave.

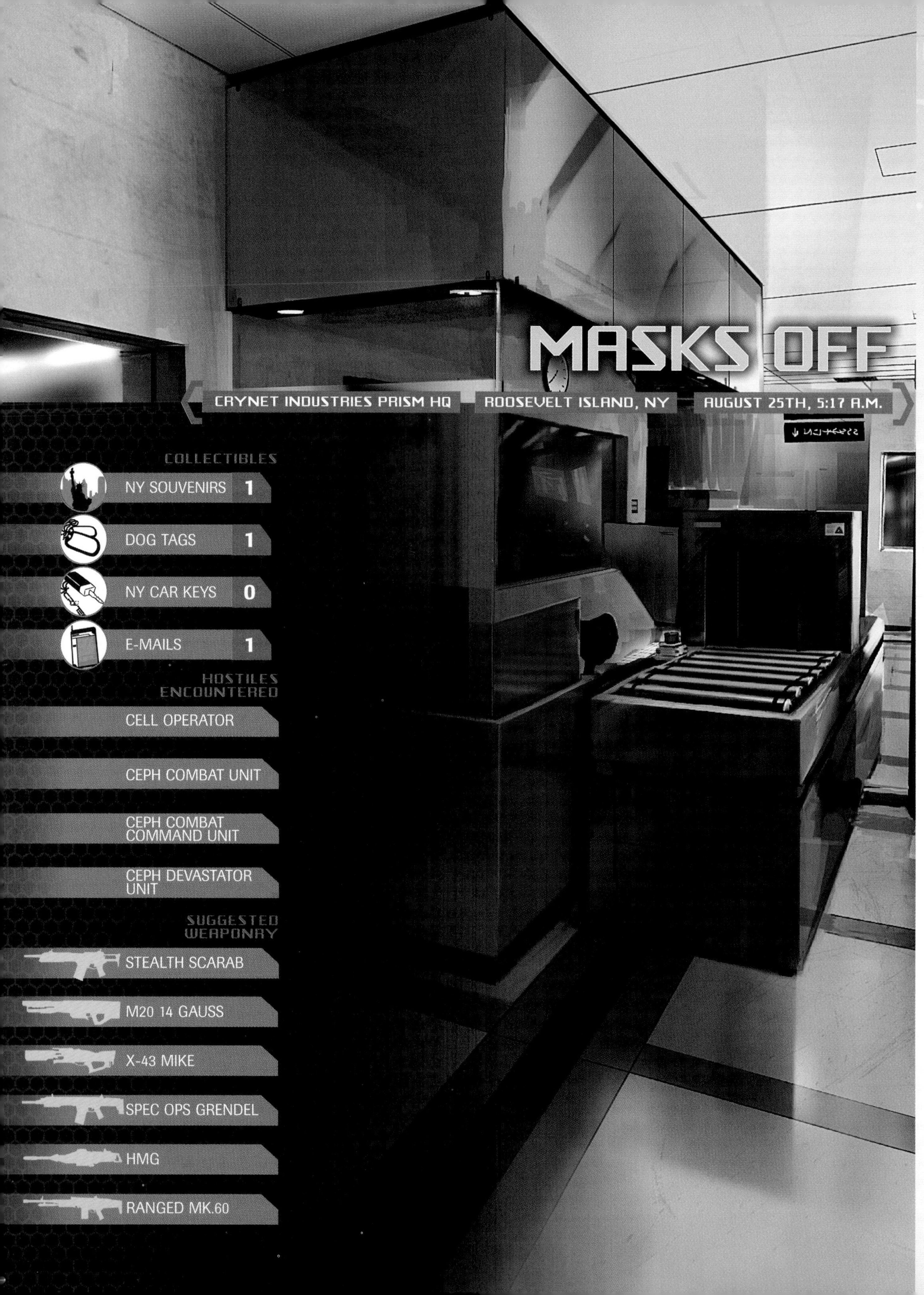

MASKS OFF

CRYNET INDUSTRIES PRISM HQ | ROOSEVELT ISLAND, NY | AUGUST 25TH, 5:17 A.M.

COLLECTIBLES

NY SOUVENIRS	1
DOG TAGS	1
NY CAR KEYS	0
E-MAILS	1

HOSTILES ENCOUNTERED

- CELL OPERATOR
- CEPH COMBAT UNIT
- CEPH COMBAT COMMAND UNIT
- CEPH DEVASTATOR UNIT

SUGGESTED WEAPONRY

- STEALTH SCARAB
- M20 14 GAUSS
- X-43 MIKE
- SPEC OPS GRENDEL
- HMG
- RANGED MK.60

LOCATE & EXTRACT HARGREAVE

FIND AND CONFRONT JACOB HARGREAVE

Alcatraz is freed from the trap and warned that the Ceph are attacking the headquarters; he must assist Tara Strickland in rescuing Hargreave, as he is the only one with specific combat knowledge of the Ceph. Follow Tara to the freight elevator and ride it up to security floor.

ENCOUNTER A

HQ SECURITY

1. **FLANK:** Avoid the security checkpoint and metal detector by moving through the room to the south.
2. **EXPLORE:** Collect the Dog Tag near the ammo crate on the second floor.
3. **STEALTH:** Use the Cloak ability to slip through the gallery undetected.

The elevator lets Alcatraz off near a security office manned by multiple CELL Operators. Locate and equip the Stealth Scarab before activating Cloak to sneak past the guards (1). Duck into a corner of the storage room to the south and eliminate any enemies in the room. Fire off an un-silenced round from the Stealth Scarab to alert the other guards, then re-attach the silencer, activate Cloak, and pick off each of the enemies as they arrive to investigate. Use the couches in the adjacent lobby for cover while the other guards descend the stairs.

Ascend the stairs to the second floor and investigate the room with the ammo crates to find a Dog Tag and more ammo for the Stealth Scarab (2). Continue to the third floor and activate Cloak before nearing the door to the gallery. Snipe the CELL Operator on the scaffolding across the room—his laser sight gives him away—and enter quietly. Take cover behind paintings or columns to allow the Energy Meter to recharge. Make the most of the stealth provided by Cloak and stay crouched to reduce the sound of Alcatraz's footsteps.

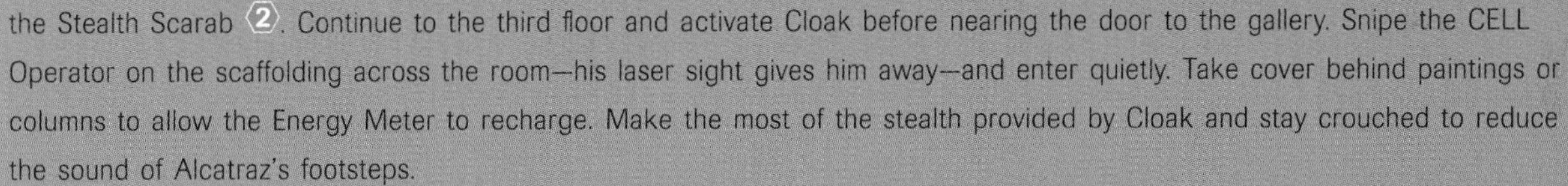

Cross the room to the northwest while Cloaked and load up on Frag Grenades. A CELL Operator is pointing a mounted HMG down the lengthy of long hallway to the west. Ready a grenade and quickly lob it down the hall then duck for cover to avoid the inevitable return fire. Watch the mini-map for indication that the enemy has been slain, then advance cautiously. Have a look around the rest of the gallery then continue down the hallway to the north to Hargreave's private office.

DOG TAG

The Dog Tag is on the floor beside the ammo crate with the Stealth Scarab on the second floor. Eliminate the enemies near the security office and in the lobby, then climb the stairs to the second floor.

BULLET DEFLECTION

This is a good time to purchase the Deflection upgrade for the Nanosuit if possible, as the action is going to increase significantly before long. The upgrade costs 12,000 Nano Catalyst.

ACHIEVEMENT

Theseus at Last

Eliminate the CELL Operators in the third floor gallery of the Prism HQ building and proceed down the hall to the north. Hargreave is just beyond those doors...

UPGRADE NANOSUIT WITH FINAL FIXING PROTOCOL

Listen to Hargreave's depiction of the events that have led Alcatraz to this room. Watch as the large table near his chamber reveals a hidden compartment and use the syringe containing the fixing protocol to upgrade the Nanosuit.

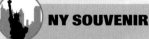

NY SOUVENIR

The small model of the Queensboro Bridge can be found on the table in front of the large world map at the north end of the room with Hargreave.

ESCAPE THE PRISM FACILITY

REACH SAFE DISTANCE FROM SELF-DESTRUCTION

The Ceph have arrived, and both the gallery and Hargreave's chamber are set to be enveloped in fiery destruction. There is no victory for Alcatraz here—run! Activate Armor mode, sprint up the stairs to the second floor bookshelves, and duck through the opening to enter a secret corridor. Power Kick the crate blocking the door on the right and hurry into the red-glowing room.

E-MAIL

The E-Mail tablet is on the floor in the room with the red lights. It's at the north end of the room, near the two large crates, left of the exit.

Unlock the metal gate using the keypad, and carefully walk onto the wooden pallet in the partially flooded room. The electrical equipment in the room is short-circuiting and electrifying the water. Enable the Nanosuit's Armor mode, wait for a lull in the sparking electrical current, then quickly move from pallet to pallet to avoid electrocution. Run and jump over the watery portions to keep safe.

Exit the room via the second locked gate and proceed down the well-lit hallway to the north. Equip the M20 14 Gauss lying against the equipment and kick open the door on the right to exit the facility.

LEGACY

FIGHT YOUR WAY TO THE BRIDGE ELEVATOR

ENCOUNTER B

ROOFTOPS AND HELIPAD

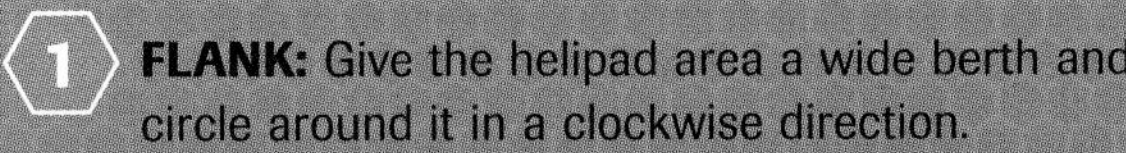

1 **FLANK:** Give the helipad area a wide berth and circle around it in a clockwise direction.

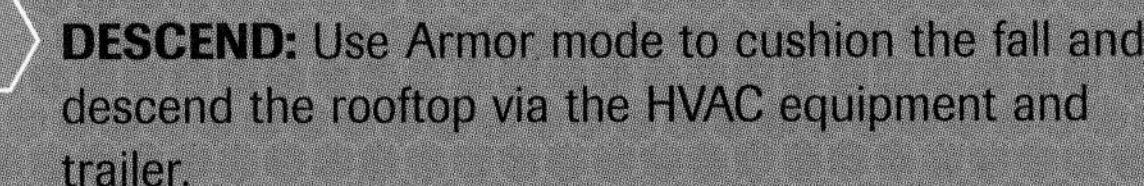

2 **DESCEND:** Use Armor mode to cushion the fall and descend the rooftop via the HVAC equipment and trailer.

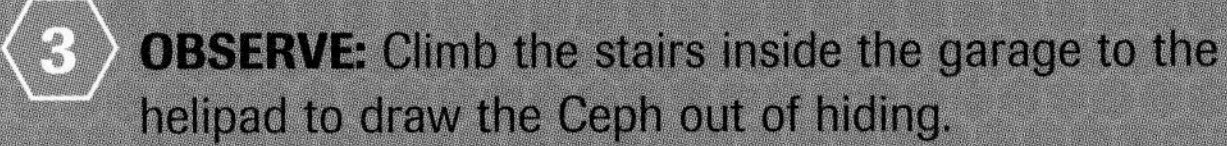

3 **OBSERVE:** Climb the stairs inside the garage to the helipad to draw the Ceph out of hiding.

Alcatraz exits onto the rooftop not far from a helipad. Activate Armor mode and descend the building by leaping down onto the air conditioning units and ductwork ②. Draw the M20 14 Gauss and snipe the Ceph Combat Units in the street below, then drop onto the trailer.

Switch to the Stealth Scarab and stealthily circle the building with the helipad to the left. Take cover behind the jersey barriers to avoid the energy based attacks from the Ceph. Enter the garage beneath the helipad and ascend the stairs ③. Equip the X-43 Mike near the ammo crates and climb onto the helipad to draw a Ceph Combat Command Unit out of hiding. Swap between ballistic weapons and the X-43 Mike to eliminate the Cephs in this area. Use traditional weapons to detonate fuel drums as the Ceph walk past them, and use the X-43 Mike to explode the tougher enemies and save ammo. Take a moment to scan the area to the south.

Drop off the helipad to the south and quickly duck into the building to the right, where the ammo crates are located. Peek through the hole in the wall to spot a Ceph Devastator Unit. Aim the X-43 Mike at it and hold the trigger to keep the beam fixed on it. Gradually back up as the Devastator Unit approaches and use Armor mode as necessary.

Dash across the street to the stairwell behind the broken glass and detach the HMG from its mount in time to open fire on multiple Cephs descending the stairs. Head to the second floor of the Hargreave-Rasch building and proceed down the hall on the left, to a locked door. Set the HMG down to use the keypad then pick it back up and continue on.

ENCOUNTER C

HARGREAVE-RASCH PARKING AREA

1. **OBSERVE:** Peer through the window atop the stairs to spot the exit across the parking lot.
2. **STEALTH:** Cross the parking area to the left and sneak up the stairs to the second floor walkway.
3. **NEUTRALIZE:** Eliminate the Cephs on the upper walkway and near the HVAC system to the right.

Take a moment to study the lay of the Hargreave-Rasch offices and inner parking area from the relative safety of the stairwell ① then break the glass and drop onto the elevated courtyard. Use the HMG to gun down the nearby Cephs, and keep an eye out for the Ceph Combat Command Unit approaching from the parking area. Use either the HMG or X-43 Mike to dispatch it then make a run for cover across the parking lot to the left.

Activate Cloak and sneak up the metal stairs to the walkway that runs left-to-right across the other half of the building ②. Use the X-43 Mike to eliminate the Cephs in the area above the rolling metal door then leap down and slide under the partially-opened door.

ENCOUNTER D

BRIDGE TOWER APPROACH

1. **FLANK:** Leap over the hedges on the right and sneak down the road to the right-hand break in the large fence.
2. **SNIPE:** Put a sniping weapon to use and eliminate the enemies on the left side of the parking area.
3. **AVOID:** There are two Devastator Units patrolling the area amongst the trailers. Stay clear of them!

Collect the ammo, grenades, and preferred weaponry from the weapons cache on the right, then hop over the hedges and sprint easterly toward the bridge. Activate Cloak as Alcatraz nears the large fence and slip through the gap on the right to flank the enemies near the main parking entrance ①. Going through the main entryway is highly unadvised without first sniping many of the enemies in that area ②.

The bridge elevator isn't far, but the area is crawling with Cephs, including a pair of Devastator Units. Making matters worse, the area is also experiencing heavy mortar fire. Don't take any chances! Wait for the Energy Meter to fully replenish then slowly and carefully sneak past all of the enemies while Cloaked and leap through the gap in the fence nearest the elevator tower. Cross the walkway at the middle of the tower and ride the second elevator up to the road surface.

▶ PUSH ACROSS THE BRIDGE

The CELL are finally on Alcatraz's side, so resist the urge to attack those on the bridge. Strafe the flaming bus near the elevator, turn north, and start running!

NO TIME TO BE A HERO!

The Queensboro Bridge is crawling with Cephs of all levels of hostility and the Prism HQ facility is rigged to blow any moment. This is not the time to be concerned with collecting Nano Catalyst; kill only those who get directly in Alcatraz's way and run past the others!

ENCOUNTER E

QUEENSBORO BRIDGE

1. **ASCEND:** Sprint past the Cephs near the elevator exit and run up the collapsed roadway to the upper deck.
2. **AVOID:** The lower level of the bridge has numerous Cephs. It's best to steer clear of them.
3. **NEUTRALIZE:** Beware the Cephs positioned high above the evacuation checkpoint.

Stay to the left-hand side of the roadway and open fire on the two lesser Cephs guarding the collapsed roadway ①. Ascend the ramp-like slab of asphalt to the upper level of the bridge and equip the Ranged MK.60 lying on the crates directly to the north.

Stay to the extreme left side of the bridge and proceed north toward the next large hole in the road surface. Wait behind cover for the Energy Meter to replenish and stay Cloaked for as long as possible. Hop onto the left-hand guardrail and carefully balance atop the white safety barrier to bypass the colossal hole in the bridge. Sneak through the evacuation checkpoint and right past the numerous Ceph Combat Units guarding the position. Alcatraz is almost to safety now!

Run a route between the abandoned cars and other obstacles for as long as possible before the bridge begins to collapse from the massive explosion. Alcatraz takes off running on his own. Watch for the on-screen button prompt that saves him from sliding off the edge of the bridge. Or does it?

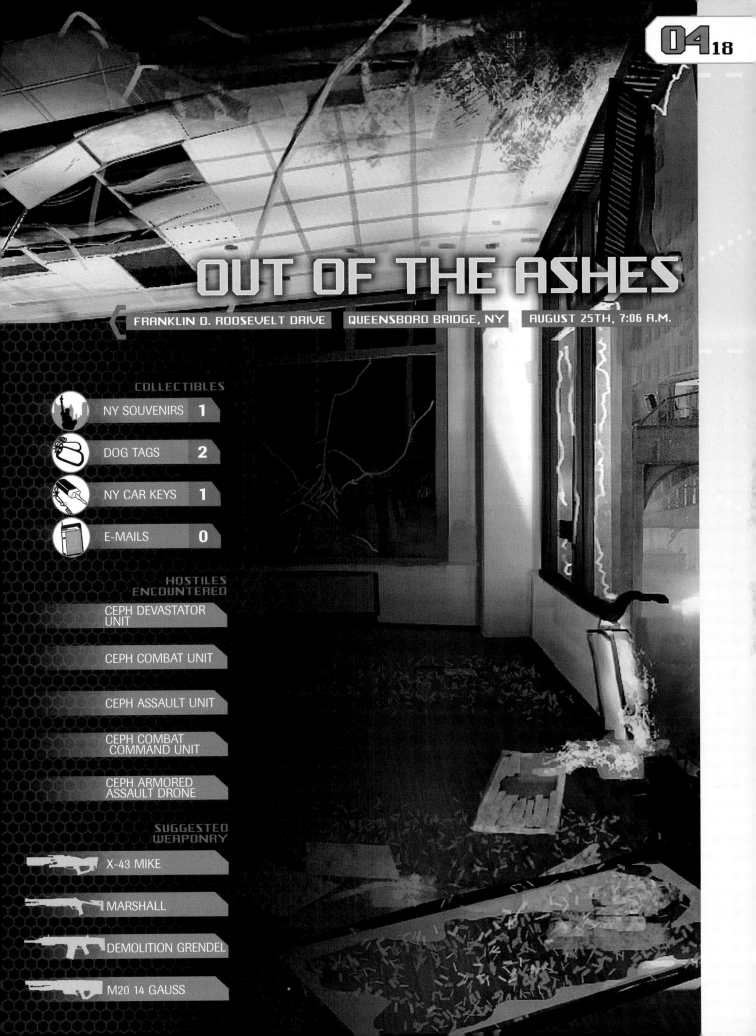

OUT OF THE ASHES

FRANKLIN D. ROOSEVELT DRIVE | QUEENSBORO BRIDGE, NY | AUGUST 25TH, 7:06 A.M.

COLLECTIBLES

NY SOUVENIRS	1
DOG TAGS	2
NY CAR KEYS	1
E-MAILS	0

HOSTILES ENCOUNTERED

- CEPH DEVASTATOR UNIT
- CEPH COMBAT UNIT
- CEPH ASSAULT UNIT
- CEPH COMBAT COMMAND UNIT
- CEPH ARMORED ASSAULT DRONE

SUGGESTED WEAPONRY

- X-43 MIKE
- MARSHALL
- DEMOLITION GRENDEL
- M20 14 GAUSS

REACH CEPH STRUCTURE AT CENTRAL PARK

MOUNT THE VEHICLE

Crawl out of the river and leap to Tara and Gould atop the highway. Swap the pistol Alcatraz has for the X-43 Mike and equip either the Marshall or K-Volt. Alcatraz is needed to man the cannon turret atop the tank; he'll be the escort for those in the other vehicles.

Listen along to Gould and Tara as the convoy trundles its way toward Central Park. A Ceph gunship attacks just after Barclay comes on the radio so be ready for action. The tank can fire cannon shells from its primary turret, as well as highly-explosive missiles from its secondary launching system.

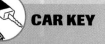

CAR KEY

The Car Key in this area is right near the starting point, on a rock beyond the vehicles. Pick it up before boarding the vehicle.

COVER THE CONVOY

It's up to Alcatraz to provide the heavy firepower to keep the Ceph at bay so the rest of the convoy can reach the rally point. Fire the primary cannon turret at the grunts, and save the missiles for the Devastator Units and Pinger. The missile launcher fires from each side of the vehicle in an alternating pattern and can be fired simultaneously with the main cannon. Rapidly fire both weapons to provide ample cover for the other vehicles as they pass the Pinger. Continue firing on the Ceph until a number of tentacles emerge from the ground and block the route, forcing Alcatraz to continue on foot from this point on.

PUSH THROUGH THE BUILDING, REJOIN THE TEAM

Load up on ammo from the piles of crates scattered amongst the road debris and drop into the trench in the middle of the street. Advance slowly toward the large building to the south. Use the X-43 Mike to destroy the Devastator Unit guarding the stairs, then fall back for a tactical assessment of the situation.

DEVASTATOR UNIT

ENCOUNTER A

BUILDING APPROACH

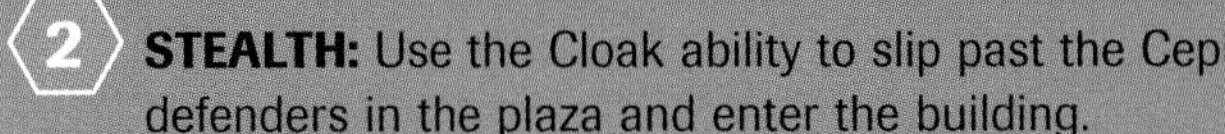

1 **RESUPPLY:** Fall back to the ammo crate across the plaza from the entrance if in need of more shells.

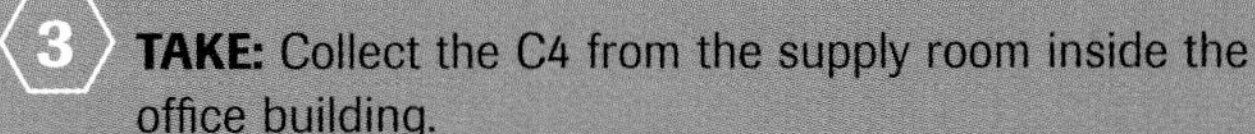

2 **STEALTH:** Use the Cloak ability to slip past the Ceph defenders in the plaza and enter the building.

3 **TAKE:** Collect the C4 from the supply room inside the office building.

It may not look like there are many Cephs in the area, but drop pods continue to rain down from the sky the longer Alcatraz stays in this area. There are too many high level enemies in the area to risk trying to annihilate them all. Remain Cloaked, move extremely slowly, and engage only those enemies that pose a direct threat. Stealthily kill those that can be killed without alarm so as to gain more Nano Catalyst.

Circle around the perimeter of the plaza, past the ammo crate (1), and toward the stairs leading into the building from the southwest while trying to avoid detection (2). Continue through the parking area, and past the kiosks to enter via the less crowded stairs leading to the room with the red lights. Proceed down the hall in the southwest corner to the table with the C4 (3). Push the call button for the elevator and ride it to the upper levels. The elevator takes a while to open after pushing the call button so make sure there aren't any Ceph in the immediate area before pushing it.

DOG TAG

The first of two Dog Tags in this area is found in the open elevator, to the left of the one that Alcatraz must ride in. It's on the floor, in the back corner of the elevator.

HEAD UPWARD TO A SUITABLE VANTAGE POINT AND MARK THE CEPH TARGETS BELOW

The marines need Alcatraz to be their eyes for them. He needs to reach a catwalk high on the building and use his visor to target a Ceph gunship patrolling the skies around the building. The marines can use their tracking systems to blast the gunship out of the sky, but only after Alcatraz fixes a target on it.

ENCOUNTER B

COLLAPSED OFFICE & HOTEL

STEALTH: Avoid detection and leap from platform to platform along the building's exterior.

USE TURRET: The mounted HMG makes it possible to take on the army of Ceph in the office building.

Exit the elevator and head down the hall to the left. Eliminate the Ceph in the cafeteria and step out onto the platform outside the window ①. Run and leap to the second platform to get a clear view of the Ceph gunships.

Another option is to turn to the right upon exiting the elevator and slip through the collapsed rooms of the hotel to reach the turret ② overlooking the office. Open fire on the Ceph to clear the room of enemies then step out onto the exterior walkway to reach the vantage point.

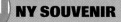

NY SOUVENIR

Approach the southeast corner of the green office room and look to the collapsed floors of the hotel. Run and leap onto the bedroom above the bathroom to find this NY Souvenir on the floor next to the bed.

MARK THE CEPH AMBUSH FOR AIRSTRIKE

Open the visor and zoom in on the Ceph gunship to the southwest. Highlight the enemy craft according to the on-screen prompt and watch as the marines launch an airstrike on the enemy. Be careful when panning for the enemy ship that Alcatraz doesn't accidentally walk off the platform.

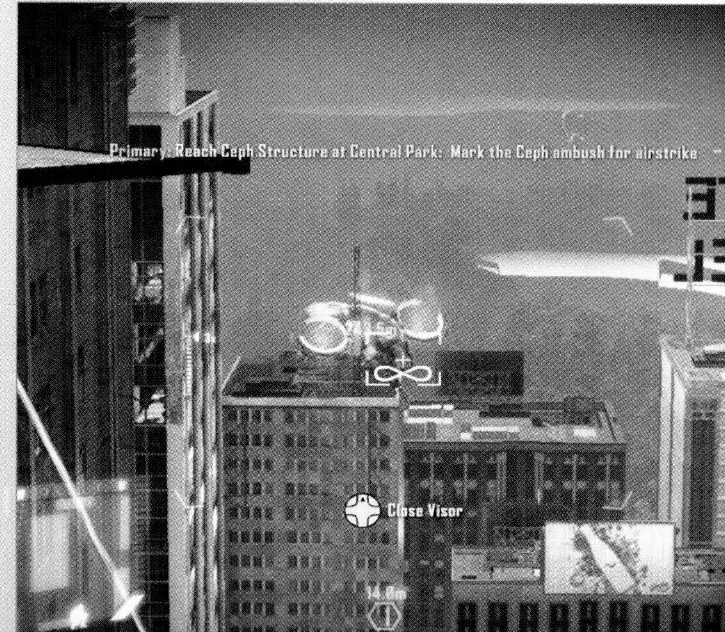

DESCEND THE BUILDING AND REGROUP WITH THE TEAM

Cross past the desks in the main office to the crumbling hotel rooms and enter the lower bedroom adjacent to the bathroom area. Head down the hall to the right to approach the stairwell where the turret is located. Follow the "running man" exit sign into the brick stairwell on the left and climb the stairs to the hole in the wall. Activate Armor mode and leap out of the building onto the mattresses placed strategically on the roof below.

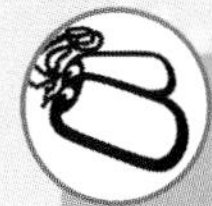

DOG TAG

The second Dog Tag is atop the tallest rooftop greenhouse. It's lying next to a body on the metal roof—climb up from the lower portion of the greenhouse.

ENCOUNTER C

ROOFTOP ESCAPE

1. **RESUPPLY:** Acquire the Demolition Grendel and ammunition from the supply crates near the air conditioning units.
2. **LEDGE GRAB:** Power Jump onto the eastern-most greenhouse then run and leap to the ledge to the south.
3. **TAKE:** Equip the M20 14 Gauss from atop the platform in the northwest corner.

Gather up the supplies near the corpse (1) before running and leaping off the southwest corner of the building to the rooftop greenhouses on the adjacent roof. Sweep through the greenhouses to the north and scale the mesh catwalk in the northwest corner to find an M20 14 Gauss (3) near a mounted HMG. There are only a couple of Cephs in this area, but they can swarm Alcatraz's position quickly. Stealth kill those that are alone, otherwise use a silenced weapon—either the Grendel or the M20 14 Gauss—and eliminate them with headshots.

Continue west across the rooftop, either via the ledge grab (2), or by climbing the stairs to the uppermost greenhouse and keep moving west. An army of Ceph is hot on Alcatraz's tail, including a Devastator Unit. Standing and fighting is not advised. Approach the western edge of the building, look down to spot the roof with the numerous solar panels, and make an Armor-protected leap of faith down to it. Survive the jump in time to watch all of Central Park rip straight out of the ground and float upwards into the sky. The team sends a helicopter to pick Alcatraz up.

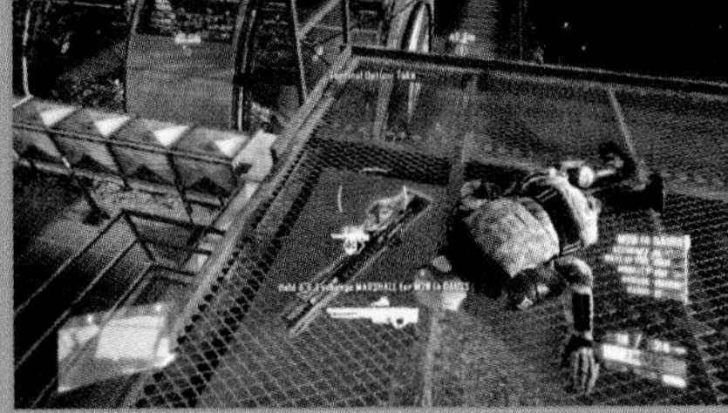

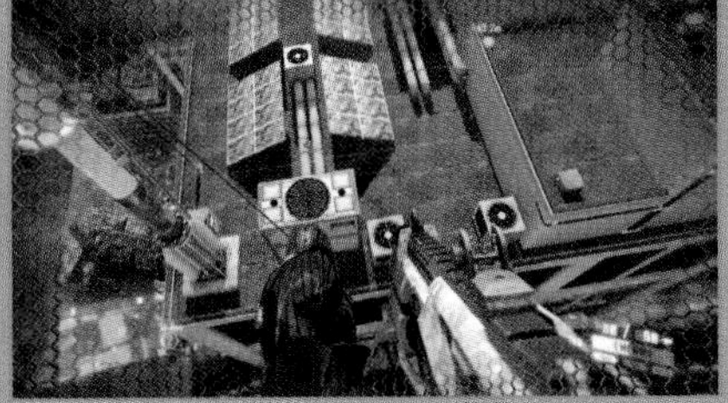

A WALK IN THE PARK

FRANKLIN D. ROOSEVELT DRIVE | QUEENSBORO BRIDGE, NY | AUGUST 25TH, 7:06 A.M.

COLLECTIBLES

NY SOUVENIRS	1
DOG TAGS	1
NY CAR KEYS	1
E-MAILS	0

HOSTILES ENCOUNTERED

- CEPH COMBAT UNIT
- CEPH ASSAULT UNIT
- CEPH COMBAT COMMAND UNIT
- CEPH ASSAULT COMMAND UNIT
- CEPH DEVASTATOR UNIT
- ADVANCED CEPH ASSAULT UNIT

SUGGESTED WEAPONRY

- MK.60 MOD 0
- RANGED GRENDEL
- JAW
- X-43 MIKE
- K-VOLT

INFILTRATE CEPH LITHO-SHIP & SUBVERT THE SPORE

REACH THE SPEAR

ACHIEVEMENT

Home Stretch

It may not have gone exactly according to plan, but Alcatraz has made it to Central Park. This is where the Ceph's assault on New York is originating from, and it's where Alcatraz is going to end this battle once and for all.

Alcatraz exits the helicopter on the southeaster edge of the floating Central Park island. The spear's tentacles continue to tear the park apart, causing it to fracture and crumble. Alcatraz must be careful not to fall from this makeshift sky island. This lower corner of the island is relatively free of Cephs; follow the cobblestone walkway as it winds its way to the northwest.

CAR KEY

Follow the walkway to the small snack stand and enter the bus dangling off the edge. The Car Key is lying on the dashboard next to the steering wheel.

Continue along the left-hand edge of the island as it wraps around to the north. The path deteriorates to little more than a sloped ledge with sheer rock cliffs on the right and a deadly plunge on the left. Hug the cliffs as closely as possible to avoid falling. Stealth kill the nearest Ceph Combat Unit where the path opens up onto solid ground, then eliminate the other Ceph in the area by detonating the fuel drum nearest it. Ascend the grassy slope past the boulders to the stack of shipping containers on the left.

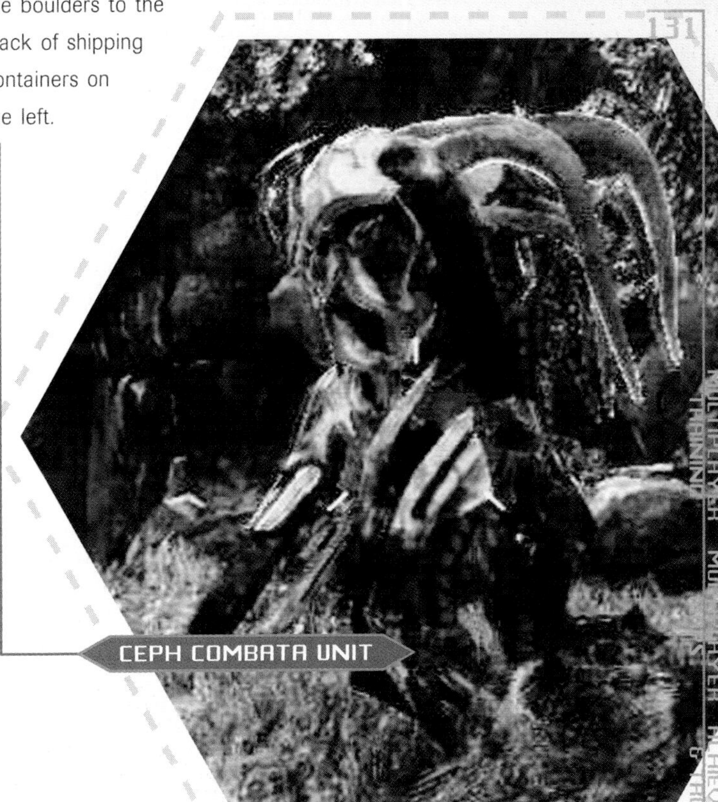

CEPH COMBATA UNIT

ENCOUNTER A

AMPHITHEATRE

1. **FLANK:** Walk along the tentacle to the far left to avoid the majority of Ceph.
2. **AMBUSH:** Use the available explosives and JAW to launch an assault on the group of Ceph.
3. **USE TURRET:** The mounted HMG can prove helpful against the lesser Ceph once the Devastator Unit has been killed.

Enter the open container to the right and load up on C4 and JAW rockets. Equip the Ranged Grendel and move into position behind the hedges to study the enemy situation. There are a number of Cephs patrolling the area directly below the ledge where Alcatraz is located, along with a Devastator Unit close to the amphitheatre stage. Firing at any of the Ceph will likely draw the attention of many more. One option is to intentionally lure the Cephs toward Alcatraz's position then toss down some C4 to detonate as they get close ②. Another is to use the JAW to take on the Devastator Unit from afar then finish it off with the turret ③.

Whether Alcatraz engages the enemy or not, it's best to ultimately loop around the area to the tentacle on the left ①. Walk carefully along the tentacle to avoid the highest concentration of Cephs, then slip past any in the rear and climb the stairs leading behind the stage.

Use any remaining explosives on the Ceph Combat Command Unit and its crony atop the stairs then set off up the slope to the left. The flags in the distance serve as a good landmark in this area. Blast the doors off the shipping container on the right and equip the X-43 Mike inside. The Spear isn't too far ahead; cross the bridge to the north and survey the scene.

NY SOUVENIR

The final NY Souvenir in *Crysis 2* is among the trickiest to find. It's locked inside the shipping container up the slope beyond the amphitheatre stage. The doors are partially open, but the only way inside is to detonate the fuel drums within the container. Doing so blows the doors off the container and grants Alcatraz access to the NY Souvenir in the rear.

SABOTAGE THE SPORE VEINS

The only way Alcatraz can reach the Spear is to first sabotage the two main veins, just as he had done at the hive. The HUD is updated to help guide Alcatraz to each of the veins. The veins are heavily guarded and require a delicate combination of stealth and high-explosive combat in order to reach them. Start the assault on the veins by walking to the left, past the vending cart to the ammo crates containing the three JAW rockets. There is more weaponry available down the stairs, in the tunnel beneath the yellow EMAT tents, but let it be for now—Alcatraz will need some ammo for the return trip.

THE FIRST TWO VEINS

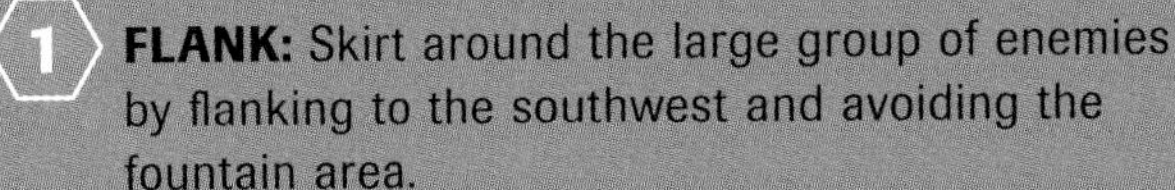

1 **FLANK:** Skirt around the large group of enemies by flanking to the southwest and avoiding the fountain area.

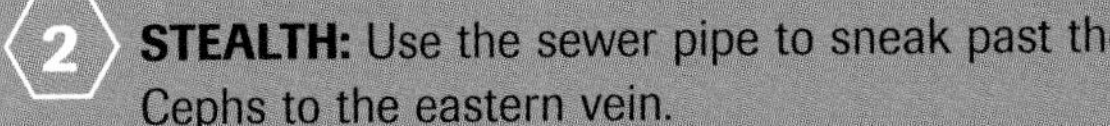

2 **STEALTH:** Use the sewer pipe to sneak past the Cephs to the eastern vein.

Tackle the eastern vein first by dropping into the trench near the yellow shipping containers and heading east into the sewer pipe ②. Continue through the pipe to the watery ditch beneath the first vein. Circle around the base of the hill to the left and leap onto the tentacle to move into position behind the Cephs guarding the vein. Move into position and fire a JAW at the three of them to take them out with a single attack. Approach the front of the vein and interact with it to sabotage it.

Now it's time to go after the second vein. Return through the pipe to the plaza near the fountain and loop high and wide to the left to avoid the major concentration of Ceph Combat Units nearest the fountain. Duck into the underpass near the tents and load up on C4 and other munitions. Eliminate any Cephs that

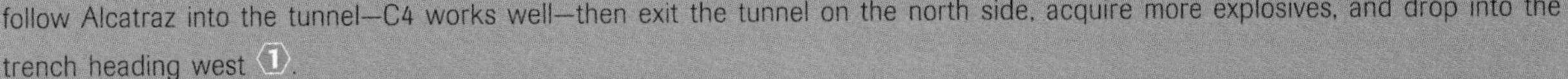

follow Alcatraz into the tunnel—C4 works well—then exit the tunnel on the north side, acquire more explosives, and drop into the trench heading west ①.

Stay low and follow the rocky trench to the west to avoid detection. Advance to the open-ended shipping container and take a moment to watch the patrol patterns of the Ceph. Deploy some C4 near the vein, de-Cloak to allow the Cephs to become alarmed, then detonate the C4 as they charge forward. Interact with the vein to sabotage it. Two down, one to go!

DOG TAG

This final Dog Tag is in the underpass tunnel beneath the yellow tents. It's on a mattress on the west side of the room. It can be very difficult to spot so look for a mattress folded against the wall.

The HUD updates with the location of the third and final vein. Continue in a southeasterly heading over the tentacle bridge to the third vein. Stealthily enter the container below the vein to load up on JAW rockets. Ensure Alcatraz is carrying the maximum allowed, then fall back behind the shields on the hill to the north. There are a number of powerful Cephs in the area, including a Ceph Assault Command Unit to the left and a Devastator Unit to the right.

Peer around the left-hand side of the blast shields to get a clear shot at the Devastator Unit in the distance and loose a JAW rocket. Duck for cover, allow the Energy Meter to recharge, then fire off a rocket at the Cephs bound to be approaching from the left. Dive for cover behind the shields again, reload the JAW, and focus on finishing off the Devastator Unit. Turn to the X-43 Mike or Mk.60 if necessary.

Stand and fight long enough to clear most of the enemies from the area, then make a run for it around the left-hand side of the hill with the vein. Set up traps behind Alcatraz's position with C4 (or just hide and open fire as they pursue), then leap onto the fountain area and sabotage the final vein.

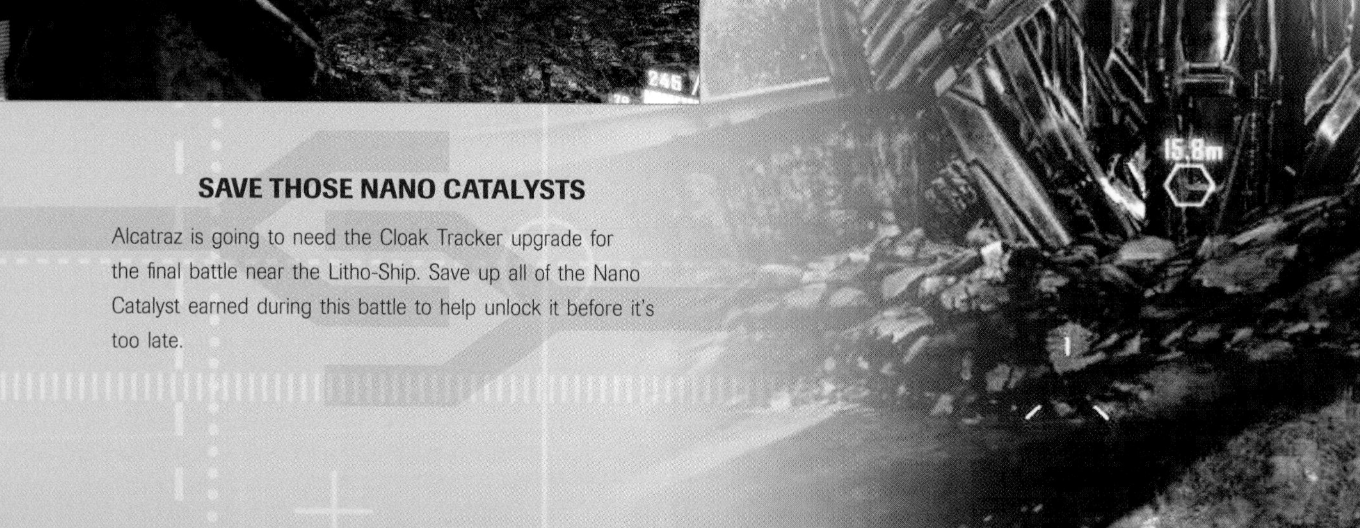

SAVE THOSE NANO CATALYSTS

Alcatraz is going to need the Cloak Tracker upgrade for the final battle near the Litho-Ship. Save up all of the Nano Catalyst earned during this battle to help unlock it before it's too late.

ENTER THE STRUCTURE

Head around back of the third vein and drop into the severed tentacle sticking out of the ground. The vein's internals are essentially a long tube; run and slide the length of the vein to drop into the darkened pit below the litho-ship.

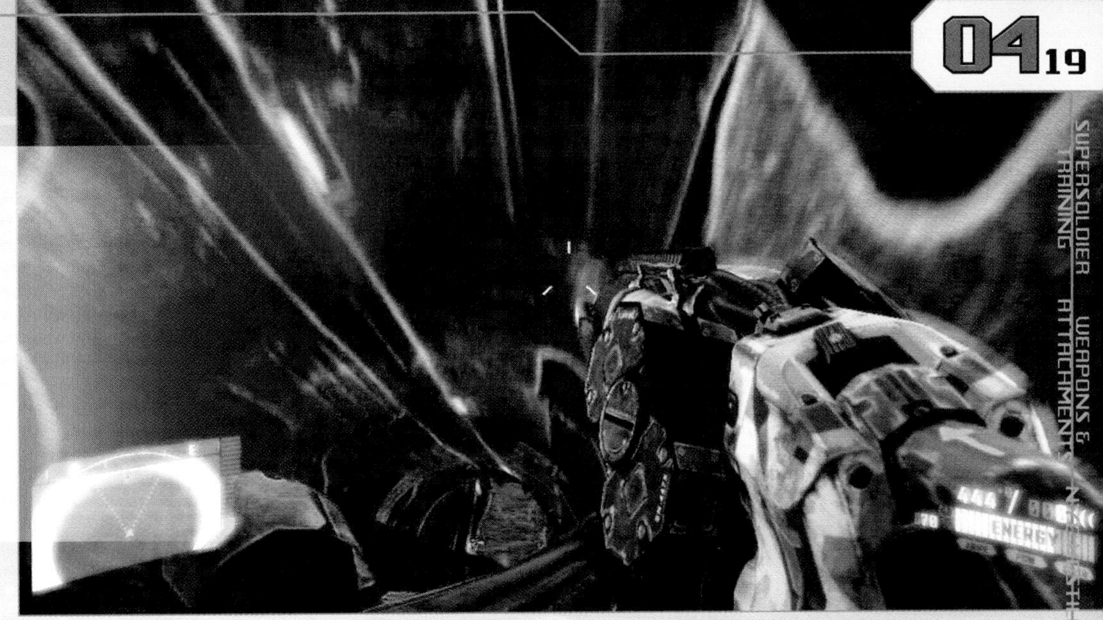

Equip a K-Volt to go along with the X-43 Mike and head north through the trench toward the massive circular entrance to the litho-ship. The large door closes as four Advanced Ceph Assault Units emerge to serve as Alcatraz's final obstacle. Alcatraz must defeat each of these four enemies to fully unlock the entrance to the litho-ship.

Unlike the other enemies Alcatraz has encountered, the Advanced Ceph Assault Units are capable of cloaking, thereby becoming much harder to spot. The K-Volt's electrically-charged shots temporarily disable the cloaking ability and render the enemies visible. They also periodically suffer an energy surge and become visible on their own. Roam the outer extent of the trench, monitoring the mini-map, and keeping an eye out for the black shadowy outline of the enemy or the sudden flash of light from a power surge. The X-43 Mike can make quick work of the Advanced Ceph Assault Unit and each one earns Alcatraz 5000 Nano Catalyst. Purchase the Cloak Tracker upgrade as soon as possible to make finding the remaining enemies easier.

Advanced Ceph Assault Units charge and slash at Alcatraz with their razor sharp claws. Back away and activate Armor should one begin to lunge forward. Defeat the last of them, climb the ledge to the small fire burning to the left of the litho-ship, and run up the hill to enter it. The force of the escaping spore is quite strong. Follow the on-screen prompts to crawl and jump into the heart of the structure. Humanity will thank you for the effort.

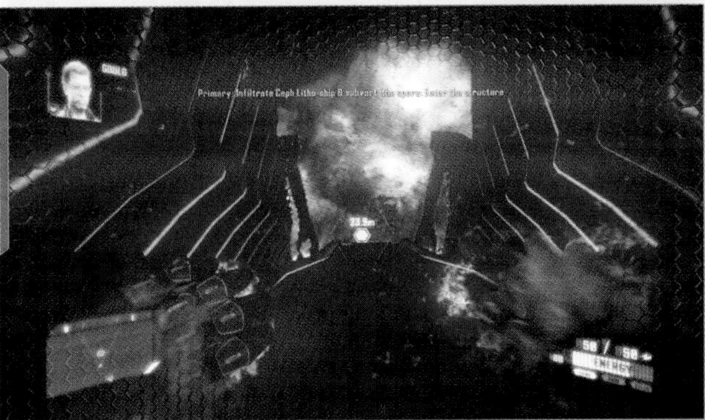

ACHIEVEMENT

Start Spreading the News

Congratulations! You've fought a long and courageous fight against the Ceph and all of humanity revels in your victory. In doing so, you became one with the Nanosuit. Prophet would be proud.

MULTIPLAYER TRAINING

The action doesn t end with the destruction of the Ceph. Take what you ve learned about the Nanosuit and revisit many of the areas explored during the single-player campaign as a member of C.E.L.L. or as a Marine in multiplayer combat. Play against friends and strangers in any of six different gameplay modes, on 13 different maps. This chapter covers all you need to know about this extremely entertaining Crysis 2 multiplayer experience.

NANOSUIT OVERVIEW

Strategic use of the Nanosuit is the key to success in *Crysis 2* multiplayer. Understanding how to harness the powers of speed, armor, and stealth granted by the Nanosuit, as well as the ability to traverse the environment in ways not found in other games, is fundamental to dominating the competition. Nanosuit powers are unavailable when the Energy Meter is depleted, so save them for the right situation. Combining suit powers, such as sprint and stealth, depletes the Energy Meter twice as fast. Nanosuit modules are available to increase the effectiveness of Nanosuit powers, or slow the energy drain when powers are used.

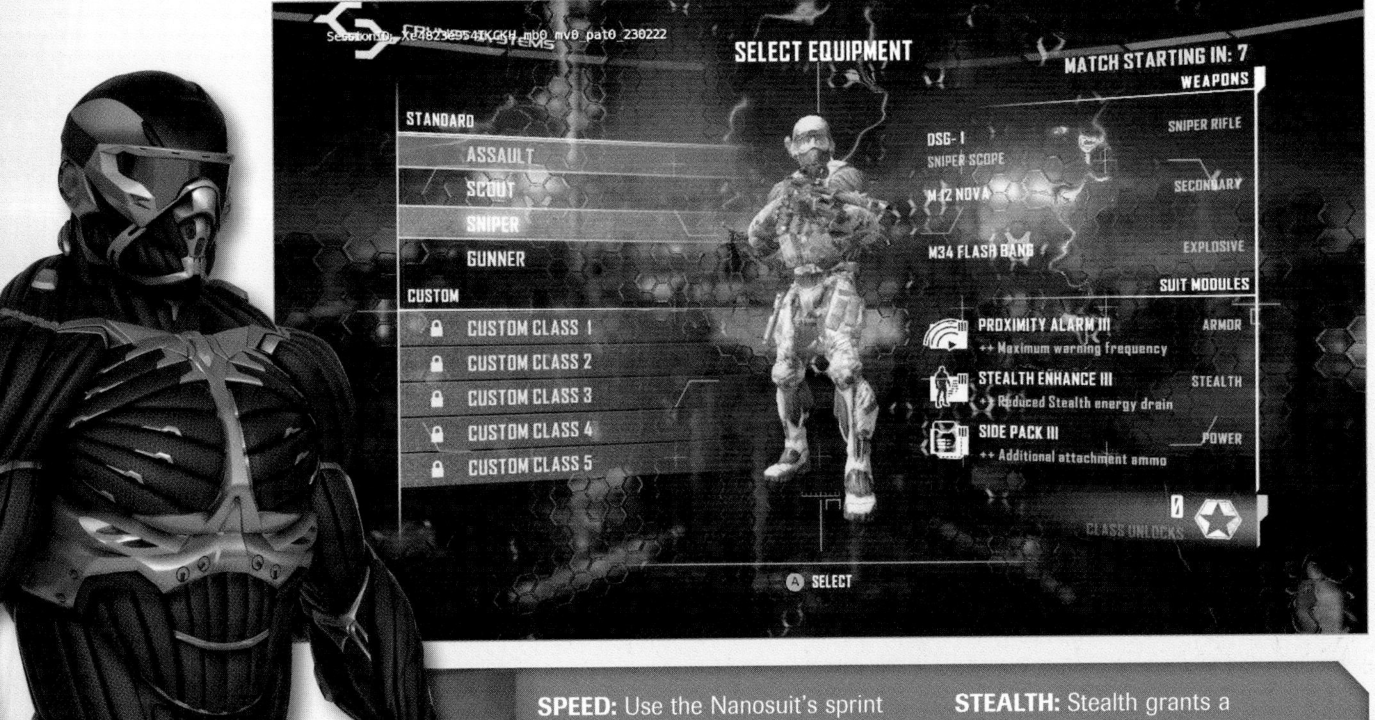

SPEED: Use the Nanosuit's sprint ability to flank enemies or move in behind an unsuspecting opponent for an assassination when combined with Stealth Mode. Sprint to cover when under fire or speed to your goal in objective-based modes.

ARMOR: Armor Mode increases the amount of damage you can absorb and grants an advantage when face to face with an unarmored opponent. Use Armor Mode when defending an objective, such as a downed alien pod in Crash Site, which is certain to be bombarded with grenades and enemy fire.

STEALTH: Stealth grants a temporary state of near invisibility. Combine with the Covert Ops module to reduce the sound of footsteps to remain undetected. This is excellent for approaching objectives or assassinating enemies.

SUIT MODULES: When creating a Custom Class choose a module from the Armor, Stealth, and Power categories to enhance your soldier. Choose modules based on your preferred style of play or to increase your chances of success in specific game modes.

MP GAME MODES

INSTANT ACTION

This is the basic death match mode, playable as either individuals or in Team Instant Action. Kill enemies to score points.

MAPS PLAYABLE **REQUIRED RANK:** CADET I (1)

MAP	INSTANT ACTION	TEAM INSTANT ACTION
CITY HALL	●	●
DOWNED BIRD	●	●
EVAC ZONE	●	●
IMPACT	●	●
LIBERTY ISLAND	●	●
LIGHTHOUSE	●	●
PARKING DECK	●	●
PIER 17	●	●
SANCTUARY	●	●
SKYLINE	●	●
TERMINAL	●	●
WALL STREET	●	●

Instant Action and Team Instant Action are two sides of the same death match coin. Objectives are non-existent and killing is the name of the game. Points are earned by killing opponents and the victor is crowned when the score limit is reached.

These two death match modes are perfect opportunities to learn the effects and uses of the various weapons and suit modules available for selection in *Crysis 2* multiplayer. Adapt your play style to incorporate those which you feel most comfortable with or which you feel are the most effective for dispatching enemies. Enhance your Stealth and Armor capabilities with related Modules and utilize your Custom Classes to assemble the ultimate death dealing class.

A balance must be struck between killing your enemies and keeping yourself alive to finish a match at the top of the scoreboard. Don't forget the tremendous benefits to be gained from earning Support Bonuses; consider this before rushing in to collect a Dog Tag if you're on the verge of earning one of the three tiers of Support Bonus available.

CRASH SITE

Capture energy from downed alien pods while preventing the enemy team from doing the same.

MAPS PLAYABLE **REQUIRED RANK:** RECRUIT III (6)

MAP	CRASH SITE
CITY HALL	⬢
DOWNED BIRD	⬢
EVAC ZONE	⬢
IMPACT	⬡
LIBERTY ISLAND	⬢
LIGHTHOUSE	⬢
PARKING DECK	⬢
PIER 17	⬢
SANCTUARY	⬢
SKYLINE	⬢
TERMINAL	⬡
WALL STREET	⬢

In Crash Site, Ceph airships drop crash pods at pre-determined locations around the map. The objective is to get to the crash site and stay within its radius to score points until reaching 150 points and victory. An off-screen indicator highlights the location of the crash site at all times so both teams will be quick to move in seeking points and kills. Be wary as the crash pod eventually explodes, killing players within its blast radius and prompting another airship to enter the map and drop the next objective.

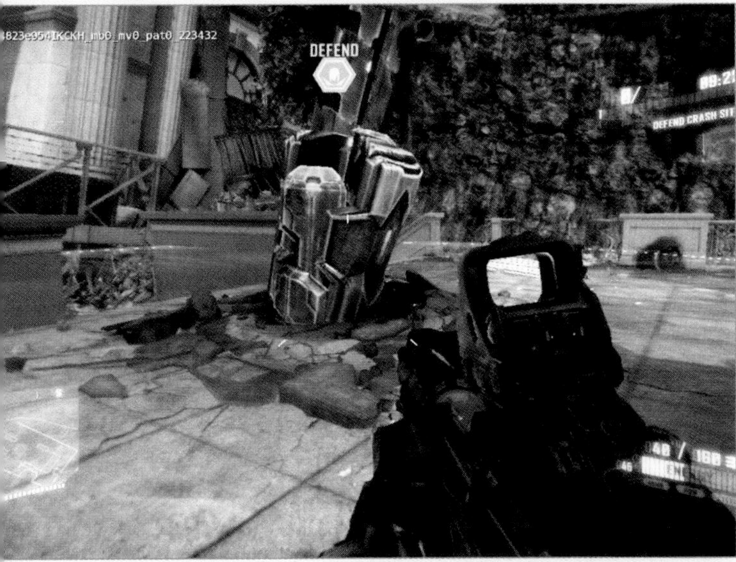

There are a finite number of locations where the crash pod can be dropped, but the order in which these locations are selected is random. Learn to watch the incoming Ceph aircraft as it flies above the map and follow its progress. Set the drop locations to memory and move in to capture the objective when the craft hovers and drops its pod.

The capture zone is both the best and worst place to be. It earns points but also comes under gunfire and a nearly constant rain of grenades. Crouch next to the pod and use it for cover from distant gunfire. Save your Nanosuit powers until enemies engage you at point blank range. Use Armor when in the capture radius to repel enemy attacks and give yourself a chance to melee the opposition. Alternatively, stay slightly outside the capture area and use Stealth to move in for an assassination.

SURVIVING THE BLAST

If Armor mode is engaged when the crash pod explodes it may save you from death. Use this to stay in the objective area as long as possible.

Crash Site is the kind of game mode that inspires players toward one of two general approaches: those who want to win the match and score points by holding the objective, and those who want to take advantage of the aforementioned team players to boost their kill-to-death ratio. Knowing this, you can decide what kind of player you want to be in any given match. Those looking to score points from the objective constantly rush in and battle it out in the red zone. Players conscious of their stats and less worried about wins often take up positions leading to the objective and set traps or seek positions overlooking the crash pod to snipe from afar.

CAPTURE THE RELAY

Capture the enemy's relay and return it to your base to score. The team with the highest number of captures wins.

MAPS PLAYABLE **REQUIRED RANK:** TROOPER III (12)

MAP	CRASH SITE
CITY HALL	⬢
DOWNED BIRD	⬢
EVAC ZONE	⬡
IMPACT	⬡
LIBERTY ISLAND	⬢
LIGHTHOUSE	⬢
PARKING DECK	⬢
PIER 17	⬡
SANCTUARY	⬢
SKYLINE	⬡
TERMINAL	⬡
WALL STREET	⬡

In Capture the Relay two teams of six defend their own relay while attempting to capture the enemy relay and bring it back to theirs. Each match consists of two rounds; teams switch sides after the first round and defend the relay they attacked in the first round. A tie at the end of the match results in a draw. Teams play both offense and defense throughout the match so teamwork is essential. When playing with a full team, assign attacker and defender roles to each player so that your relay is properly defended while you attempt to infiltrate the enemy's defenses and bring their relay to your home base. Create custom classes prior to playing that utilize the best modules for each role and, if possible, create multiple classes so that you change your approach from that of an attacker to a defender as necessary.

Relay locations often have nearby turrets for use in defense or high vantage points from which to fire upon attackers. Use the nearby environment to your advantage, whether waiting to ambush would be attackers or attempting to sneak into a relay location and get away with the enemy relay.

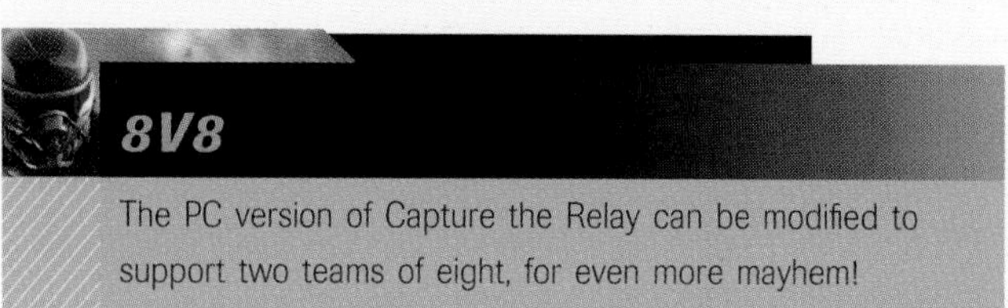

8V8

The PC version of Capture the Relay can be modified to support two teams of eight, for even more mayhem!

Approach the relay and hold the Interact button to take it from its base. When your relay is taken, an on-screen "KILL" indicator tracks the enemy player carrying the relay. If your relay is dropped, you can return it immediately by touching it. While holding the relay you cannot fire your primary weapon but may utilize your secondary weapon. Since the relay is in your off-hand, you are unable to aim down the sights of your weapon.

FASTER SWAPPING

On-screen instructions tell you to hold the Interact button to drop the relay, allowing full use of your weapons. Instead tap the Change Weapon button once to more quickly drop the relay and switch to the last weapon equipped before you picked up the relay.

Sprinting and overcoming the environment are both possible while holding the relay. Consider allowing the Energy Meter to fully charge before grabbing it so you can run and move as effectively as possible. Even then, sprint in short bursts so as to not drain the Energy Meter completely and be left moving too slowly.

ASSAULT

Nanosuit operatives must download data from terminals defended by black ops soldiers. This is a single life mode with no respawns.

MAPS PLAYABLE **REQUIRED RANK:** SPECIALIST III (18)

MAP	CRASH SITE
CITY HALL	⬡
DOWNED BIRD	⬢
EVAC ZONE	⬡
IMPACT	⬡
LIBERTY ISLAND	⬢
LIGHTHOUSE	⬡
PARKING DECK	⬢
PIER 17	⬢
SANCTUARY	⬢
SKYLINE	⬡
TERMINAL	⬡
WALL STREET	⬢

Assault pits a team of defenders against a team of attackers attempting to upload data from either of five data terminals (A, B, C, D, & E). However, when the session has fewer players, it reduces the number of terminals to two. Each round ends in victory for the attackers when 100% of the data has been uploaded. Data uploaded from either terminal counts toward the collective upload percentage. Defenders emerge victorious by preventing 100% data upload within a given round. This can be achieved by either holding the assaulting team off until time expires or by killing all the attackers. The round continues if all defenders are killed, giving the attackers an opportunity to upload 100% of the data before time runs out. There are four rounds total, the team with more round victories wins. In the event of a tie, the team with the most overall data uploaded wins. If this amount is the same for both teams the match ends in a draw.

Defenders begin each round in close proximity to the data terminals while the attackers begin farther away. This allows the defense to prepare for the upcoming onslaught. Assault is unique in several ways. There is no use of custom classes. Instead, teams pick from one of three offensive and defensive classes. When on offense your soldier is equipped with a Nanosuit with predetermined modules per class but carries only a pistol. Conversely, the soldiers on defense have no Nanosuit and lack all related powers. However, defenders come equipped with a primary weapon as well as a pistol to compensate for the lack of special abilities.

BEHOLD! NANO-STRENGTH!

Turrets can be manned by attackers and defenders alike, but only attackers can detach the mounted HMGs using their Nanosuit powers. Ordinary soldiers don't have the strength to rip these heavy weapons off their mounts.

ASSAULT: OFFENSE

When on offense, take advantage of your Nanosuit abilities to approach the data terminals without detection. All modules reflect the amount of upgrades you have earned in your multiplayer progression. Consider the following roles:

- The **Predator** class has increased tracking capabilities, enabling you to act as a spotter calling out defender locations to teammates.
- The **Ghost** class utilizes stealth capabilities. Use this class to flank defenders undetected and attempt assassination attempts from the rear and to provide cover for teammates downloading data from terminals.
- The **Infiltrator** class has increased health restoration abilities. This class is an ideal option to upload data, utilizing its ability to heal faster while trying to withstand the defender's attacks.

OFFENSIVE CLASSES

CLASS	PRIMARY WEAPON	SECONDARY WEAPON	NANOSUIT MODULES
PREDATOR	—	HAMMER	THREAT TRACER, TRACKER, AND AIM ENHANCE
GHOST	—	M 12 NOVA WITH SUPPRESSOR	PROXIMITY ALARM, STEALTH ENHANCE, AND POINT FIRE ENHANCE
INFILTRATOR	—	M 12 NOVA	NANO RECHARGE, COVERT OPS, AND MOBILITY ENHANCE

ASSAULT: DEFENSE

The three defensive classes vary much less due to the lack of Nanosuit modules. Choosing your class on defense comes down to personal preference; choose the weapons you prefer. Take up positions with eyes on both data upload positions but be wary of flanking attackers. The offense may attempt to eliminate all defenders using their Nanosuit abilities before even approaching the data terminals. Keep this is mind and assign at least one teammate to watch the team's back. The success of the defense is going to largely be determined based on the accuracy of the defenders' shots fired.

DEFENSIVE CLASSES

CLASS	PRIMARY WEAPON	SECONDARY WEAPON	NANOSUIT MODULES
SENTINEL	SCAR WITH LASER SIGHT	HAMMER WITH LASER SIGHT	N/A
ENFORCER	SCARAB WITH LASER SIGHT	M 12 NOVA WITH LASER SIGHT	N/A
PROTECTOR	FELINE WITH LASER SIGHT	M 12 NOVA WITH LASER SIGHT	N/A

EXTRACTION

Extract Nanosuit-enhancing alien bio-ticks from defended locations. Capture all of the ticks to win.

MAPS PLAYABLE **REQUIRED RANK:** GUARD I (22)

MAP	CRASH SITE
CITY HALL	○
DOWNED BIRD	●
EVAC ZONE	○
IMPACT	○
LIBERTY ISLAND	●
LIGHTHOUSE	○
PARKING DECK	●
PIER 17	●
SANCTUARY	●
SKYLINE	○
TERMINAL	○
WALL STREET	●

In Extraction, there are two alien bio-ticks that must be taken from their positions to an awaiting helicopter for extraction. The extraction helicopter has an EMP radius that disables the Nanosuit energy and powers of the defending team to prevent camping of the extraction point. One team defends the bio-ticks while the other seeks to extract them. When held, the bio-ticks enhance the carrier's Armor or Stealth abilities by slowing the rate at which each depletes your Energy Meter. The team that captures the most bio-ticks wins the match.

A custom class including Stealth Enhance or Covert Ops can increase your ability to approach the bio-tick locations without being detected. When you obtain a bio-tick, immediately activate the associated power to take advantage of the bonus it bestows. Focus on making your way back to the extraction helicopter while teammates cover your retreat. You are restricted to firing a pistol while carrying the bio-tick and your movement rate is slightly decreased. You are, however, still able to sprint and mantle objects in the environment.

CAPTURE THE TICKS!

If both teams are successful in capping the ticks, the decision of winner is then based on the time. The team that extracts the ticks in the quickest time is victorious!

As is the case in Capture the Relay, you are instructed to hold the Interact button to drop the bio-tick. Instead, tap the Change Weapon button to quickly change back to the last equipped weapon. Once a bio-tick is dropped an on-screen timer around the object indicator counts down the time remaining until the bio-tick resets to its original position.

WHEN WHIRLYBIRDS ATTACK

Beware the helicopter blades when nearing the extraction point. They can and will kill you if you jump into them!

When on defense divide your forces between the two bio-tick capture points. The attackers will likely focus on one of the two capture locations. If this happens, send reinforcements from the other bio-tick but don't leave it completely unguarded. Create custom classes that emphasize defensive abilities such as Armor Enhance or Proximity Alarm to increase your ability to withstand attacks as well as to detect enemies in the vicinity of the bio-ticks. Consider planting C4 near the bio-tick locations and detonate it as soon as an enemy takes control of a bio-tick. A "KILL" prompt pops up to indicate the location of the enemy player once a bio-tick is taken.

CUSTOM CLASSES

Over the course of your *Crysis 2* multiplayer career you are able to unlock up to five Custom Classes on your way to the maximum multiplayer rank of 50. You also earn Weapon, Armor Module, Stealth Module, and Power Module Unlocks (i.e. Tokens) to be used to select from the numerous weapons and Nanosuit enhancements to be used in matches. Weapon Tokens are used to customize each weapon to your liking.

WEAPONS AND ATTACHMENTS

The following pages detail each of the customization options for primary and secondary weapons, including their weapon stats, default attachments, and available unlocks. Purchase attachments with Weapon Tokens, received every other rank increase, beginning with Recruit II (Rank 5).

SCOPE ATTACHMENTS	TYPE	DESCRIPTION
	ASSAULT SCOPE	ADVANCED OPTICAL 2.5X ZOOM.
	PISTOL LASER	SOLID STATE LASER PROJECTOR FOR ENHANCED ACCURACY.
	REFLEX SIGHT	REFRACTIVE OPTICAL RED DOT SIGHT FOR ENHANCED TARGET ACQUISITION.
	RIFLE LASER	SOLID STATE LASER PROJECTOR FOR ENHANCED ACCURACY.
	SNIPER SCOPE	ADVANCED OPTICAL 4X OR 12X ZOOM DEPENDING ON ZOOM LEVEL.

BARREL ATTACHMENTS	TYPE	DESCRIPTION
	SUPPRESSOR	NOISE SUPPRESSOR FOR ENHANCED STEALTH.

UNDER-BARREL ATTACHMENTS	TYPE	DESCRIPTION
	EXTENDED	INCREASED MAGAZINE CAPACITY.
	GAUSS	A MINIATURIZED ELECTROMAGNETIC SOLID SLUG PROJECTOR.
	GRENADE	FIRES 30MM ADVANCED EXPLOSIVE ANTI-PERSONNEL PERCUSSION GRENADES.
	HOLOGRAM	PROJECTS A DECOY IMAGE TO FOOL ENEMIES.
	SHOTGUN	A MINIATURIZED LIGHTWEIGHT SHOTGUN ATTACHMENT.
	SINGLE SHOT	SINGLE SHOT MODE FOR INCREASED ACCURACY.

FELINE

Type: Sub-Machine Gun

ACCURACY

RATE OF FIRE

RANGE

DAMAGE

MOBILITY

ATTACHMENTS AVAILABLE

CATEGORY	DEFAULT	UNLOCK #1	UNLOCK #2	UNLOCK #3
SCOPE	IRONSIGHT	REFLEX SIGHT	ASSAULT SCOPE	RIFLE LASER
BARREL	—	SUPPRESSOR	—	—
UNDER-BARREL	SINGLE SHOT	EXTENDED	HOLOGRAM	—
WEAPON SKIN	—	C.E.L.L.	—	—

K-VOLT

Type: Sub-Machine Gun

ACCURACY

RATE OF FIRE

RANGE

DAMAGE

MOBILITY

ATTACHMENTS AVAILABLE

CATEGORY	DEFAULT	UNLOCK #1	UNLOCK #2	UNLOCK #3
SCOPE	IRONSIGHT	REFLEX SIGHT	ASSAULT SCOPE	PISTOL LASER
BARREL	—	—	—	—
UNDER-BARREL	—	EXTENDED	—	—
WEAPON SKIN	—	C.E.L.L.	—	—

SCAR

Type: Assault Rifle

ACCURACY

RATE OF FIRE

RANGE

DAMAGE

MOBILITY

ATTACHMENTS AVAILABLE

CATEGORY	DEFAULT	UNLOCK #1	UNLOCK #2	UNLOCK #3	UNLOCK #4	UNLOCK #5
SCOPE	—	REFLEX SIGHT	ASSAULT SCOPE	RIFLE LASER	—	—
BARREL	—	—	—	—	—	—
UNDER-BARREL	SINGLE SHOT	EXTENDED	GRENADE	GAUSS	SHOTGUN	HOLOGRAM
WEAPON SKIN	—	URBAN CAMO	DESERT CAMO	C.E.L.L.	—	—

GRENDEL

Type: Assault Rifle

ACCURACY

RATE OF FIRE

RANGE

DAMAGE

MOBILITY

ATTACHMENTS AVAILABLE

CATEGORY	DEFAULT	UNLOCK #1	UNLOCK #2	UNLOCK #3	UNLOCK #4	UNLOCK #5
SCOPE	IRONSIGHT	REFLEX SIGHT	ASSAULT SCOPE	RIFLE LASER	—	—
BARREL	—	SUPPRESSOR	—	—	—	—
UNDER-BARREL	SINGLE SHOT	EXTENDED	GRENADE	SHOTGUN	HOLOGRAM	—
WEAPON SKIN	—	—	—	—	—	—

SCARAB

Type: Assault Rifle

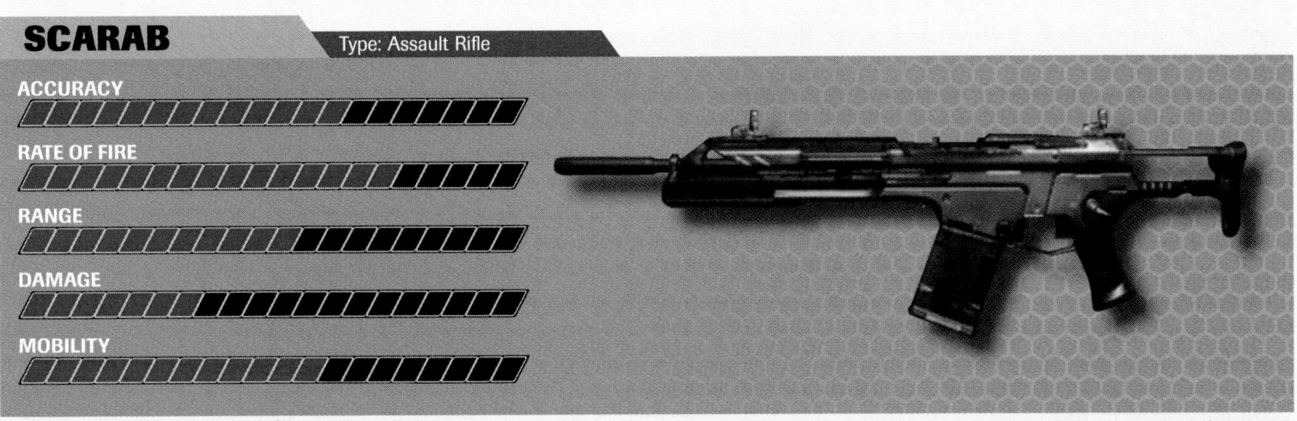

ATTACHMENTS AVAILABLE

CATEGORY	DEFAULT	UNLOCK #1	UNLOCK #2	UNLOCK #3	UNLOCK #4	UNLOCK #5
SCOPE	IRONSIGHT	REFLEX SIGHT	RIFLE LASER	—	—	—
BARREL	—	SUPPRESSOR	—	—	—	—
UNDER-BARREL	SINGLE SHOT	EXTENDED	GRENADE	GAUSS	SHOTGUN	HOLOGRAM
WEAPON SKIN	—	C.E.L.L.	—	—	—	—

DSG-1

Type: Sniper Rifle

ACCURACY

RATE OF FIRE

RANGE

DAMAGE

MOBILITY

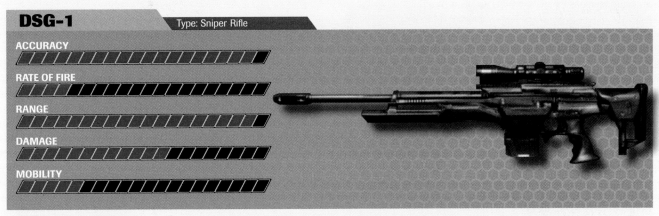

ATTACHMENTS AVAILABLE

CATEGORY	DEFAULT	UNLOCK #1	UNLOCK #2	UNLOCK #3	UNLOCK #4	UNLOCK #5
SCOPE	SNIPER SCOPE	REFLEX SIGHT	ASSAULT SCOPE	—	—	—
BARREL	—	SUPPRESSOR	—	—	—	—
UNDER-BARREL	—	EXTENDED	—	—	—	—
WEAPON SKIN	—	—	—	—	—	—

M20 14 GAUSS

Type: Sniper Rifle

ACCURACY

RATE OF FIRE

RANGE

DAMAGE

MOBILITY

ATTACHMENTS AVAILABLE

CATEGORY	DEFAULT	UNLOCK #1	UNLOCK #2	UNLOCK #3	UNLOCK #4	UNLOCK #5
SCOPE	SNIPER SCOPE	REFLEX SIGHT	ASSAULT SCOPE	—	—	—
BARREL	—	—	—	—	—	—
UNDER-BARREL	—	EXTENDED	HOLOGRAM	—	—	—
WEAPON SKIN	—	C.E.L.L.	—	—	—	—

JACKAL

Type: Shotgun

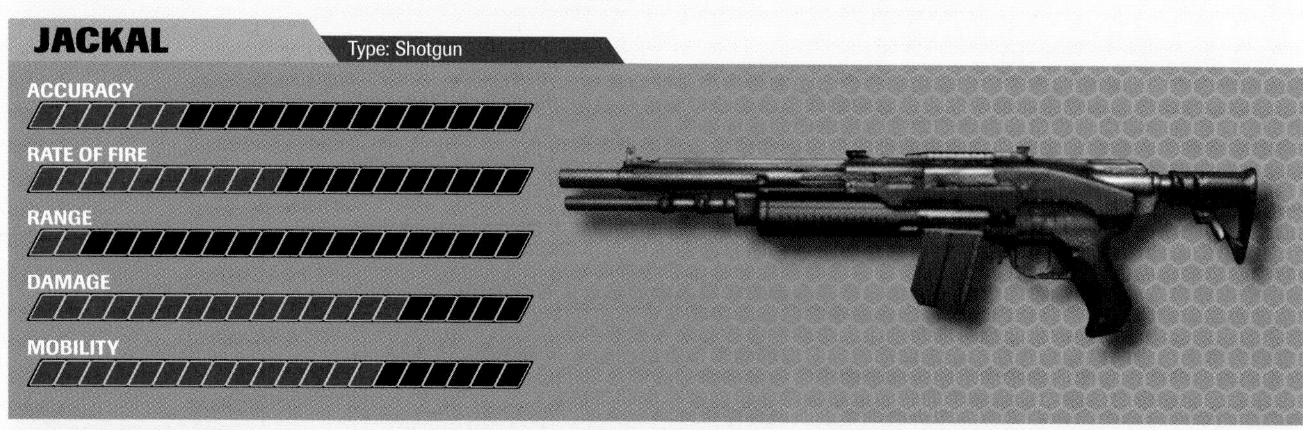

ATTACHMENTS AVAILABLE

CATEGORY	DEFAULT	UNLOCK #1	UNLOCK #2	UNLOCK #3	UNLOCK #4	UNLOCK #5
SCOPE	—	REFLEX SIGHT	—	—	—	—
BARREL	—	—	—	—	—	—
UNDER-BARREL	SINGLE SHOT	EXTENDED	HOLOGRAM	—	—	—
WEAPON SKIN	—	—	—	—	—	—

MARSHALL

Type: Shotgun

ACCURACY

RATE OF FIRE

RANGE

DAMAGE

MOBILITY

ATTACHMENTS AVAILABLE

CATEGORY	DEFAULT	UNLOCK #1	UNLOCK #2	UNLOCK #3	UNLOCK #4	UNLOCK #5
SCOPE	—	REFLEX SIGHT	—	—	—	—
BARREL	—	SUPPRESSOR	—	—	—	—
UNDER-BARREL	—	EXTENDED	—	—	—	—
WEAPON SKIN	—	—	—	—	—	—

MK.60 MOD 0

Type: Heavy

ACCURACY

RATE OF FIRE

RANGE

DAMAGE

MOBILITY

ATTACHMENTS AVAILABLE

CATEGORY	DEFAULT	UNLOCK #1	UNLOCK #2	UNLOCK #3	UNLOCK #4	UNLOCK #5
SCOPE	IRONSIGHT	REFLEX SIGHT	ASSAULT SCOPE	—	—	—
BARREL	—	—	—	—	—	—
UNDER-BARREL	—	EXTENDED	HOLOGRAM	—	—	—
WEAPON SKIN	—	—	—	—	—	—

L-TAG

Type: Heavy

ACCURACY

RATE OF FIRE

RANGE

DAMAGE

MOBILITY

ATTACHMENTS AVAILABLE

CATEGORY	DEFAULT	UNLOCK #1	UNLOCK #2	UNLOCK #3	UNLOCK #4	UNLOCK #5
SCOPE	—	—	—	—	—	—
BARREL	—	—	—	—	—	—
UNDER-BARREL	—	—	—	—	—	—
WEAPON SKIN	—	—	—	—	—	—

X-43 MIKE

Type: Heavy

ACCURACY

RATE OF FIRE

RANGE

DAMAGE

MOBILITY

ATTACHMENTS AVAILABLE

CATEGORY	DEFAULT	UNLOCK #1	UNLOCK #2	UNLOCK #3	UNLOCK #4	UNLOCK #5
SCOPE	—	—	—	—	—	—
BARREL	—	—	—	—	—	—
UNDER-BARREL	—	—	—	—	—	—
WEAPON SKIN	—	C.E.L.L.	—	—	—	—

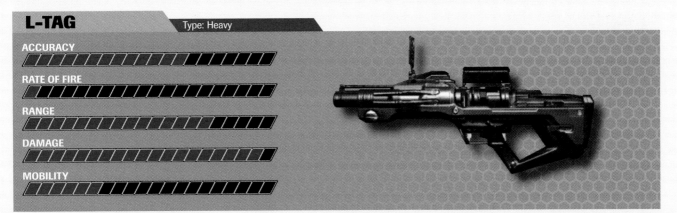

SECONDARY WEAPONS

M 12 NOVA

Type: Semi-Automatic Pistol

ACCURACY

RATE OF FIRE

RANGE

DAMAGE

MOBILITY

ATTACHMENTS AVAILABLE

CATEGORY	DEFAULT	UNLOCK #1	UNLOCK #2	UNLOCK #3	UNLOCK #4	UNLOCK #5
SCOPE	–	LASER SIGHT	–	–	–	–
BARREL	–	SUPPRESSOR	–	–	–	–
UNDER-BARREL	–	EXTENDED	–	–	–	–
WEAPON SKIN	–	–	–	–	–	–

HAMMER

Type: Pistol

ACCURACY

RATE OF FIRE

RANGE

DAMAGE

MOBILITY

ATTACHMENTS AVAILABLE

CATEGORY	DEFAULT	UNLOCK #1	UNLOCK #2	UNLOCK #3	UNLOCK #4	UNLOCK #5
SCOPE	–	LASER SIGHT	–	–	–	–
BARREL	–	SUPPRESSOR	–	–	–	–
UNDER-BARREL	–	EXTENDED	–	–	–	–
WEAPON SKIN	–	C.E.L.L.	–	–	–	–

AY69

Type: Machine Pistol

ACCURACY

RATE OF FIRE

RANGE

DAMAGE

MOBILITY

ATTACHMENTS AVAILABLE

CATEGORY	DEFAULT	UNLOCK #1	UNLOCK #2	UNLOCK #3	UNLOCK #4	UNLOCK #5
SCOPE	IRONSIGHT	LASER SIGHT	–	–	–	–
BARREL	–	SUPPRESSOR	–	–	–	–
UNDER-BARREL	–	EXTENDED	–	–	–	–
WEAPON SKIN	–	–	–	–	–	–

MAJESTIC

Type: Heavy Revolver

ACCURACY

RATE OF FIRE

RANGE

DAMAGE

MOBILITY

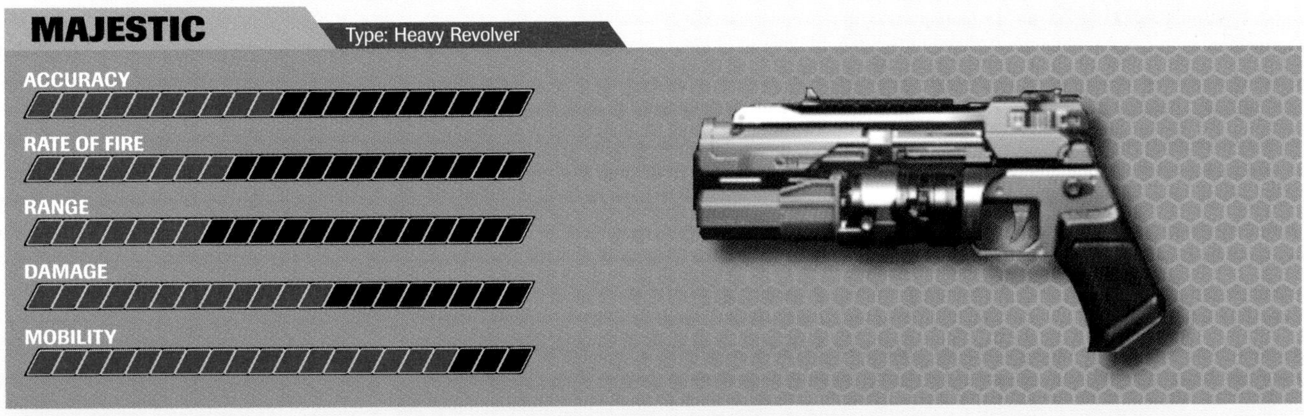

ATTACHMENTS AVAILABLE

CATEGORY	DEFAULT	UNLOCK #1	UNLOCK #2	UNLOCK #3	UNLOCK #4	UNLOCK #5
SCOPE	–	LASER SIGHT	–	–	–	–
BARREL	–	–	–	–	–	–
UNDER-BARREL	–	–	–	–	–	–
WEAPON SKIN	–	–	–	–	–	–

EXPLOSIVES

There are also four types of explosives to be used, including M17 Frag Grenades, M34 Flash Bang grenades, remote-detonating C4, and the JAW shoulder-held missile launcher.

M17 FRAG GRENADE

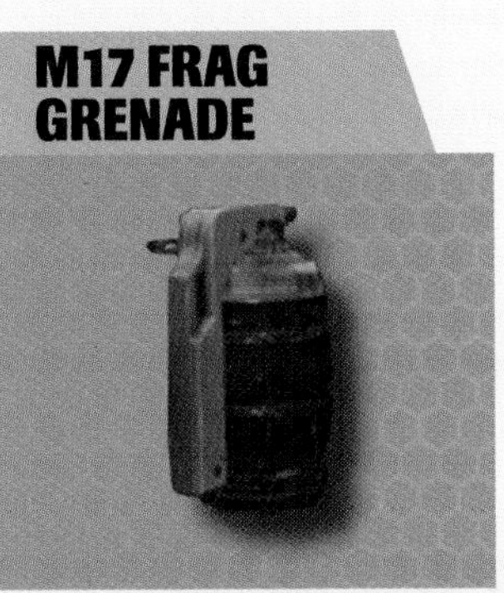

M34 FLASH BANG GRENADE

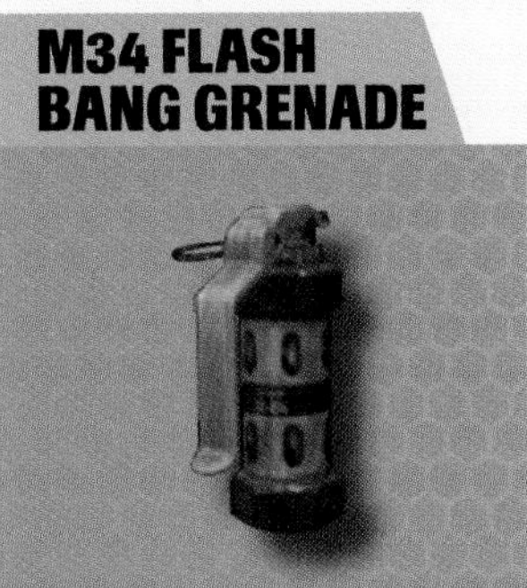

REMOTE-DETONATING C4

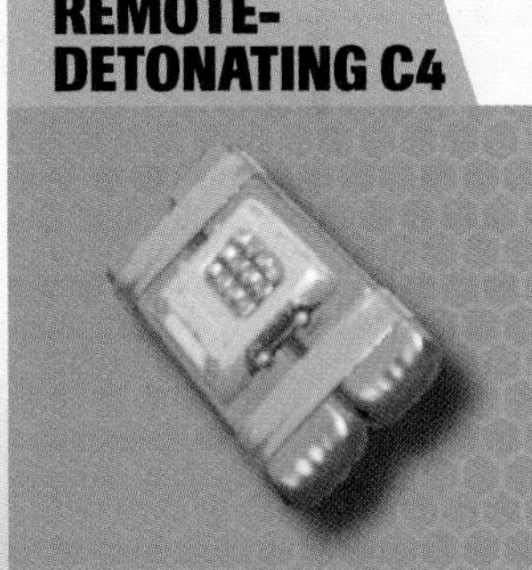

JAW MISSILE LAUNCHER

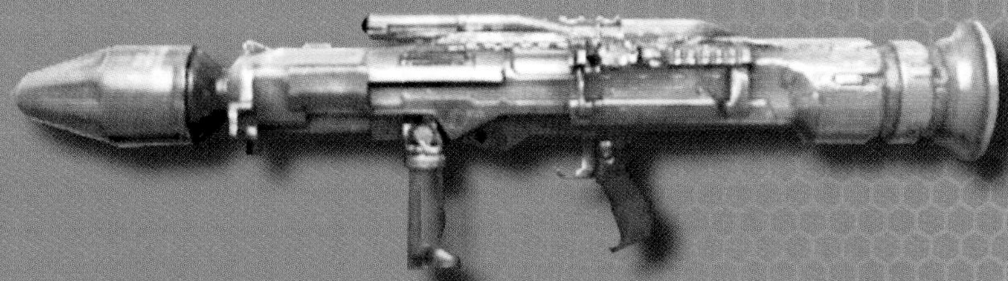

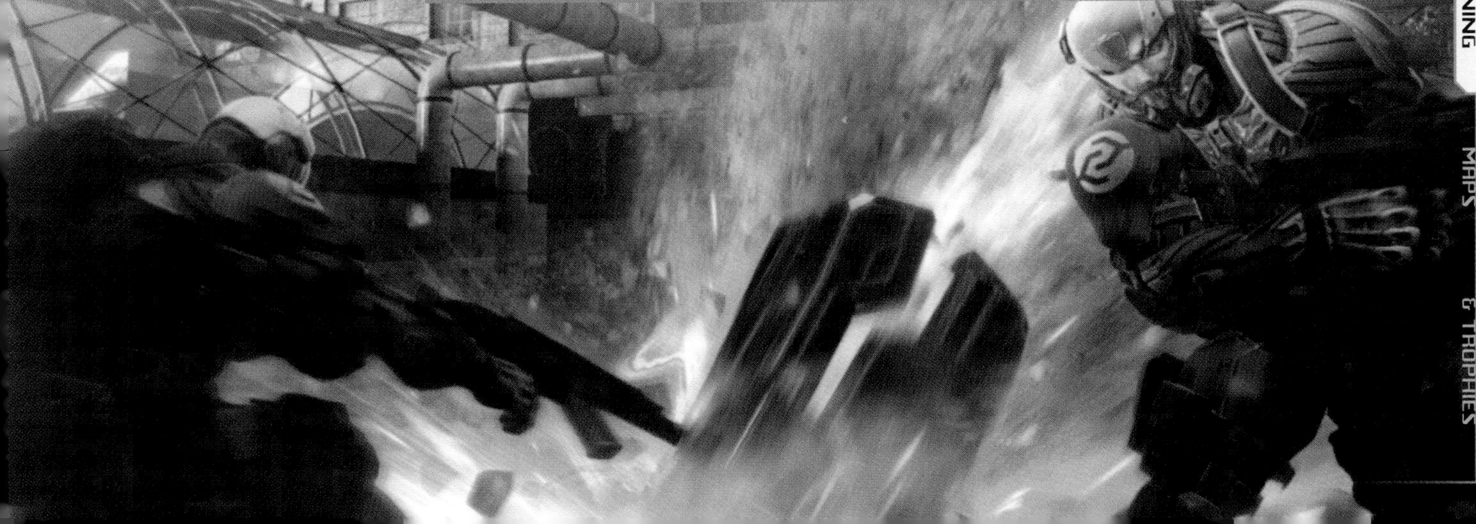

NANOSUIT MODULES

Each module in the Armor, Stealth, and Power categories has three levels of effectiveness. The latter two must be unlocked by fulfilling specific requirements while a previous module is attached. The following tables detail the module's effects in the progression. Consult this table to determine which types of modules you want to invest time into unlocking, so as to not work toward unlocks that you don't best fit your style of play.

ARMOR MODULES

SUIT MODULE	BASE DESCRIPTION	UPGRADE #2 DESCRIPTION	UPGRADE #3 DESCRIPTION
AIR STOMP	PERFORM A POWERFUL DOWNWARDS ATTACK WHEN IN THE AIR.	NO DAMAGE SUFFERED FROM FALLING LONG DISTANCES.	FASTER RECOVERY AFTER AIR STOMP ATTACKS.
THREAT TRACER	HIGHLIGHTS INCOMING BULLET PATHS.	HIGHLIGHTS INCOMING GRENADES.	HIGHLIGHTS NEARBY EXPLOSIVES.
PROXIMITY ALARM	AUTOMATIC WARNING WHEN AN ENEMY IS NEARBY.	INCREASED WARNING FREQUENCY WHEN AN ENEMY IS NEARBY.	MAXIMUM WARNING FREQUENCY WHEN AN ENEMY IS NEARBY.
ARMOR ENHANCE	REDUCES DRAIN SPEED OF ENERGY IN ARMOR MODE.	INCREASES MOVEMENT SPEED IN ARMOR MODE.	PROTECTS AGAINST THE NANOSUIT JAMMER BONUS.
NANO RECHARGE	FASTER HEALTH RECHARGE.	FASTER SUIT ENERGY RECHARGE.	SHORTER DELAY BEFORE HEALTH STARTS RECHARGING.
DETONATION DELAY	DELAYS THE DETONATION OF NEARBY ENEMY GRENADES.	DELAYS THE DETONATION OF ENEMY EXPLOSIVES.	PROVIDES AN AUTOMATIC DEFENSE AGAINST MISSILE ATTACKS.
ENERGY TRANSFER	RESTORES NANOSUIT ENERGY WITH EACH KILL.	RESTORES ADDITIONAL NANOSUIT ENERGY WITH EACH KILL.	RESTORES FULL NANOSUIT ENERGY WITH EACH KILL.

STEALTH MODULES

SUIT MODULE	BASE DESCRIPTION	UPGRADE #2 DESCRIPTION	UPGRADE #3 DESCRIPTION
STEALTH ENHANCE	FASTER TRANSITION IN AND OUT OF STEALTH MODE.	NO SHADOW CAST IN STEALTH MODE.	REDUCES ENERGY DRAIN IN STEALTH MODE.
BLIND SPOT	PROVIDES PROTECTION FROM ENEMY MAXIMUM RADAR BONUS.	PROVIDES PROTECTION FROM ENEMY TAGGING.	BECOME LESS VISIBLE TO ENEMIES IN NANOVISION.
COVERT OPS	REDUCES THE SOUND OF FOOTSTEPS.	PROVIDES PROTECTION FROM THE CEPH AIRSTRIKE BONUS.	ENEMY FOOTSTEPS ARE LOUDER WITHIN RANGE.
JAMMER	SCRAMBLES THE RADAR OF ENEMIES WITHIN RANGE.	PROVIDES PROTECTION AGAINST ENEMY RADAR JAMMER ATTACKS.	SCRAMBLES THE RADAR OF ENEMIES WITHIN AN INCREASED RANGE.
TRACKER	HIGHLIGHTS THE FOOTSTEPS OF NEARBY ENEMIES.	HIGHLIGHTS ENEMY ROUTES WITH DIRECTION.	HIGHLIGHTS ENEMY ROUTES WITH INCREASED FREQUENCY.
CLOAK TRACKER	IDENTIFIES WHERE NEARBY ENEMIES ENTER STEALTH MODE.	INCREASES THE VISIBILITY OF CLOAKED ENEMIES.	MAXIMUM VISIBILITY OF CLOAKED ENEMIES.
VISOR ENHANCE	HIGHLIGHTS ENEMIES THROUGH WEAPON SCOPES.	PROVIDES PROTECTION AGAINST FLASH BANG GRENADES.	REDUCES ENERGY COST OF NANOVISION.

POWER MODULES

SUIT MODULE	BASE DESCRIPTION	UPGRADE #2 DESCRIPTION	UPGRADE #3 DESCRIPTION
SIDE PACK	ALLOWS AN ADDITIONAL MAGAZINE OF PRIMARY AMMUNITION TO BE CARRIED.	ALLOWS AN ADDITIONAL GRENADE OR EXPLOSIVE TO BE CARRIED.	ALLOWS ADDITIONAL ATTACHMENT AMMUNITION TO BE CARRIED.
POINT FIRE ENHANCE	REDUCES THE SPREAD OF PRIMARY WEAPONS WHEN SHOOTING FROM THE HIP.	REDUCES THE SPREAD OF SECONDARY WEAPONS WHEN SHOOTING FROM THE HIP.	REDUCES THE SPREAD OF MOUNTED WEAPONS WHEN SHOOTING FROM THE HIP.
AIM ENHANCE	DECREASES WEAPON RECOIL WHEN AIMING DOWN SIGHTS.	REDUCES AIM SHAKE FROM EXPLOSIVES.	INCREASES MOBILITY WHEN AIMING DOWN SIGHTS.
WEAPON PRO	FASTER WEAPON RELOADING.	FASTER AIMING DOWN SIGHTS.	FASTER SWITCHING BETWEEN WEAPONS.
LOADOUT PRO	ALLOWS AN ADDITIONAL PRIMARY WEAPON TO BE CARRIED IN PLACE OF A SECONDARY.	REMOVES THE WEIGHT PENALTY FROM WEAPON ATTACHMENTS.	INCREASES MOBILITY SPEED WHEN CARRYING HEAVY WEAPONS.
RAPID FIRE	FASTER FIRE RATE ON PRIMARY WEAPONS.	FASTER FIRE RATE ON SECONDARY WEAPONS.	FASTER FIRE RATE ON MOUNTED WEAPONS.
MOBILITY ENHANCE	REDUCED ENERGY DRAIN FROM SPRINTING AND JUMPING.	INCREASES LEDGE GRAB SPEED.	FASTER FIRING AFTER SPRINTING.
RETRIEVER SUIT	AUTOMATICALLY COLLECT DOG TAGS FROM KILLED ENEMIES	SUPPORT BONUSES REQUIRE ONE LESS DOG TAG TO ACTIVATE	SUPPORT BONUSES REMIAN ACTIVE FOR LONGER

CUSTOM CLASS RECOMMENDATIONS

Players can eventually unlock five Custom Class slots that can be used to save pre-configured custom classes that fit different styles of play. We recommend using each of these to not only fit different playing styles, but tailor them to fit different roles for specific game types. Here are a few custom class recommendations to get you started. Be sure to experiment to find which configurations work best for you!

SPEED DEMON

Speed class with emphasis on constant, fast movement to take advantage of the deadly Feline sub-machine gun at short range or to score melee kills before enemies can react.

PRIMARY: Feline sub-machine gun with Reflex Sight and Single Shot

SECONDARY: AY69 machine pistol with Laser Sight and M34 Flash Bang

SUIT MODULES: Nano Recharge, Covert Ops, and Mobility Enhance

RIFLEMAN

Well-rounded assault rifle class. Engage enemies at medium to long range with ability to detect enemy field of fire and return fire with high accuracy while staying off of Maximum Radar screens.

PRIMARY: Grendel assault rifle with Assault Scope and Shotgun attachment

SECONDARY: Hammer semi-automatic pistol with M 17 Frag Grenade

SUIT MODULES: Threat Tracer, Blind Spot, and Aim Enhance

WALKING TANK

The title says it all, an explosive bad ass of a kit. Not fast or sneaky, packs plenty of bullets, and thrives in Armor mode.

PRIMARY: MK.60 MOD 0 medium machine gun with Reflex Sight and Extended Magazine

SECONDARY: Majestic heavy revolver with JAW (Joint Anti-Tank Weapon)

SUIT MODULES: Armor Enhance, Cloak Tracker, and Side Pack

NINJA SNIPER

Master at dealing silent, long-range kills while remaining undetected. Utilizes Proximity Alarm to alert you to enemies while camping invisibly and Retriever to make Support Bonuses not only possible but frequent!

PRIMARY: DSG-1 sniper rifle with Sniper Scope, Suppressor and Extended Magazine

SECONDARY: M 12 Nova semi-automatic pistol with Pistol Laser Sight, Suppressor and Extended Magazine and C4 explosives.

SUIT MODULES: Proximity Alarm, Stealth Enhance, and Retriever

SUPPORT BONUSES

Support Bonuses are game-changing rewards that are earned by collecting dog tags from fallen enemies. Dog tags must be collected within one life to count toward earning the three Support Bonuses available on each map. Your dog tag meter resets each time you are killed. Dog tags are only visible to the player who earned them, so have no fears about teammates or opponents stealing them from you! There are just three individual Support Bonuses per map (out of six total) and the Support Bonuses are pre-fixed, meaning all players have access to the same three bonuses.

SUPPORT BONUSES DEFINED

SUPPORT BONUS	DOG TAGS REQ'D	DESCRIPTION
MAXIMUM RADAR	3	HIGHLIGHT ENEMIES ON THE RADAR
COUNTER RADAR	5	SCRAMBLE THE RADAR OF ALL ENEMIES
ORBITAL STRIKE	5	DEVASTATING ORBITAL BEAM ATTACK
NANOSUIT JAMMER	5	DEPLOY A NANOSUIT DISRUPTION CAPSULE
CEPH AIRSTRIKE	7	SUMMON A CEPH GUNSHIP
MAXIMUM NANOSUIT	7	OVERCHARGE YOUR NANOSUIT ARMOR

SUPPORT BONUSES PER MAP

MAP NAME	3 DOG TAGS	5 DOG TAGS	7 DOG TAGS
SKYLINE	MAXIMUM RADAR	ORBITAL STRIKE	CEPH AIRSTRIKE
DOWNED BIRD	MAXIMUM RADAR	NANOSUIT JAMMER	CEPH AIRSTRIKE
PARKING DECK	MAXIMUM RADAR	COUNTER RADAR	MAXIMUM NANOSUIT
SANCTUARY	MAXIMUM RADAR	ORBITAL STRIKE	MAXIMUM NANOSUIT
CITY HALL	MAXIMUM RADAR	ORBITAL STRIKE	MAXIMUM NANOSUIT
IMPACT	MAXIMUM RADAR	COUNTER RADAR	MAXIMUM NANOSUIT
LIBERTY ISLAND	MAXIMUM RADAR	NANOSUIT JAMMER	CEPH AIRSTRIKE
STATUE	MAXIMUM RADAR	NANOSUIT JAMMER	CEPH AIRSTRIKE
EVAC ZONE	MAXIMUM RADAR	NANOSUIT JAMMER	CEPH AIRSTRIKE
WALL STREET	MAXIMUM RADAR	ORBITAL STRIKE	MAXIMUM NANOSUIT
LIGHTHOUSE	MAXIMUM RADAR	ORBITAL STRIKE	CEPH AIRSTRIKE
PIER 17	MAXIMUM RADAR	ORBITAL STRIKE	CEPH AIRSTRIKE

3 Dog Tags: Maximum Radar is always rewarded for collecting three dog tags and benefits not only you but your entire team by highlighting enemies on the mini-map for a limited time period. Counter Radar, earned at five dog tags, scrambles the radar of all enemies. Save this bonus until an enemy Maximum Radar is called in to nullify its effects.

5 Dog Tags: The other two second tier support bonuses are Nanosuit Jammer and Orbital Strike. Nanosuit Jammer takes away all Nanosuit abilities from enemy players for a limited time by completely draining their energy within its EMP radius. Orbital Strike calls in a devastating laser strike that affects an area of the map. Triggering the Support Bonus calls up a mini map; target an area of the map heavily populated by enemy soldiers for maximum results!

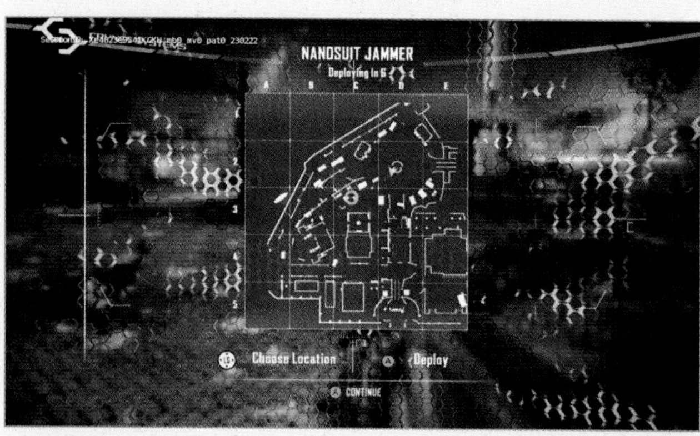

7 Dog Tags: The third tier of Support Bonuses, earned by collecting seven dog tags, consists of Maximum Nanosuit and the Ceph Airstrike. The Nanosuit Overcharge unleashed by Maximum Nanosuit allows you to sprint without loss of energy for a limited time while in an enhanced Armor mode. The Ceph Airstrike calls in a Ceph gunship that flies around the map and rains continuous fire on your foes for a limited time. The airship can eventually be destroyed if hit with enough gunfire; step out of cover briefly to fire upon its vulnerable generator before taking shelter from its retaliatory fire.

THE GAME CHANGER

The Retriever module is, by far, the most valuable when it comes to making the most of Support Bonuses. By default it automatically collects dog tags from fallen enemies. Once upgraded, Support Bonuses require one less dog tag to activate and once Support Bonuses remain active longer once this module has been fully upgraded. Don't overlook this awesome module!

There are several Nanosuit Modules that can provide protection from Support Bonuses. Decide whether you consider these valuable enough compared to the other Suit Modules choices available to you. While they can neutralize some of the most devastating aspects of multiplayer, they only serve a purpose when Support Bonuses are active.

BLIND SPOT LEVEL 1: Provides protection from enemy Maximum Radar bonus.

COVERT OPS LEVEL 2: Provides protection from the Ceph Airstrike bonus

JAMMER LEVEL 2: Provides protection against enemy Radar Jammer attacks

ARMOR ENHANCE LEVEL 3: Protects against the Nanosuit Jammer bonus

OPERATIVE STATUS

The Operative Status menu is the main multiplayer hub where you can track your progress via Service Record, compare your skills to others on the Leaderboards, view game Unlocks, monitor your Skill Assessments, browse your collected Dog Tags, and set your Clan Tag.

SERVICE RECORD

Service Record is where you can view your overall rank from 1 to 50 as well as your Armor, Power and Stealth Levels from 1 to 12. Overall stats, Support Bonus totals, Suit Usage, Weapons Usage, and Game Types results can all be viewed in Service Record

RANKING REQUIREMENTS & BONUSES

MP RANK NO.	EMBLEM	RANK NAME	XP REQUIRED	COMPLETION REWARD
1		CADET I	0	—
2		CADET II	500	CLASS TOKEN
3		CADET III	1500	CLASS TOKEN
4		RECRUIT I	3000	CLASS TOKEN
5		RECRUIT II	5100	CUSTOM CLASS 1 WEAPON TOKEN
6		RECRUIT III	7800	GAME TYPE: CRASH SITE
7		PRIVATE I	11,200	WEAPON TOKEN
8		PRIVATE II	15,300	SKILL ASSESSMENTS: ARMOR
9		PRIVATE III	20,200	WEAPON TOKEN
10		TROOPER I	25,900	CUSTOM CLASS 2
11		TROOPER II	32,500	SKILL ASSESSMENTS: STEALTH
12		TROOPER III	40,000	GAME TYPE: CTR
13		PRIVATE FIRST CLASS I	48,500	WEAPON TOKEN
14		PRIVATE FIRST CLASS II	58,000	SKILL ASSESSMENTS: POWER
15		PRIVATE FIRST CLASS III	68,600	WEAPON TOKEN
16		SPECIALIST I	80,300	CUSTOM CLASS 3
17		SPECIALIST II	93,200	WEAPON TOKEN
18		SPECIALIST III	107,300	GAME TYPE: ASSAULT
19		RANGER I	122,600	WEAPON TOKEN
20		RANGER II	139,200	CUSTOM CLASS 4
21		RANGER III	157,100	WEAPON TOKEN
22		GUARD I	176,400	GAME TYPE: EXTRACTION
23		GUARD II	197,100	SKILL ASSESSMENTS: SUPPORT BONUS I
24		GUARD III	219,300	WEAPON TOKEN
25		OPERATIVE I	243,000	CUSTOM CLASS 5
26		OPERATIVE II	268,300	SKILL ASSESSMENTS: SUPPORT BONUS II
27		OPERATIVE III	295,200	WEAPON TOKEN
28		CORPORAL I	323,800	GAME TYPE: CLASSIC
29		CORPORAL II	354,100	WEAPON TOKEN
30		CORPORAL IIII	386,200	SKILL ASSESSMENTS: TRAVELER I
31		SERGEANT I	420,100	WEAPON TOKEN
32		SERGEANT II	455,900	SKILL ASSESSMENTS: TRAVELER II
33		SERGEANT III	493,600	WEAPON TOKEN

MP RANK NO.	EMBLEM	RANK NAME	XP REQUIRED	COMPLETION REWARD
34		VETERAN I	533,300	GAME TYPE: SINGLE LIFE
35		VETERAN II	575,000	SKILL ASSESSMENTS: SKILL KILL I
36		VETERAN III	618,700	—
37		MAJOR I	664,500	WEAPON TOKEN
38		MAJOR II	712,400	SKILL ASSESSMENTS: SKILL KILL II
39		MAJOR III	762,500	GAME TYPE: PRO
40		ENFORCER I	814,800	WEAPON TOKEN
41		ENFORCER II	869,400	SKILL ASSESSMENTS: ALTERNATIVE KILLS
42		ENFORCER III	926,300	SKILL ASSESSMENTS: CHALLENGE I
43		COLONEL I	985,600	WEAPON TOKEN
44		COLONEL II	1,047,300	SKILL ASSESSMENTS: CHALLENGE II
45		COLONEL I	1,111,500	WEAPON TOKEN
46		GENERAL I	1,178,200	SKILL ASSESSMENTS: MARKSMAN I
47		GENERAL II	1,247,500	SKILL ASSESSMENTS: MARKSMAN II
48		GENERAL III	1,319,400	SKILL ASSESSMENTS: DOMINATION I
49		GROUP COMMANDER	1,394,000	SKILL ASSESSMENTS: DOMINATION II
50		FORCE COMMANDER	1,471,300	RANK 50 ACHIEVEMENT
BONUS		—	1,551,400	SUIT REBOOT ABILITY CELL SCAR, CELL FELINE

NANOSUIT: POWER MODE UPGRADES

POWER RANK	COMPLETION REWARD	SUIT XP REQUIRED
1	—	0
2	MYSTERY DOG TAG TOKEN	1200
3	POWER MODULE TOKEN	3400
4	MYSTERY DOG TAG TOKEN	6900
5	POWER MODULE TOKEN	13,300
6	POWER MODULE TOKEN	22,200
7	MYSTERY DOG TAG TOKEN	33,500
8	POWER MODULE TOKEN	47,100
9	MYSTERY DOG TAG TOKEN	63,200
10	POWER MODULE TOKEN	82,000
11	MYSTERY DOG TAG TOKEN	103,500
12	POWER MODULE TOKEN	127,900

NANOSUIT: STEALTH MODE UPGRADES

POWER RANK	COMPLETION REWARD	SUIT XP REQUIRED
1	—	0
2	MYSTERY DOG TAG TOKEN	800
3	STEALTH MODULE TOKEN	2200
4	MYSTERY DOG TAG TOKEN	4500
5	MYSTERY DOG TAG TOKEN	8700
6	STEALTH MODULE TOKEN	14,500
7	MYSTERY DOG TAG TOKEN	21,900
8	STEALTH MODULE TOKEN	30,800
9	MYSTERY DOG TAG TOKEN	41,300
10	STEALTH MODULE TOKEN	53,600
11	MYSTERY DOG TAG TOKEN	67,700
12	STEALTH MODULE TOKEN	83,600

NANOSUIT: ARMOR MODE UPGRADES

POWER RANK	COMPLETION REWARD	SUIT XP REQUIRED
1	—	0
2	MYSTERY DOG TAG TOKEN	800
3	ARMOR MODULE TOKEN	2200
4	MYSTERY DOG TAG TOKEN	4500
5	MYSTERY DOG TAG TOKEN	8700
6	ARMOR MODULE TOKEN	14,500
7	MYSTERY DOG TAG TOKEN	21,900
8	ARMOR MODULE TOKEN	30,800
9	MYSTERY DOG TAG TOKEN	41,300
10	ARMOR MODULE TOKEN	53,600
11	MYSTERY DOG TAG TOKEN	67,700
12	ARMOR MODULE TOKEN	83,600

LEADERBOARDS

See where you rank both globally and amongst your friends. Compare your Kill to Death Ratio, Weapon Accuracy, Win/Loss Ratio and total Skill Kills.

UNLOCKS

The Unlocks page shows your total progress toward unlocking 150 total possible unlocks spread across the categories of Weapons, Modules, Classes, Attachments and Game Types.

SKILL ASSESSMENTS

Track your progress in Skill Assessments from numerous categories such as Game Type, Weapons and Modules. Rewards for completing Skill Assessments are XP bonuses as well as Attachment and Module unlocks for use in Custom Classes.

DOG TAGS

View the number of times you've collected General Dog Tags, any Mystery Dog Tags you've revealed using Dog Tag unlocks, Medals awarded for meeting specified criteria and Awards given for exceptional performance during multiplayer matches.

GENERAL DOG TAGS

The following Dog Tags are all available at the start of your multiplayer career.

DOG TAG NAME	STYLE
WELCOME TO CRYSIS	
PARKING DECK	
SANCTUARY	
CITY HALL	
IMPACT	
LIBERTY ISLAND	
WALL STREET	
LIGHTHOUSE	

DOG TAG NAME	STYLE
ALBANIA	
ARGENTINA	
AUSTRALIA	
AUSTRIA	
BELARUS	
BELGIUM	
BRAZIL	
BULGARIA	

DOG TAG NAME	STYLE
CANADA	
CHINA	
CROATIA	
CUBA	
CYPRUS	
CZECH REPUBLIC	
DENMARK	
ENGLAND	

DOG TAG NAME	STYLE
ESTONIA	
FINLAND	
FRANCE	
GERMANY	
GREECE	
HUNGARY	
ICELAND	
IRELAND	
INDIA	
ITALY	
JAPAN	
LATVIA	
LITHUANIA	
LUXEMBOURG	
MACEDONIA	
MALAYSIA	
MEXICO	
MOLDOVA	
NETHERLANDS	
NEW ZEALAND	
NORWAY	
PAKISTAN	
PERU	
PHILIPPINES	
POLAND	
PORTUGAL	
ROMANIA	
RUSSIA	
SCOTLAND	
SLOVAKIA	
SPAIN	
SOUTH AFRICA	
SOUTH KOREA	
SWEDEN	
SWITZERLAND	
TURKEY	
UKRAINE	
UNITED KINGDOM	
UNITED STATES OF AMERICA	
WALES	

MYSTERY DOG TAGS

Mystery Dog Tags are unlocked with Mystery Dog Tag Tokens earned by utilizing the Nanosuit's Power, Stealth, and Armor abilities to earn experience in each discipline. Rank up each of the three Nanosuit modes to earn the tokens to unlock these special Dog Tags.

DOG TAG NAME	STYLE
MARINE NANOSUIT	
COMBAT READY	
NANOSUIT CONCEPT	
MARINE CONCEPT	
NYPD CONCEPT	
CITY CONCEPT	
ALIEN CONCEPT	
MARINE NANOSUIT CONCEPT	
C.E.L.L. NANOSUIT CONCEPT	
CHURCH CONCEPT	
RUSH HOUR	
STORM	
FRACTURE	
CITY HALL	
CRYTEK	
I LOVE NY	
ALCATRAZ	
RIPPED	
MOLECULAR PULSE	

DOG TAG NAME	STYLE
STRUCTURE	
HELIX	
NERVE ENDING	
CELL SCAN	
BLOOD STREAM	
HIDDEN MENACE	
CRYSTALLIZED	
STEALTH MODE ACTIVATED	
POWER MODE ACTIVATED	
SYMBIOTIC	
EYE SPY	
ARMOR MODE ACTIVATED	
CRYSIS®2	
BIOHAZARD	
EA	
NANOSUIT 2.0	
HEADSHOT	
STARS AND STRIPES	
NANOVISION	

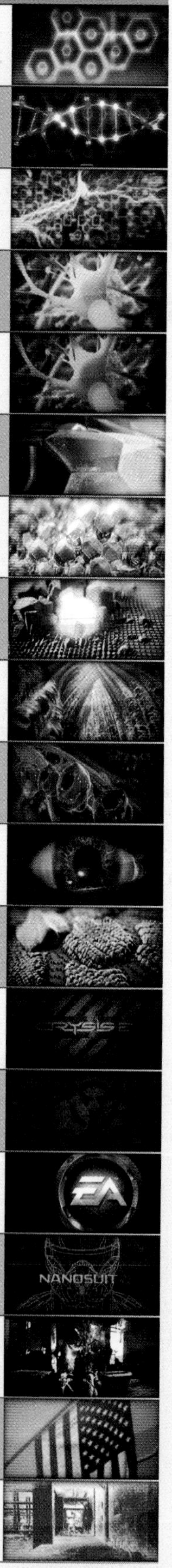

DOG TAG NAME	STYLE
OVERVIEW	
KNUCKLE SANDWICH	
FIRE AND FORGET	
OPEN WATER	
FARE DODGER	
SPLASH DOWN	
EAGLE EYE	
PIER 17	
DETONATOR	
SHOCKWAVE	
ROOFTOP	
CRASH SITE	
WATCH YOUR SIX	
TSUNAMI	
FIRST CONTACT	
KILOTON	
BE THE WEAPON	
STATUE OF LIBERTY	
SHRAPNEL	

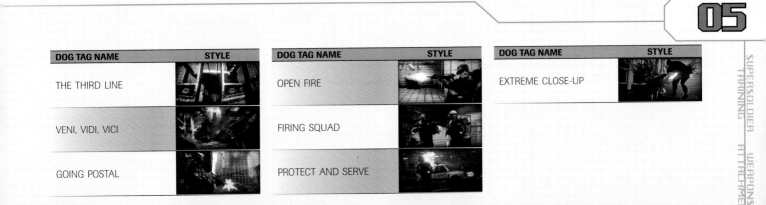

DOG TAG NAME	STYLE
THE THIRD LINE	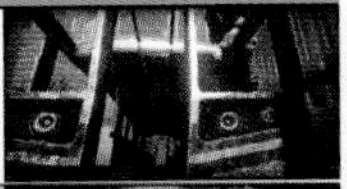
VENI, VIDI, VICI	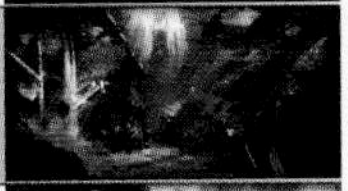
GOING POSTAL	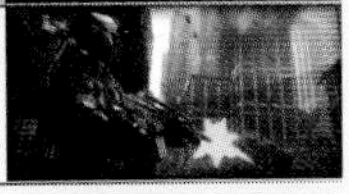
OPEN FIRE	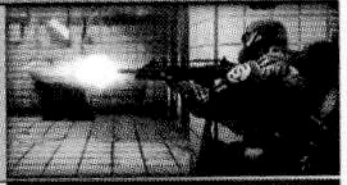
FIRING SQUAD	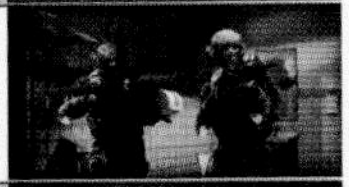
PROTECT AND SERVE	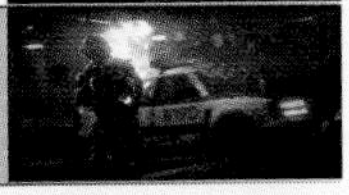
EXTREME CLOSE-UP	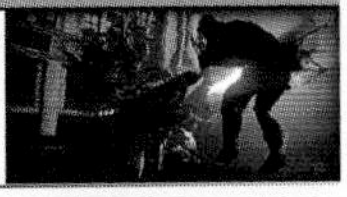

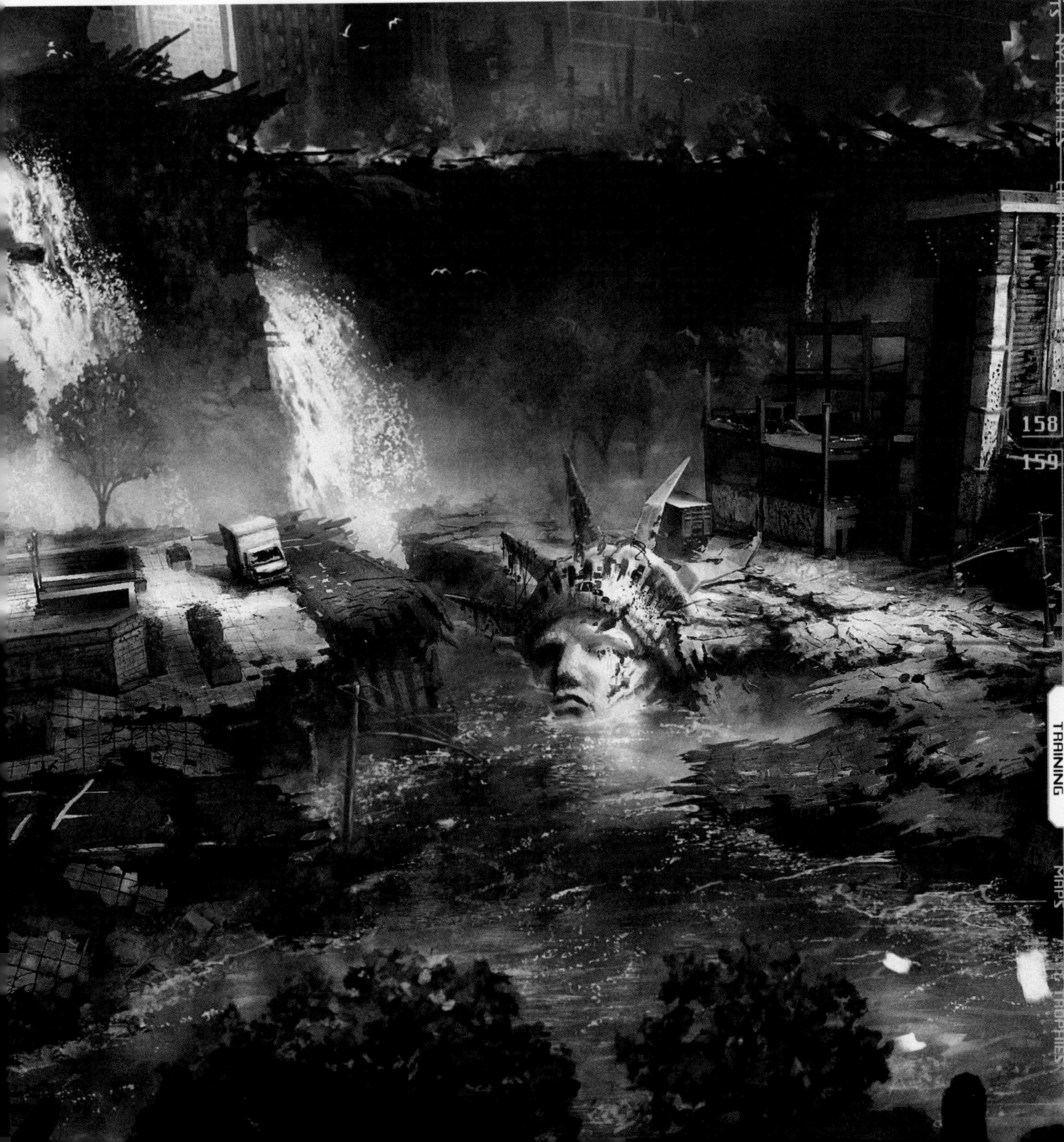

DOG TAG MEDALS

Dog Tag Medals are unlocked over the course of the player's multiplayer career. Many are unlocked as a reward for long-term efforts while others can be unlocked for very specific actions made on individual maps.

DOG TAG NAME	MP CAREER MILESTONE	STYLE
KILL 5,000	KILL 5,000 PLAYERS ONLINE	
DEAD INSIDE	KILL 10,000 PLAYERS ONLINE	
BORN AGAIN!	NANOSUIT REBOOT FOR THE FIRST TIME	
ETERNAL WARRIOR	NANOSUIT REBOOT 5 TIMES	
LEMMING	FALL TO YOUR DEATH 10 TIMES	
FOOL	BLOW YOURSELF UP 10 TIMES	
HIGH FLYER	FINISH TOP OF THE END GAME SCOREBOARD 10 TIMES	
MIDGET WRESTLER	GET A MELEE KILL WHILE CROUCHED	
WHITE STICK	BLIND YOURSELF 10 TIMES	
THE INCREDIBLE BULK	RIP OFF A MOUNTED WEAPON	
FOOT FETISH	SNIPE SOMEONE IN THE FOOT	
YOU'VE BEEN FRAMED	BE THE VICTIM IN THE FINAL KILL REPLAY AT THE END OF A GAME	
VIEW TO A KILL	STAND AT THE HIGHEST POINT OF SKYLINE	
STOCKBROKER RETIREMENT PARTY	FALL OUT OF A WINDOW IN IMPACT	
WET AND WILD	GO SWIMMING IN PIER 17	
NEVER FLAGGING	GET THE WINNING SCORE IN CAPTURE THE RELAY WITH LESS THAN 10 SECONDS REMAINING	
THERE IS NO SPOON	UPLOAD THE FINAL BIT OF INTEL WITH LESS THAN 5 SECONDS REMAINING	
FORT KNOX	PERSONALLY KILL ALL THE ATTACKERS IN ASSAULT	
NIGHT OWL	PLAY AFTER 2AM	

DOG TAG NAME	MP CAREER MILESTONE	STYLE
DRUNK AND DISORDERLY	PLAY AFTER 11:30PM AND FINISH IN THE BOTTOM THIRD 3 TIMES IN A ROW	
VOYEUR	WHILE CLOAKED SEE AN ENEMY BE KILLED WITHIN 8M	
AFTERNOON TEA	TEABAG 10 VICTIMS	
GRADUATION DAY	GRADUATE FROM NEW RECRUITS	
SCARRED FOR LIFE	COMPLETE ALL ASSESSMENTS FOR THE SCAR	
PURRRRRRRFECT	COMPLETE ALL ASSESSMENTS FOR THE FELINE	
MARSHALL LAW	COMPLETE ALL ASSESSMENTS FOR THE MARSHALL	
DAY OF THE JACKAL	COMPLETE ALL ASSESSMENTS FOR THE JACKAL	
BEETLE JUICE	COMPLETE ALL ASSESSMENTS FOR THE SCARAB	
MONSTER HUNTER	COMPLETE ALL ASSESSMENTS FOR THE GRENDEL	
SUPER SHARP SHOOTER	COMPLETE ALL ASSESSMENTS FOR THE DSG-1	
MAXIMUM ACCELERATION	COMPLETE ALL ASSESSMENTS FOR THE M20 14 GAUSS	
H.S.M.	COMPLETE ALL ASSESSMENTS FOR THE MK.60 MOD 0	
WHIZZBANGER	COMPLETE ALL ASSESSMENTS FOR THE L-TAG	
HMMMM DING!	COMPLETE ALL ASSESSMENTS FOR THE X-43 MIKE	
SHOCKING	COMPLETE ALL ASSESSMENTS FOR THE K-VOLT	
SUPER NOVA	COMPLETE ALL ASSESSMENTS FOR THE NOVA	
RAPID RESPONSE	COMPLETE ALL ASSESSMENTS FOR THE AY69	
HAMMER DOWN	COMPLETE ALL ASSESSMENTS FOR THE HAMMER	

DOG TAG NAME	MP CAREER MILESTONE	STYLE
FEELING LUCKY	COMPLETE ALL ASSESSMENTS FOR THE MAJESTIC	
WALKING TANK	COMPLETE ALL ASSESSMENTS FOR THE HMG.	
FRAGGER	COMPLETE ALL ASSESSMENTS FOR THE FRAG GRENADES	
STICKY DEATH	COMPLETE ALL ASSESSMENTS FOR THE C4	
ROCKET MAN	COMPLETE ALL ASSESSMENTS FOR THE JAW	
THICK SKINNED	COMPLETE ASSESSMENT SET "ARMOR MODULES"	
ON THE DOWN-LOW	COMPLETE ASSESSMENT SET "STEALTH MODULES"	
RUN AND GUN	COMPLETE ASSESSMENT SET "POWER MODULES"	
TEAM PLAYER	COMPLETE ASSESSMENT SET "SUPPORT BONUS"	
CLIP ON, CLIP OFF	COMPLETE ASSESSMENT SET "ATTACHMENTS"	
IN IT TO WIN IT	COMPLETE ASSESSMENT SET "GAME TYPE"	
ALTERNATIVE LIFESTYLE	COMPLETE ASSESSMENT SET "ALTERNATIVE KILLS"	
WHY THE LONG FACE?	COMPLETE ASSESSMENT SET "CHALLENGE"	

DOG TAG NAME	MP CAREER MILESTONE	STYLE
DEADEYE	COMPLETE ASSESSMENT SET "MARKSMAN"	
THE BIG BOSS	COMPLETE ASSESSMENT SET "DOMINATION"	
MAD SKILLS	COMPLETE ASSESSMENT SET "SKILL KILLS"	
UP FOR MORE	COMPLETE ASSESSMENT SET "NANOSUIT REBOOT"	
FULL PASSPORT	COMPLETE ASSESSMENT SET "TRAVELER"	
WARMING UP	KILL 1,000 PLAYERS ONLINE	
ARMS OF STEEL	RIP OFF 100 MOUNTED WEAPONS	
MARATHON MAN	CARRY THE RELAY FOR 10 MINUTES	
LONE WOLF	KILL 100 ENEMIES WITHOUT ASSISTANCE FROM YOUR TEAM	
CROUCHING WARRIOR	SPEND A TOTAL OF AN HOUR CROUCHED IN-GAME	
ARMOR PLATING	ACTIVATE ARMOR MODE 1000 TIMES	
CLOAK ADDICT	ACTIVATE STEALTH MODE 1000 TIMES	
IT'S ALL OVER...	REACH 100% OPERATIVE STATUS COMPLETE	

AFTER MATCH AWARDS

After Match Awards are unlocked for doing the most or least of a specific action out of all players in the match. Consult the requirements for each award and make your mark.

DOG TAG NAME	AFTER MATCH AWARD	STYLE
MOST VALUABLE	HIGHEST KILL DEATH RATIO	
MOST MOTIVATED	HIGHEST OBJECTIVE SCORE	
MOST SNEAKY	MOST ENEMIES SHOT IN THE BACK	
MOST COWARDLY	GET SHOT IN THE BACK MOST	
NINJA	LONGEST TIME IN STEALTH MODE	
SPEED DEMON	MOST TIME SPRINTING	
ARMOR PLATING	MOST TIMES SHOT WHILE IN ARMOR MODE	
ADVANCED RECON	MOST TIME SPENT IN VISOR	
ASSASSIN	MOST STEALTH TAKEDOWNS	
ADAPTABLE	MOST SUIT MODE CHANGES	
MURDERIZER	MOST MELEE KILLS	
GLASS JAW	BE MELEE KILLED THE MOST	
UNTOUCHABLE	FEWEST DEATHS	
RAMPAGE	LONGEST KILL STREAK	
DEMOLITION MAN	MOST KILLS USING C4	
KEEP YOUR HEAD DOWN	MOST TIME SPENT CROUCHED	
LEAP OF FAITH	HIGHEST FALL WITHOUT DYING	
AIDING RADAR	MOST RADARS CALLED IN	
IS IT A BIRD?	MOST TIME SPENT IN THE AIR	
VENDETTA	MOST KILLS OF THE SAME PLAYER	
GENOCIDE	KILL THE ENTIRE ENEMY TEAM	
EXHIBITIONIST	HIGHEST NUMBER OF SKILL KILLS	
MAGPIE	MOST NUMBER OF DOG TAGS COLLECTED	
CLAY PIGEON	MOST TIMES KILLED IN THE AIR	

DOG TAG NAME	AFTER MATCH AWARD	STYLE
X-RAY	MOST BULLET PENETRATION KILLS	
STANDARD BEARER	MOST TIME CARRYING A RELAY	
DUG IN	HOLD A CRASH SITE FOR THE LONGEST TIME	
ALIENATED	MOST ALIEN BIO-TICKS EXTRACTED	
TECHNOMANCER	UPLOAD THE MOST INTEL	
BING!	MOST HEADSHOT KILLS	
BANG ON	MOST ACCURATE	
BULLETS COST MONEY	LEAST SHOTS FIRED	
BATTLEFIELD SURGERY	MOST TIMES HEALTH RESTORED TO FULL	
MOST SELFISH	MOST KILLS WITHOUT ASSISTS EARNED BY TEAMMATES	
TOOLS OF THE TRADE	AT LEAST 3 KILLS WITH 4 DIFFERENT WEAPONS	
SPRAY AND PRAY	MOST SHOTS FIRED	
BIG BANGER	MOST KILLS WITH A SINGLE EXPLOSIVE	
ROBBED	MOST KILL ASSISTS	
MONEY SHOT	GET THE WINNING KILL	
SINGLE MINDED	MOST KILLS	
DON'T PANIC!	MOST FRIENDLIES SHOT (NUMBER OF HITS)	
LONE WOLF	MOST KILLS WITH NO FRIENDLY PLAYER WITHIN 15M	
NEVER SAY DIE	LONGEST DEATHSTREAK	
ENERGETIC BUNNY	MOST ENERGY USED UP	

DOG TAG NAME	AFTER MATCH AWARD	STYLE
WAR BIRD	MOST KILLS WITHIN 5 SECONDS OF DECLOAKING	
IMPREGNABLE	MOST FIGHTS WON IN ARMOR MODE	
TARGET LOCKED	MOST ENEMIES SPOTTED	
SAFETY IN NUMBERS	MOST KILLS WITH A FRIENDLY WITHIN 15M	
SPANKED	NO KILLS	
PARDON?	MOST GRENADES SURVIVED	
DIRTY DOZEN	SCORE 12 KILLS WITHOUT DYING	
CODPIECE	MOST GROIN SHOTS	
MOUNTIE	MOST KILLS WITH MOUNTED WEAPONS	
RIP OFF	MOST KILLS WITH RIPPED OFF MOUNTED WEAPONS	
PRO TIPS	MOST CLOAKED RELOADS	
WRONG PLACE, WRONG TIME	BE THE WINNING KILL	
OBSERVER	MOST TIME WATCHING THE KILLCAM	
INVINCIBLE	NO DEATHS	
GOOD CONDITION	LEAST DAMAGE RECEIVED	
PUNISHER	MOST DAMAGE DEALT	
BULLET MAGNET	MOST DAMAGE RECEIVED	
PACIFIST	LEAST DAMAGE DEALT	
ICY	GREATEST DISTANCE SLID	
BOING!	MOST ENEMIES KILLED BY AIR STOMP	

MULTIPLAYER
MAPS

CITY HALL

TACTICAL OVERVIEW

VITAL INTELLIGENCE

RECOMMENDED PLAYERS: 6-10

PLAYABLE GAME MODES

INSTANT ACTION

TEAM INSTANT ACTION

CRASH SITE

CAPTURE THE RELAY

SUPPORT BONUSES

DOG TAGS	SUPPORT BONUS
3	MAXIMUM RADAR
5	ORBITAL STRIKE
7	MAXIMUM NANOSUIT

POTENTIAL CRASH SITES

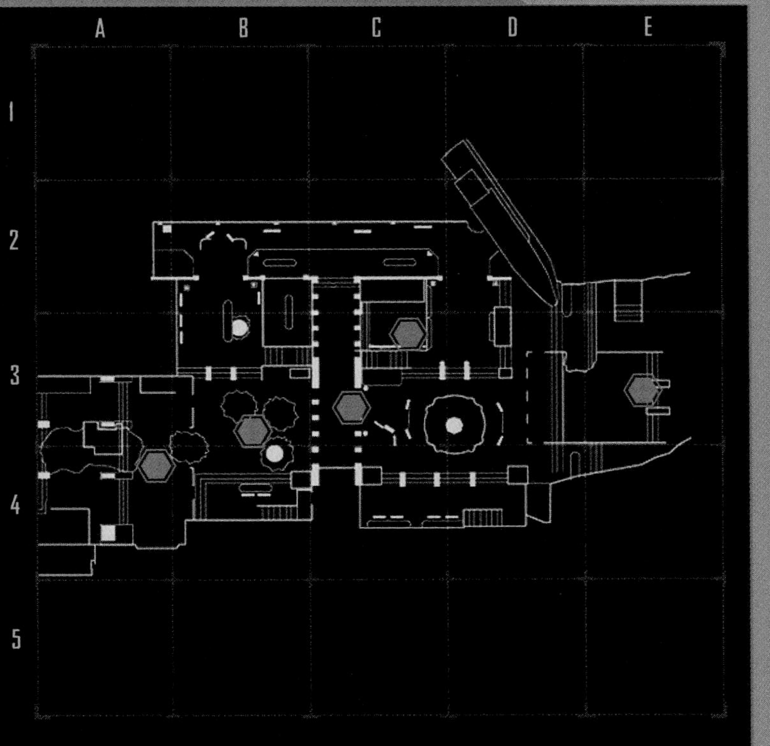

ALTERNATE GAME MODES

GENERAL TACTICS

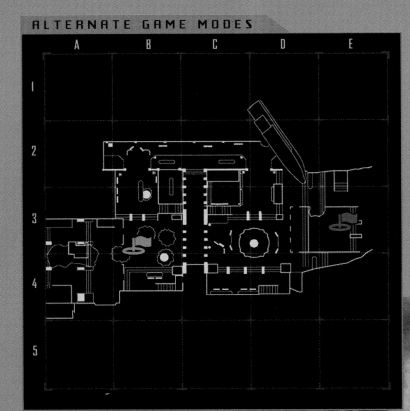

The Sky Bridge is a good position from which to snipe, as most of this outdoor map is visible from this position and has limited access points.

Use the Stranded Boat to hop onto the broken brick wall adjacent to it. Crouch and use the tree for concealment while you fire upon enemies in the highly trafficked Central Fountain.

The metal cover on the Café Balcony (D4) provides a great overlook to the Central Fountain and the Vantage Point.

The Underpass in the middle of the map provides a perfect spot to take refuge from an Orbital Strike and is one of the limited areas on this map in which to do so.

MODE-SPECIFIC TIPS

Crash Site: When the alien pod lands in sector C3, throw your C4 on the objective and drop to the terrace below leading toward the Stranded Boat. Detonate the C4 as soon as enemies enter the pod's radius before jumping back up to start earning points.

Capture the Relay: When defending the Relay in sector E3, fall back to the far right edge of the mini-map and crouch in Stealth mode while checking your left and right corners. This position has a clear view of the Relay and cannot be flanked from behind.

DOWNED BIRD

TACTICAL OVERVIEW

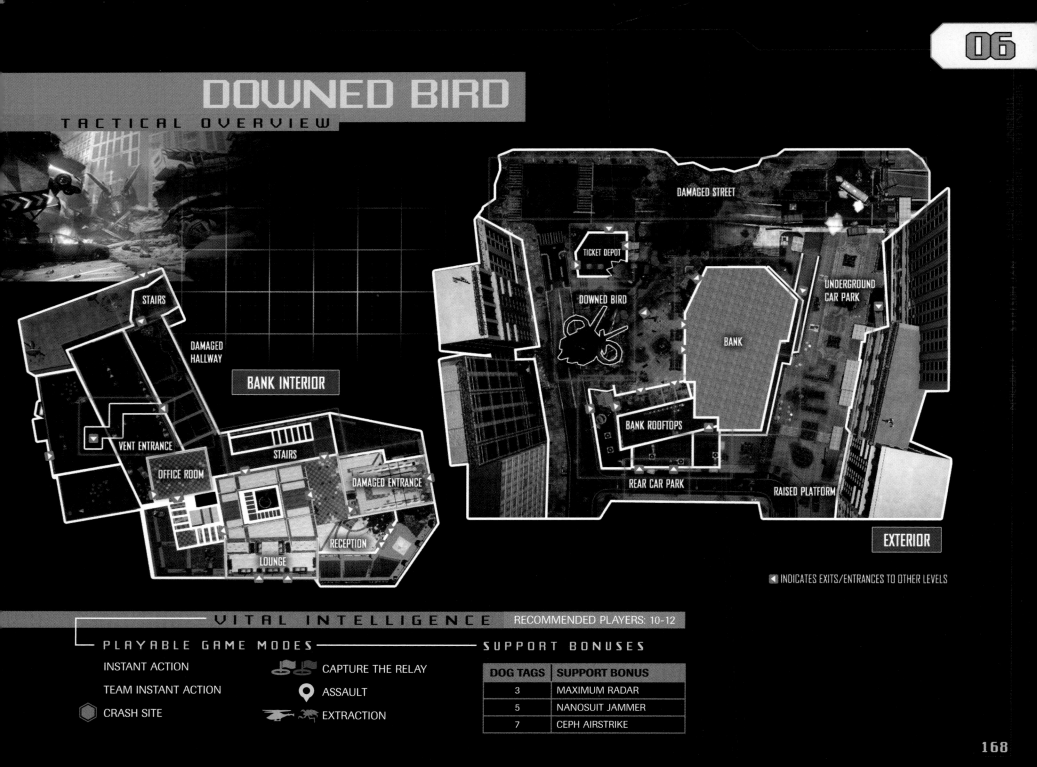

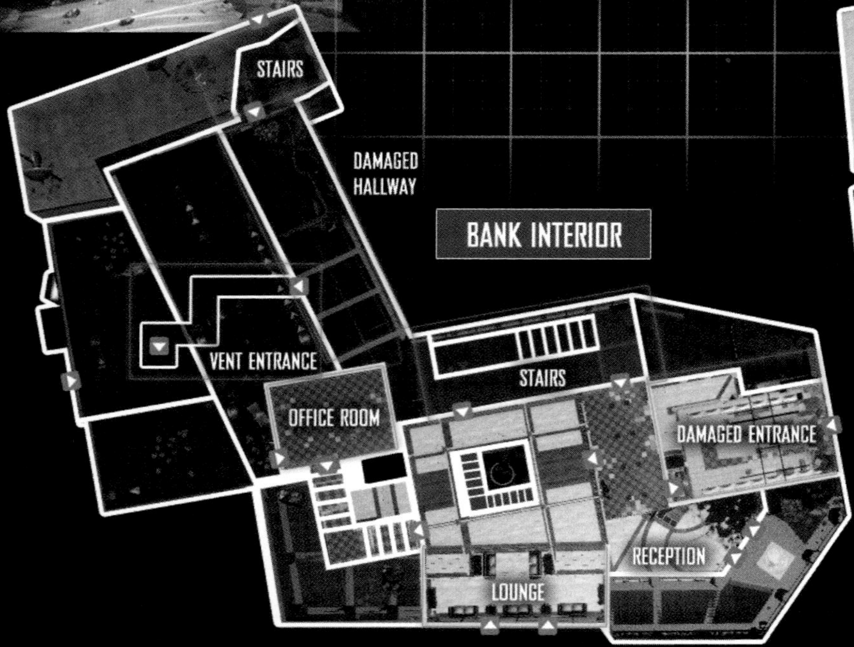

BANK INTERIOR

STAIRS
DAMAGED HALLWAY
VENT ENTRANCE
OFFICE ROOM
STAIRS
DAMAGED ENTRANCE
RECEPTION
LOUNGE

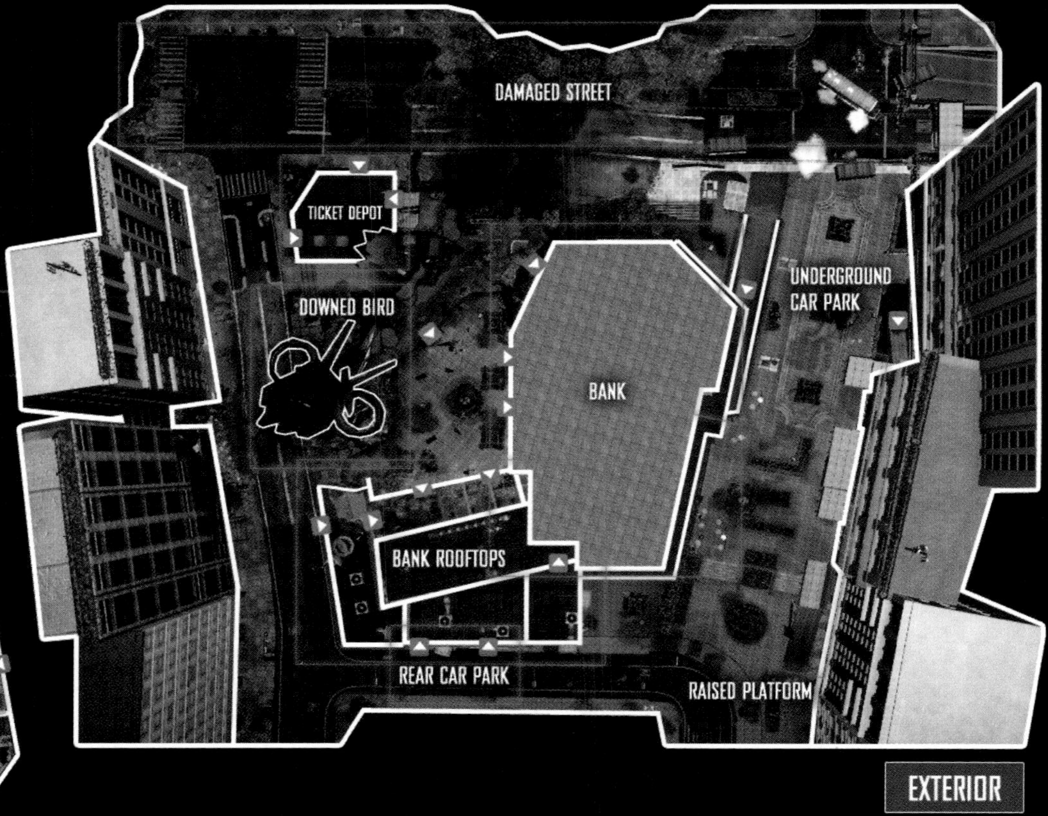

EXTERIOR

DAMAGED STREET
TICKET DEPOT
DOWNED BIRD
BANK
UNDERGROUND CAR PARK
BANK ROOFTOPS
REAR CAR PARK
RAISED PLATFORM

INDICATES EXITS/ENTRANCES TO OTHER LEVELS

VITAL INTELLIGENCE

RECOMMENDED PLAYERS: 10-12

PLAYABLE GAME MODES

INSTANT ACTION

TEAM INSTANT ACTION

CRASH SITE

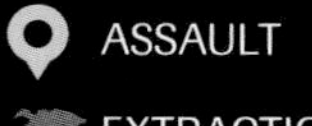

CAPTURE THE RELAY

ASSAULT

EXTRACTION

SUPPORT BONUSES

DOG TAGS	SUPPORT BONUS
3	MAXIMUM RADAR
5	NANOSUIT JAMMER
7	CEPH AIRSTRIKE

POTENTIAL CRASH SITES

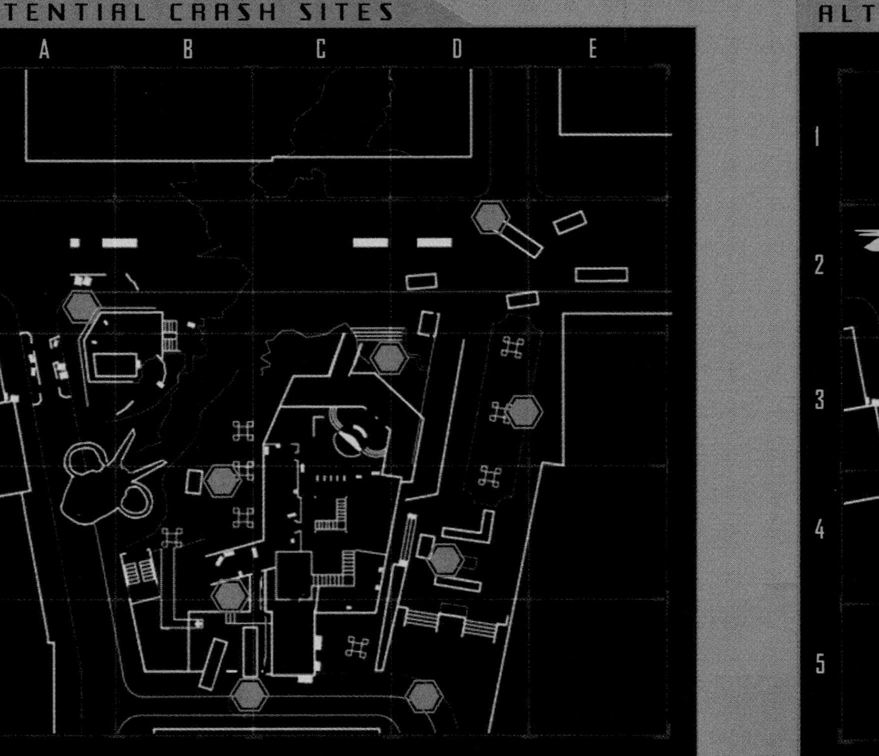

ALTERNATE GAME MODES

A B C D E
1 2 3 4 5

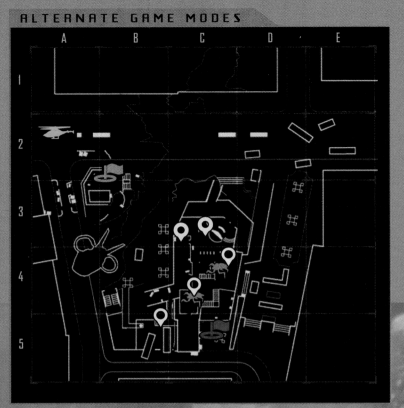

▶ GENERAL TACTICS

Hop onto the exposed steel beams of the Bank Rooftop in sector B4 and crouch to slowly make your way to the middle beam. This is an excellent spot from which to fire upon the Downed Bird area or enemies in the hallway below. Back up against the wall to capture the Crash Site on the Bank Rooftops from this position.

The bank interior can serve not only as a refuge from the Ceph Airstrike, but can also serve as a shortcut between the Downed Bird area and the street on the opposite side of the bank.

Don't forget to utilize the many cars in the streets. When the opportunity presents itself, perform a Power Kick to smash one of the vehicles into an incoming squad of enemies. Similarly, be wary not to let yourself wind up on the receiving end of a vehicular slaughter.

▶ MODE-SPECIFIC TIPS

Assault: When defending the terminal in sector C3, have one player stand in the corner next to the terminal and cover the broken external wall while another player stands in the opposite corner diagonally covering the internal doorway beneath the ramp formed from debris.

Extraction: On offense, make an immediate dash for the bio-tick in sector C4. It's not that far from the spawn area; if you're quick enough, you may be able to grab it and sprint all the way to the extraction helicopter before the defense has time to respond.

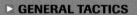

EVAC ZONE

TACTICAL OVERVIEW

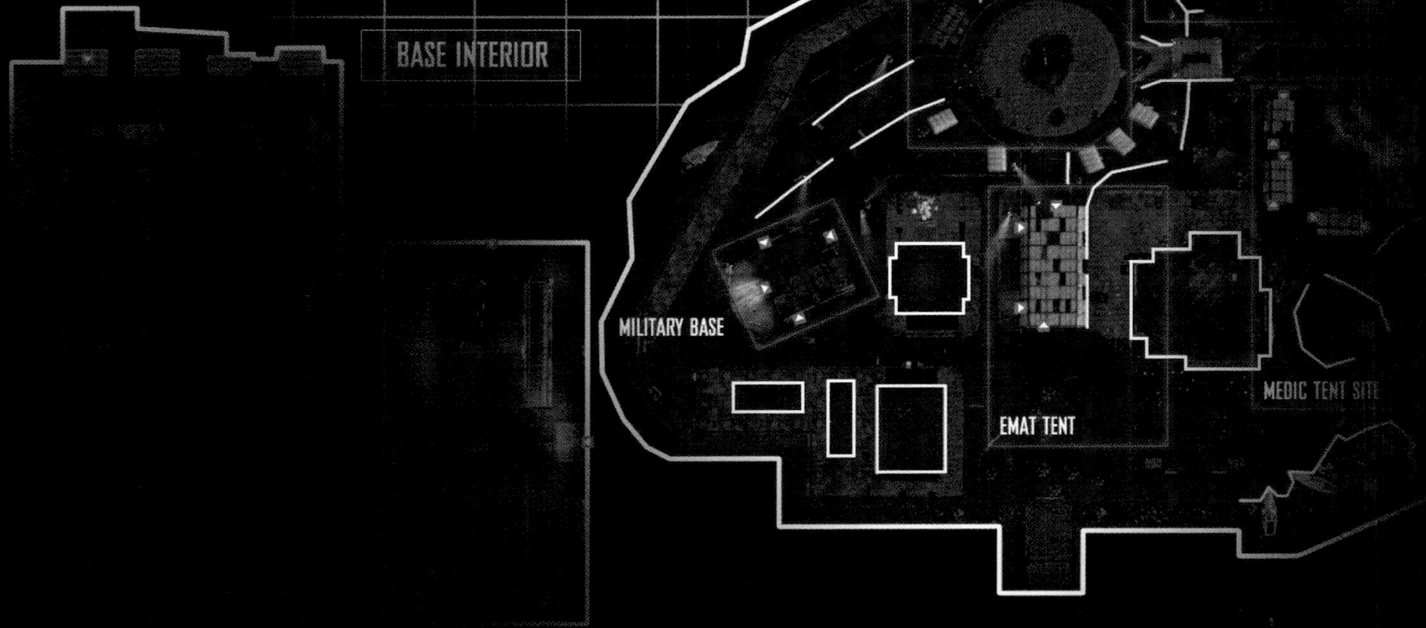

VITAL INTELLIGENCE

RECOMMENDED PLAYERS: 6-10

PLAYABLE GAME MODES

INSTANT ACTION

TEAM INSTANT ACTION

CRASH SITE

SUPPORT BONUSES

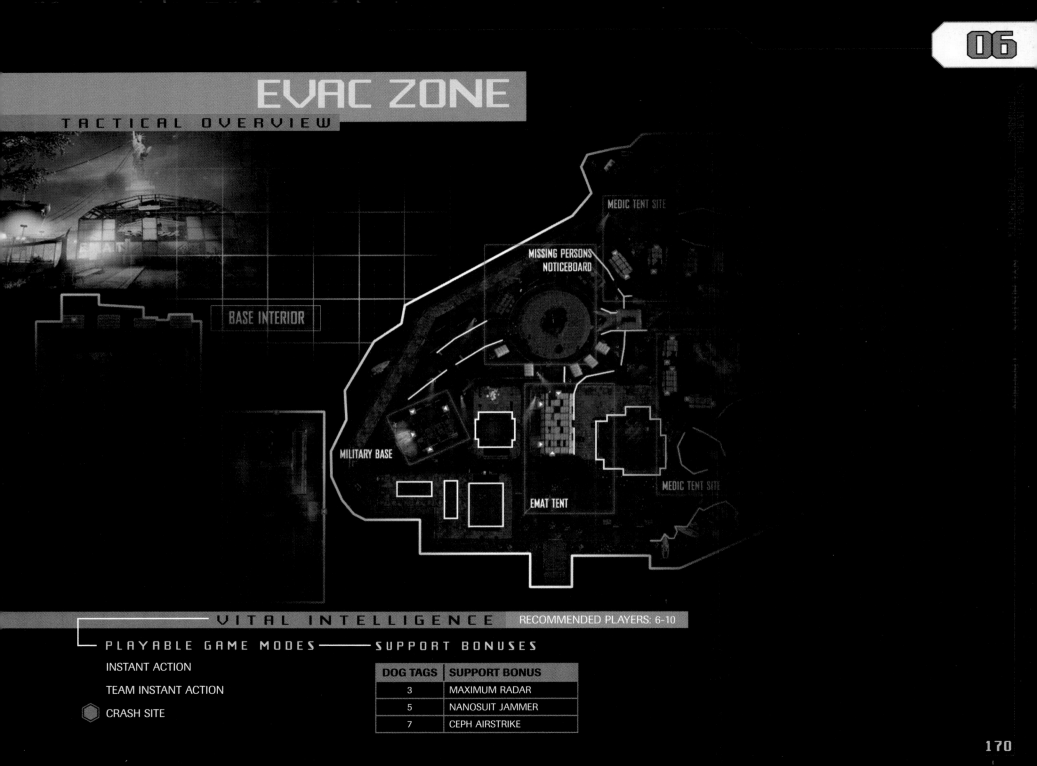

DOG TAGS	SUPPORT BONUS
3	MAXIMUM RADAR
5	NANOSUIT JAMMER
7	CEPH AIRSTRIKE

POTENTIAL CRASH SITES

▶ GENERAL TACTICS

Utilize the rooftops of the buildings in the corner of the map near A5 to fire upon enemies on the ground.

The yellow rooftops in sectors D3 and D4 provide good spots from which to snipe. Crouch in the back part of the roof against the stone wall and creep forward to snipe targets on other buildings or on the ground.

A watchtower in sector C2 contains a turret that can be fired on the lighted circular area beneath the American flag.

▶ MODE-SPECIFIC TIPS

Crash Site: When your team controls the alien pod in sector D5, have one or more teammates hide underwater just outside the capture area ready to counterattack when the enemy takes control.

Crash Site: Take position on the roof of the building with "Help" painted on it when defending the alien pod in sector C3, or toss grenades into the capture area from this location when attempting to dislodge enemy forces.

IMPACT

TACTICAL OVERVIEW

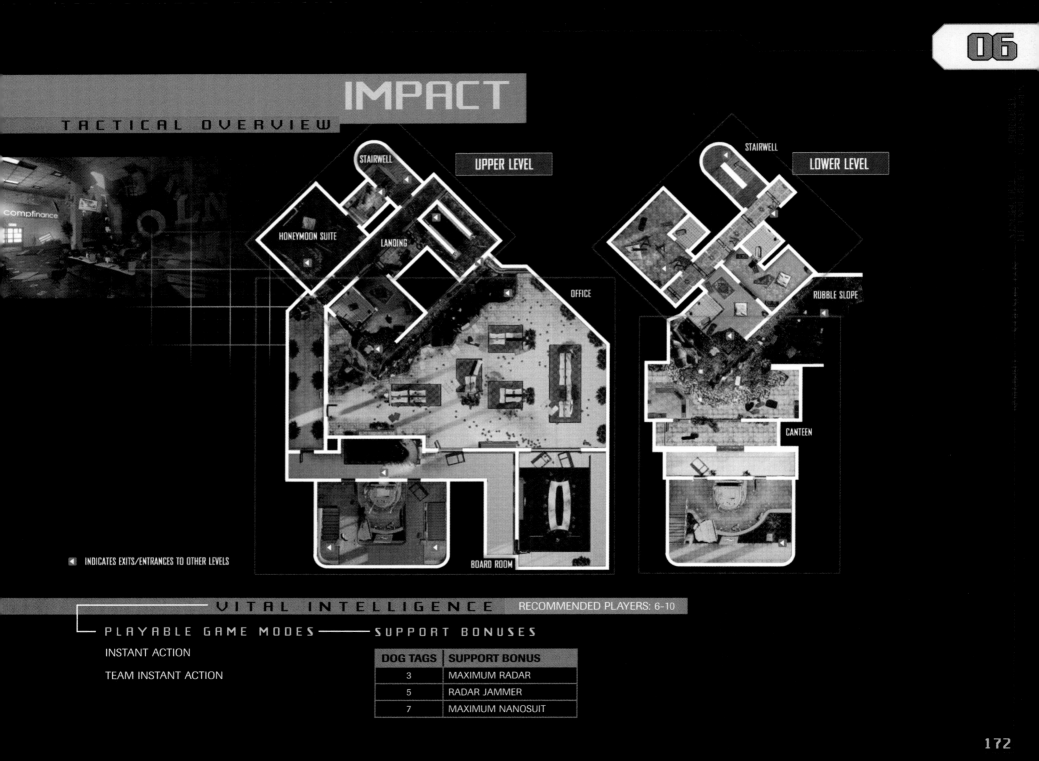

UPPER LEVEL

STAIRWELL

HONEYMOON SUITE

LANDING

OFFICE

BOARD ROOM

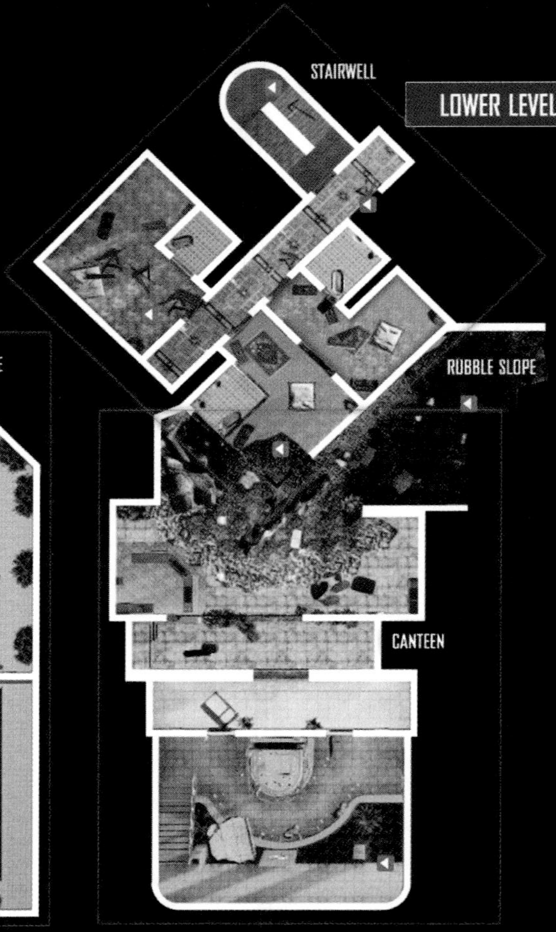

LOWER LEVEL

STAIRWELL

RUBBLE SLOPE

CANTEEN

◄ INDICATES EXITS/ENTRANCES TO OTHER LEVELS

VITAL INTELLIGENCE

RECOMMENDED PLAYERS: 6-10

PLAYABLE GAME MODES

INSTANT ACTION

TEAM INSTANT ACTION

SUPPORT BONUSES

DOG TAGS	SUPPORT BONUS
3	MAXIMUM RADAR
5	RADAR JAMMER
7	MAXIMUM NANOSUIT

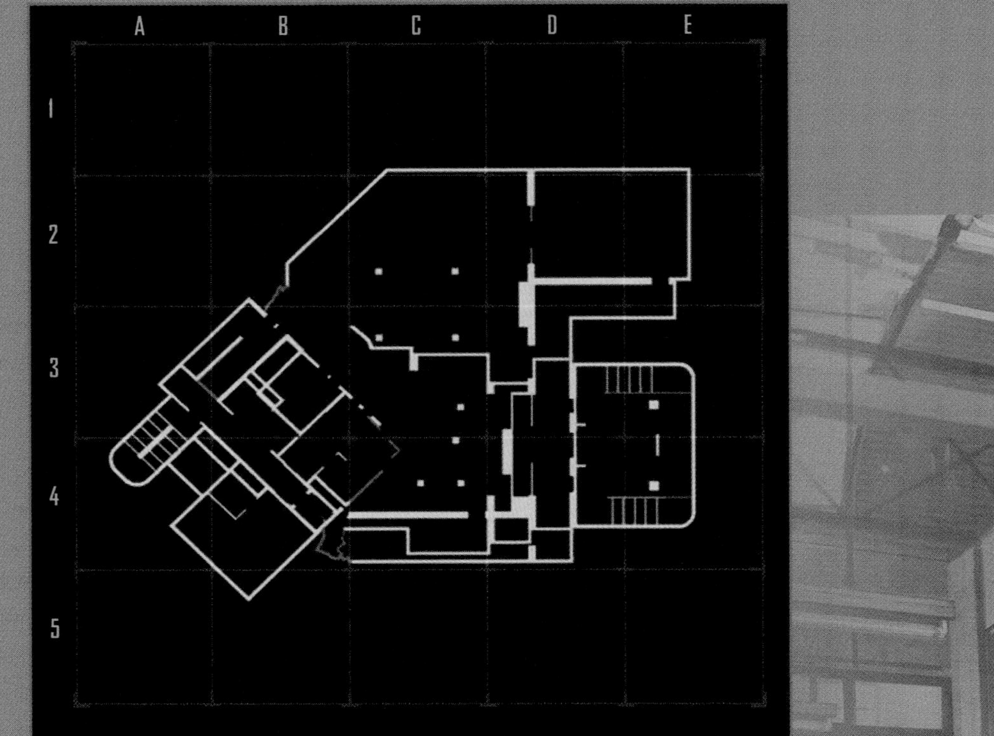

GENERAL TACTICS

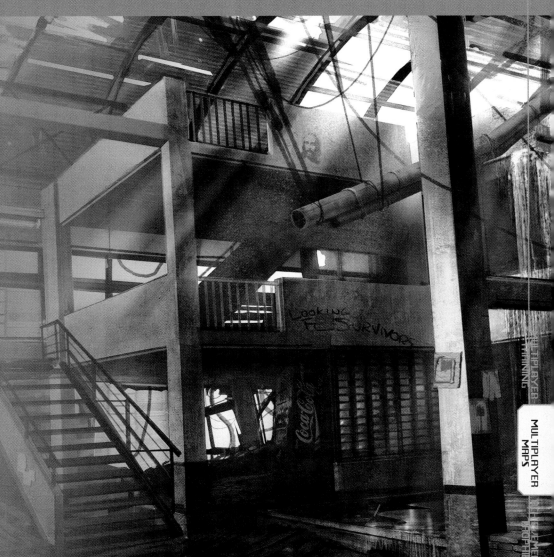

Utilize a class with the Mobility Enhance Suit Module and a shotgun to take advantage of the many corners and confined spaces of the map.

There's a room in the lower-right corner of sector B3 with a bed on a downward slope. The room has only one access point; hide behind the bed and peek out occasionally at foes running by for some easy camping kills.

Hop onto the partially destroyed window-washing platform outside the building in sector B2. Crouch and pick off unsuspecting foes as they make their way past you.

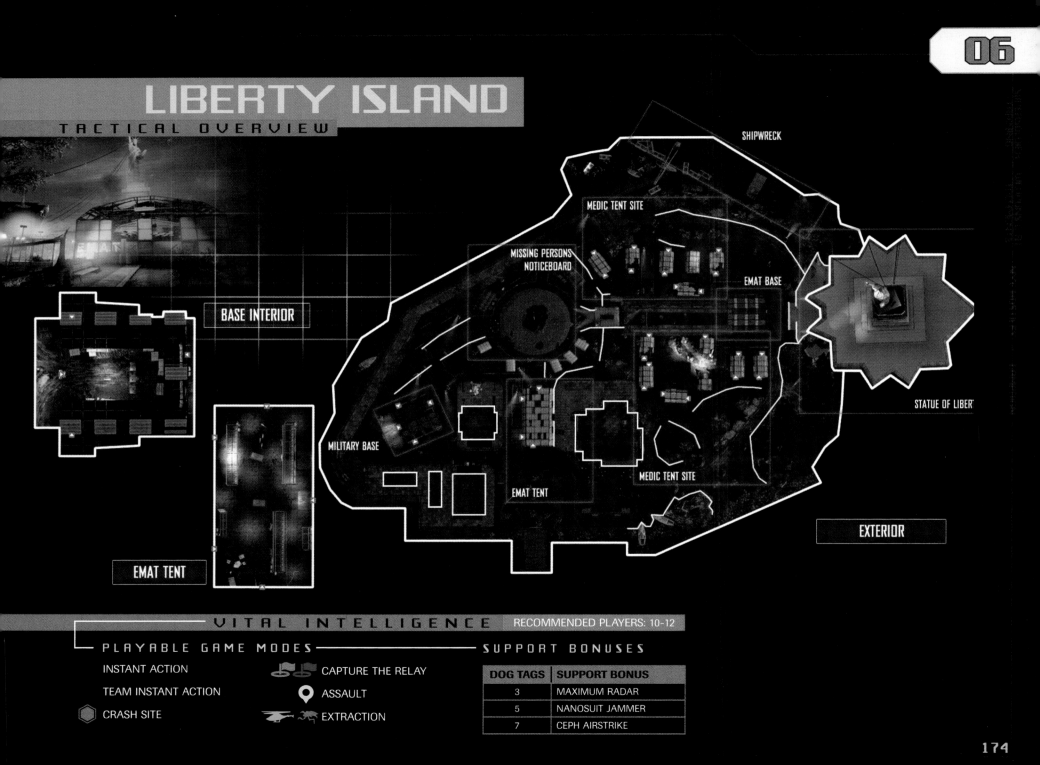

LIBERTY ISLAND

TACTICAL OVERVIEW

VITAL INTELLIGENCE

RECOMMENDED PLAYERS: 10-12

PLAYABLE GAME MODES

- INSTANT ACTION
- TEAM INSTANT ACTION
- CRASH SITE
- CAPTURE THE RELAY
- ASSAULT
- EXTRACTION

SUPPORT BONUSES

DOG TAGS	SUPPORT BONUS
3	MAXIMUM RADAR
5	NANOSUIT JAMMER
7	CEPH AIRSTRIKE

POTENTIAL CRASH SITES

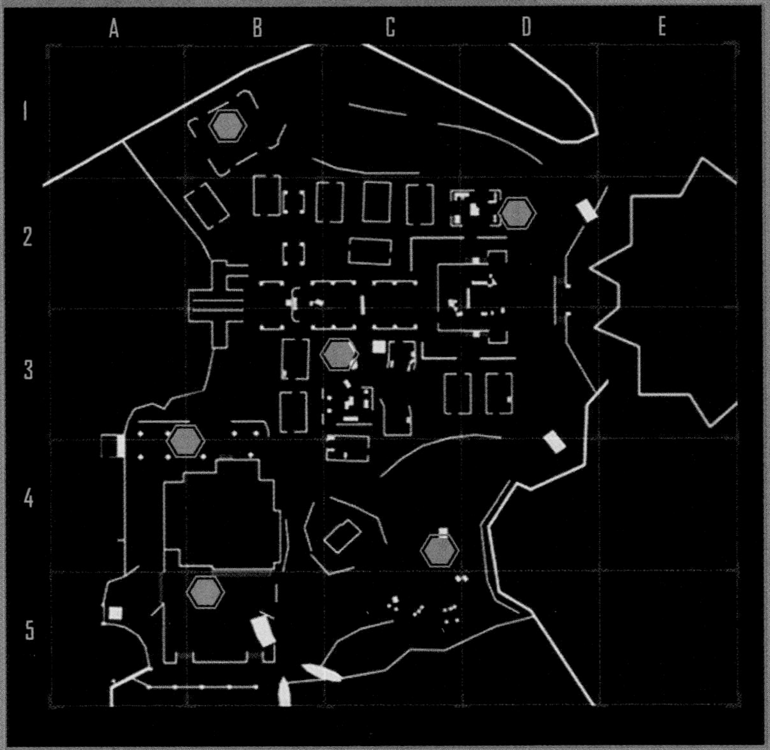

ALTERNATE GAME MODES

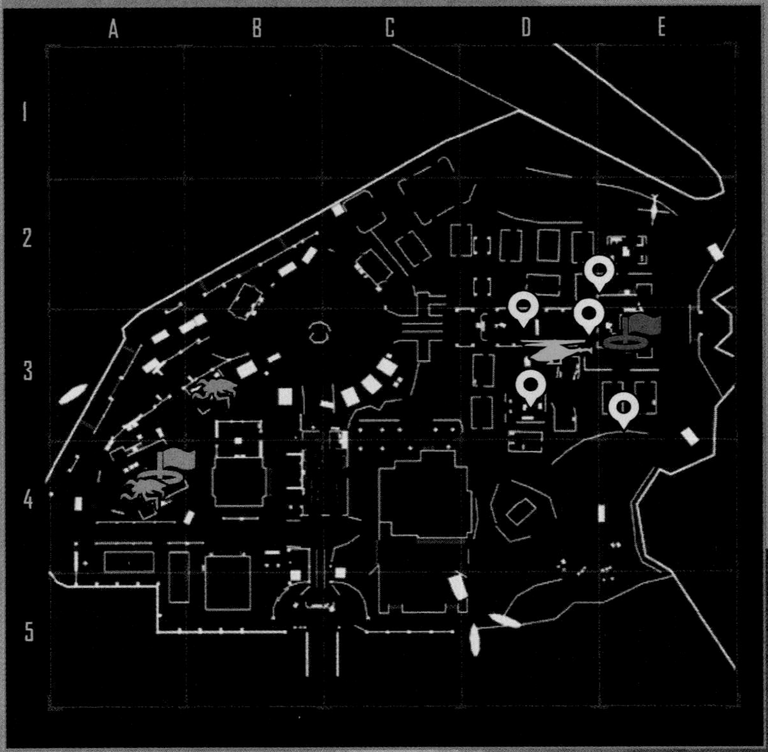

▶ GENERAL TACTICS

Use the roof of one of the short yellow E.M.A.T. buildings to hop into the gun tower in sector D3 equipped with a turret.

Climb to the top of the rubble in the lower-right corner of sector E3 for a good sniping vantage point.

There's an area at the bottom of sector D1 where the rubble slopes down to the Atlantic Trade freighter which has run ashore. Use this area to hide out and run to the top of the rubble to fire on enemies in the direction of the base of the Statue of Liberty.

▶ MODE-SPECIFIC TIPS

Capture the Relay: When defending, utilize the upstairs turret facing the middle of the map in each of the buildings housing the relay.

Assault: Hide behind the construction vehicle in sector E3 when defending data terminal B until the enemy starts a data upload, then slowly strafe to your left and fire upon the position through the leaning chain link fence.

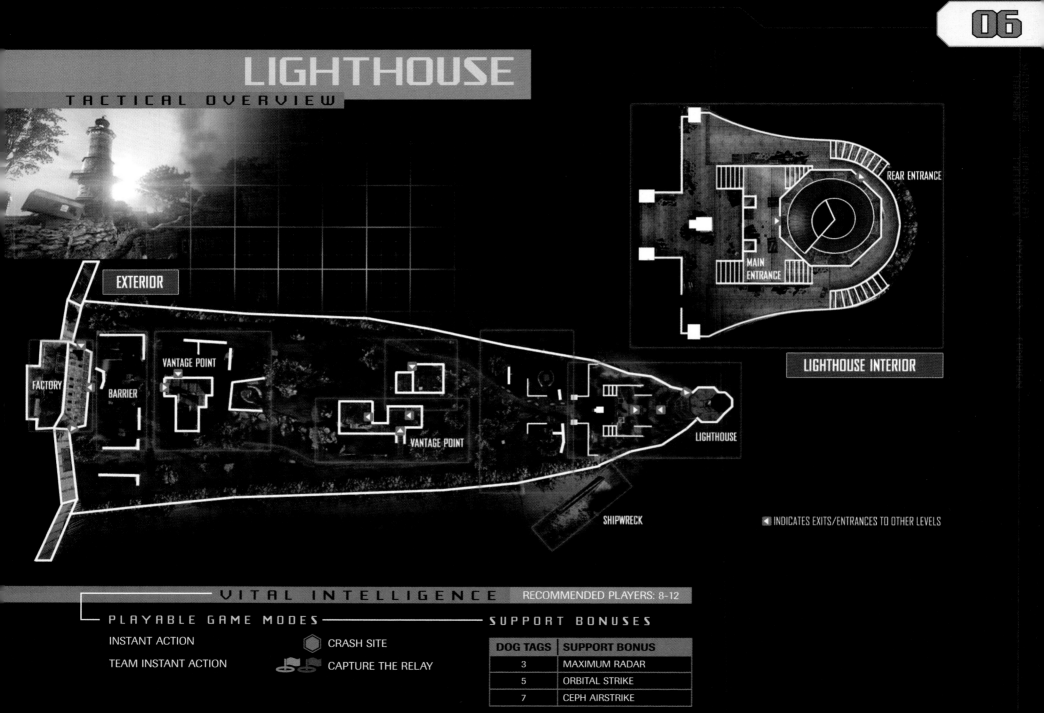

LIGHTHOUSE

TACTICAL OVERVIEW

VITAL INTELLIGENCE

RECOMMENDED PLAYERS: 8-12

PLAYABLE GAME MODES

- INSTANT ACTION
- TEAM INSTANT ACTION
- CRASH SITE
- CAPTURE THE RELAY

SUPPORT BONUSES

DOG TAGS	SUPPORT BONUS
3	MAXIMUM RADAR
5	ORBITAL STRIKE
7	CEPH AIRSTRIKE

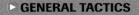

POTENTIAL CRASH SITES

ALTERNATE GAME MODES

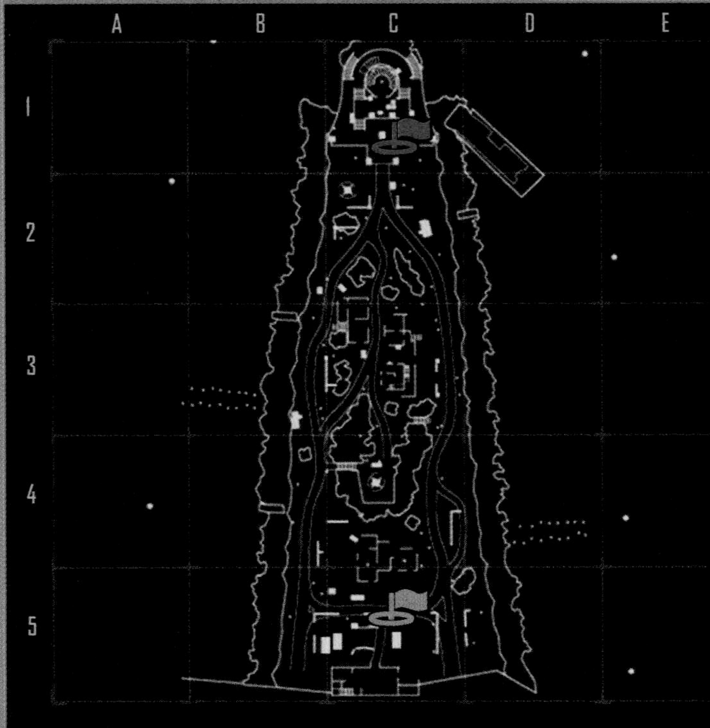

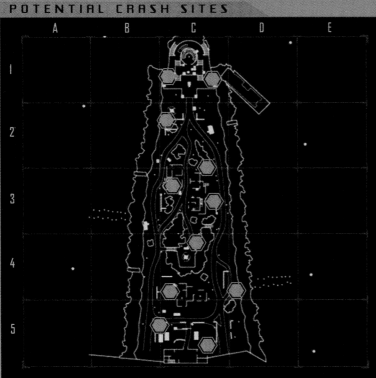

▶ GENERAL TACTICS

The Lighthouse area is a popular sniping roost. Turn the tables and creep along either coastline to snipe opponents who can't resist the lure of the high vantage point afforded by the lighthouse.

The factory on the opposite side of the map has a third floor with several windows. It is a fantastic sniper's perch. This spot is an incredible lure for snipers, so use the Proximity Alarm Suit Module to warn you against potential assassins once you've taken it.

Perch on the metal wall in the water in sector D2 and crouch with Stealth Mode engaged to stay out of the action and fire upon distracted enemies on the island.

▶ MODE-SPECIFIC TIPS

Crash Site: Activate Stealth mode and crouch with your back against the anti-air battery inside the sandbags when defending the alien pod in sector C4.

Capture The Relay: Both relay locations have ample overhead perches from which to defend. Knowing this, flush out and kill defenders before rushing into the kill zone seeking the relay.

PARKING DECK

TACTICAL OVERVIEW

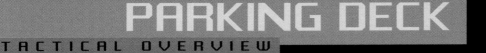

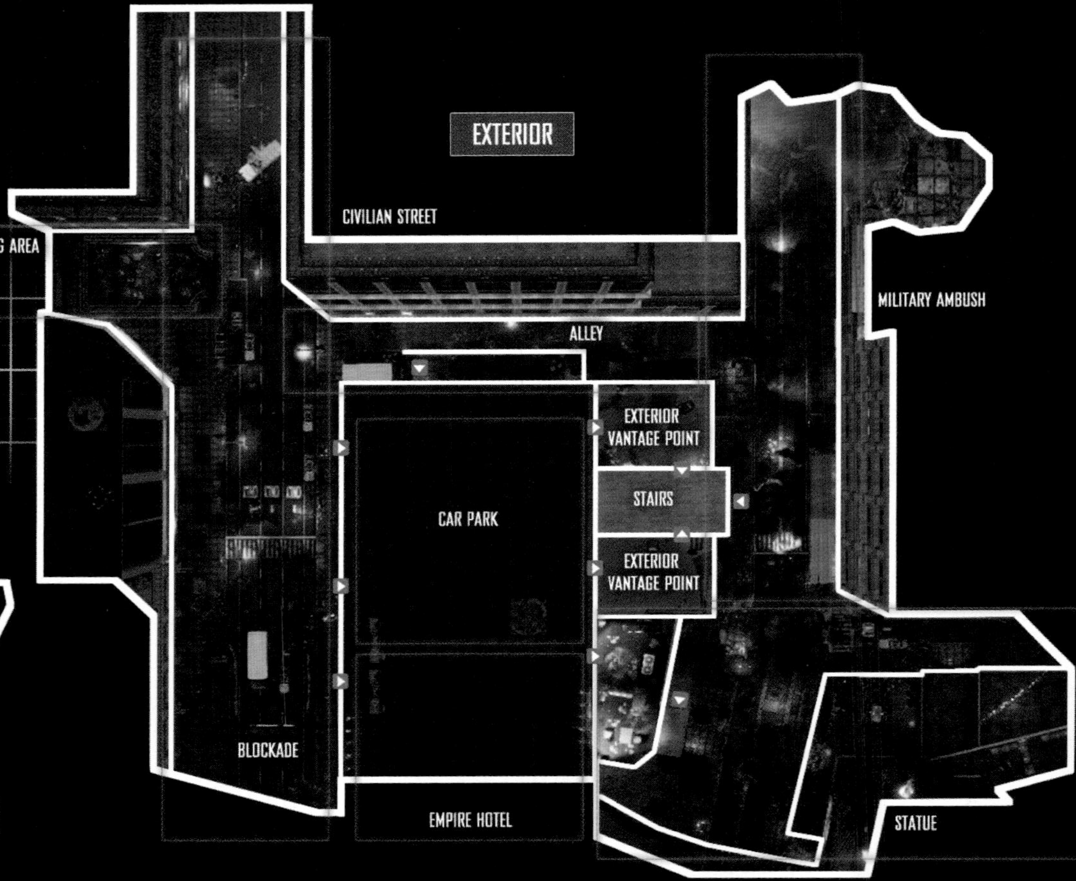

EXTERIOR

MEETING AREA

CIVILIAN STREET

MILITARY AMBUSH

ALLEY

EXTERIOR VANTAGE POINT

STAIRS

CAR PARK

EXTERIOR VANTAGE POINT

BLOCKADE

EMPIRE HOTEL

STATUE

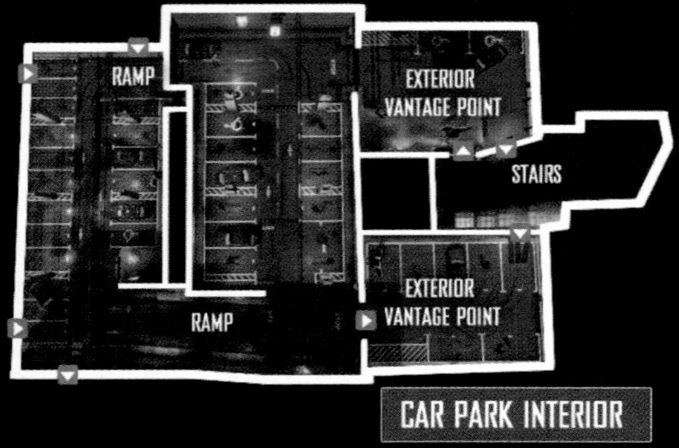

RAMP

EXTERIOR VANTAGE POINT

STAIRS

EXTERIOR VANTAGE POINT

RAMP

CAR PARK INTERIOR

INDICATES EXITS/ENTRANCES TO OTHER LEVELS

VITAL INTELLIGENCE

RECOMMENDED PLAYERS: 8-12

PLAYABLE GAME MODES

INSTANT ACTION

TEAM INSTANT ACTION

CRASH SITE

CAPTURE THE RELAY

ASSAULT

EXTRACTION

SUPPORT BONUSES

DOG TAGS	SUPPORT BONUS
3	MAXIMUM RADAR
5	RADAR JAMMER
7	MAXIMUM NANOSUIT

POTENTIAL CRASH SITES

ALTERNATE GAME MODES

▶ GENERAL TACTICS

In sector C2, hop onto the roof of the building with the "Food" sign and break through a window to enter the hotel to escape a firefight if you're outnumbered.

Locate the parking deck on the borders of sectors B2 and C2, above the "Save A Green Future" sign. It provides decent sightlines to the surrounding areas while minimizing flanking opportunities. This location also features a turret.

Use C4 on cars in the parking deck and fall back, waiting to blow up unsuspecting enemies as they pass by.

▶ MODE-SPECIFIC TIPS

Assault: Hop in the dumpster near data terminal A and crouch when defending, keeping your laser pointer low enough so that it doesn't leave the dumpster and give away your position. This location offers good concealment and may catch unsuspecting attackers off guard.

Extraction: Take position on the dumpster outside the window when defending the bio-tick in sector C2. Enemies may approach from above but the position cannot be flanked and most attackers will likely jump down in front of you for an easy melee kill.

PIER 17

TACTICAL OVERVIEW

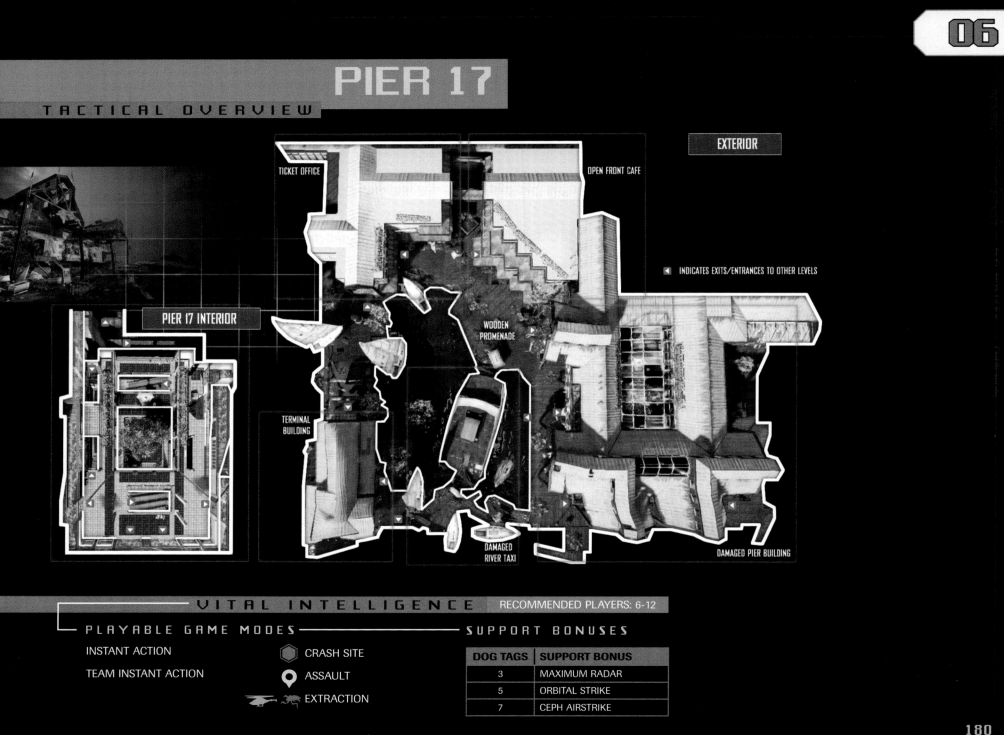

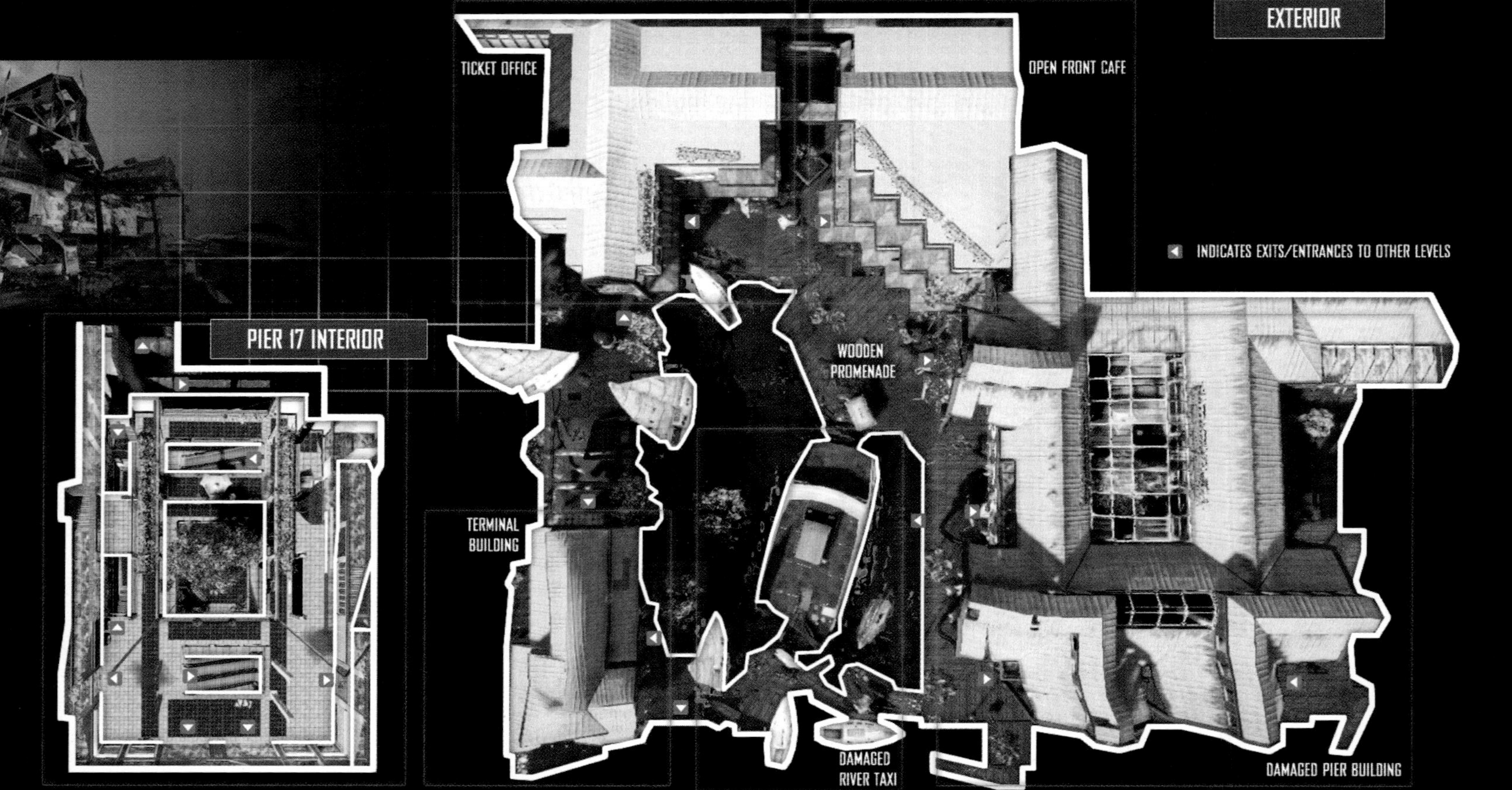

VITAL INTELLIGENCE

RECOMMENDED PLAYERS: 6-12

PLAYABLE GAME MODES

INSTANT ACTION

TEAM INSTANT ACTION

CRASH SITE

ASSAULT

EXTRACTION

SUPPORT BONUSES

DOG TAGS	SUPPORT BONUS
3	MAXIMUM RADAR
5	ORBITAL STRIKE
7	CEPH AIRSTRIKE

POTENTIAL CRASH SITES

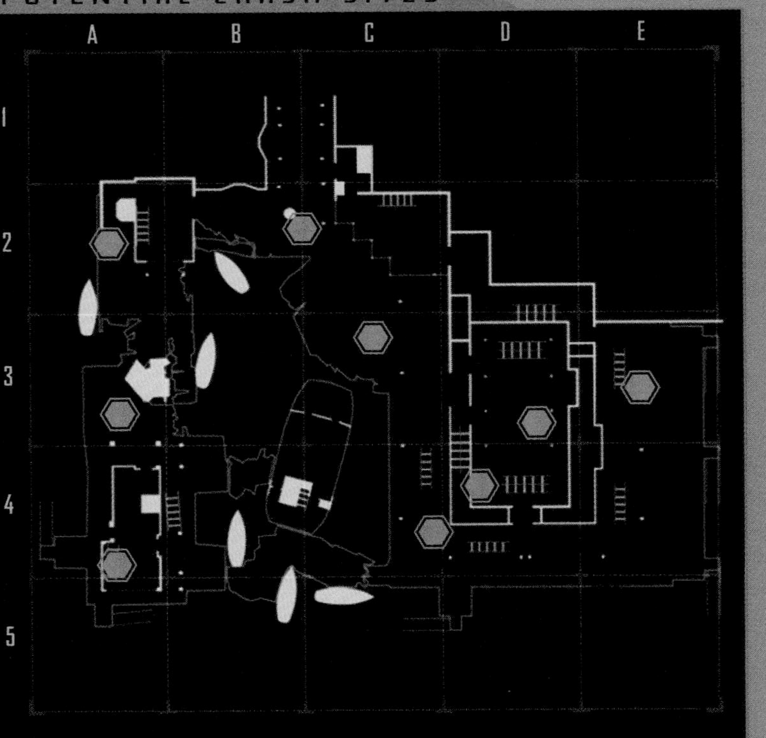

ALTERNATE GAME MODES

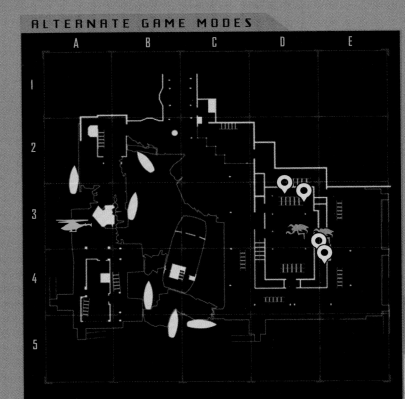

▸ GENERAL TACTICS

Enter the captain's perch of the damaged River Taxi in sectors B and C3 for a good hiding spot from which most of the map is visible. The location provides decent cover and makes you hard to spot from a distance.

Climb to the top of building 17B in sectors A4 and B4. Jump to the back of the building across the broken floor. The windows of this building provide a decent view of the damaged River Taxi and surrounding areas.

The upstairs of the diner in sector A2 features tight quarters and a mounted HMG. Lure enemies in with turret fire and fall back to finish them off with a shotgun at short range as they climb the interior stairs to flank you.

There's a dead end in the top left corner of sector E3. It's on the top floor of the back side of the mall near the deli. This is an ideal spot to utilize Stealth mode and lay in wait for opponents climbing the stairs directly ahead or exiting the doorway ahead on the right.

▸ MODE-SPECIFIC TIPS

Crash Site: When defending the alien pod in sector A4, have a teammate stay in the corner upstairs next to the potted tree, ready to fire upon attackers below.

Assault: When on offense flank the mall and use Stealth to approach the upstairs entrance near data terminal B in sector E3. Most defenders will likely be covering the front entrances of the mall.

SANCTUARY

TACTICAL OVERVIEW

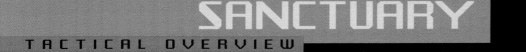

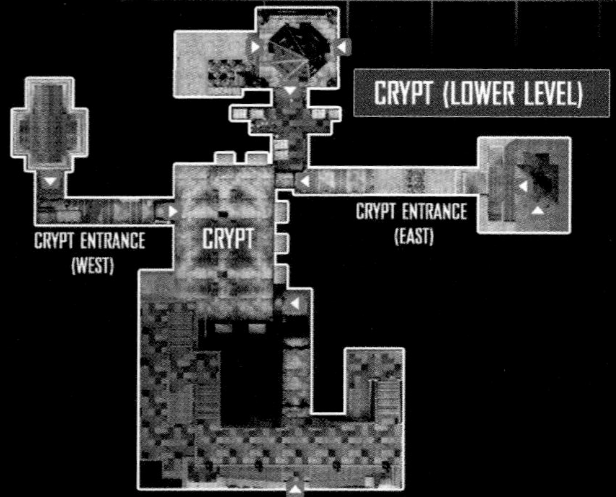

EXTERIOR

CABIN ZONE
VANTAGE POINT
VANTAGE POINT
CRYPT ENTRANCE (WEST)
CHURCH
CRYPT ENTRANCE (EAST)
CABIN ZONE
CRYPT ENTRANCE
BLOCKADE
BLOCKADE
RAMP

CRYPT (LOWER LEVEL)

CRYPT ENTRANCE (WEST)
CRYPT
CRYPT ENTRANCE (EAST)

◄ INDICATES EXITS/ENTRANCES TO OTHER LEVELS

VITAL INTELLIGENCE

RECOMMENDED PLAYERS: 10-12

PLAYABLE GAME MODES

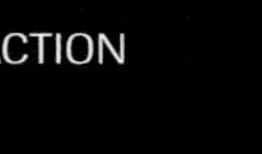

- INSTANT ACTION
- TEAM INSTANT ACTION
- CRASH SITE
- CAPTURE THE RELAY
- ASSAULT
- EXTRACTION

SUPPORT BONUSES

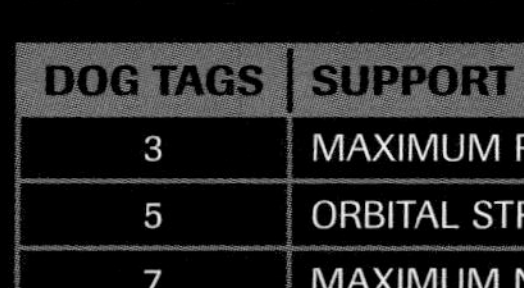

DOG TAGS	SUPPORT BONUS
3	MAXIMUM RADAR
5	ORBITAL STRIKE
7	MAXIMUM NANOSUIT

POTENTIAL CRASH SITES

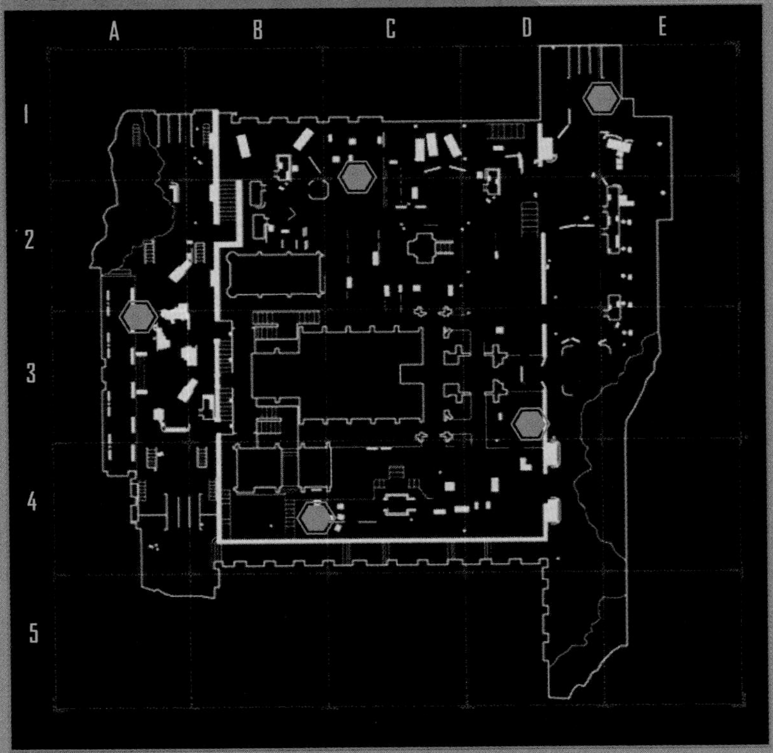

A B C D E
1 2 3 4 5

ALTERNATE GAME MODES

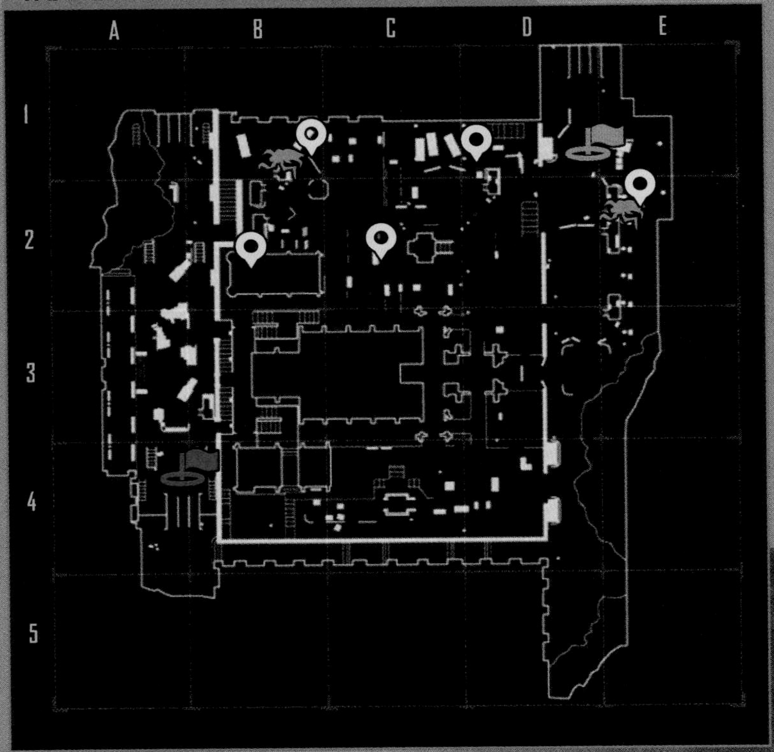

A B C D E
1 2 3 4 5

GENERAL TACTICS

The Blockade in sector A4 provides an elevated location with good sight lines down the street. It cannot be attacked from directly behind, minimizing the chances of being assassinated in this location.

The lower level of the Crypt is a confined space ideal for short-range shotgun battles. There are three entrances to this area so watch your corners.

The tower in the top of the building outside the church in sector C4 provides views in every direction and is difficult for enemies to spot as they pass by. Toss grenades into this location to dislodge any enemies encamped in this location.

In sector C1, the room with the electrical sparks above the ramps provides an excellent view of the nearby street and graveyard near the West Crypt Entrance. A turret on the ramps below can provide additional firepower.

MODE-SPECIFIC TIPS

Crash Site: When defending the alien pod bordering sectors A2 and A3 utilize the nearby subway entrances. While one teammate earns points wait in this position for the enemy team to attack and ambush them.

Assault: When on offense take to the underground crypts and emerge from the crypt entrance in sector C2 to get behind enemy lines and assassinate defenders before moving in on the data terminals.

SKYLINE

TACTICAL OVERVIEW

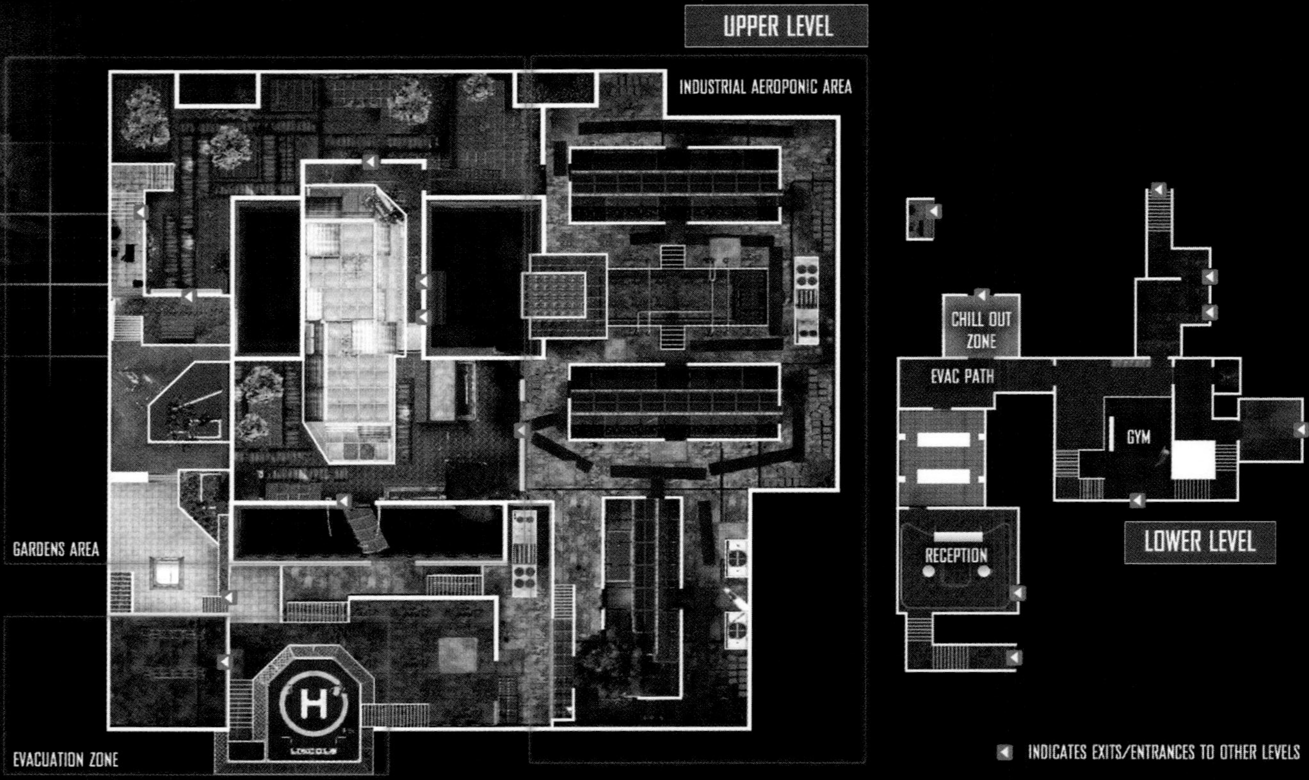

UPPER LEVEL

INDUSTRIAL AEROPONIC AREA

GARDENS AREA

EVACUATION ZONE

CHILL OUT ZONE

EVAC PATH

GYM

RECEPTION

LOWER LEVEL

◄ INDICATES EXITS/ENTRANCES TO OTHER LEVELS

VITAL INTELLIGENCE

RECOMMENDED PLAYERS: 8-12

PLAYABLE GAME MODES

INSTANT ACTION

TEAM INSTANT ACTION

CRASH SITE

SUPPORT BONUSES

DOG TAGS	SUPPORT BONUS
3	MAXIMUM RADAR
5	ORBITAL STRIKE
7	CEPH AIRSTRIKE

POTENTIAL CRASH SITES

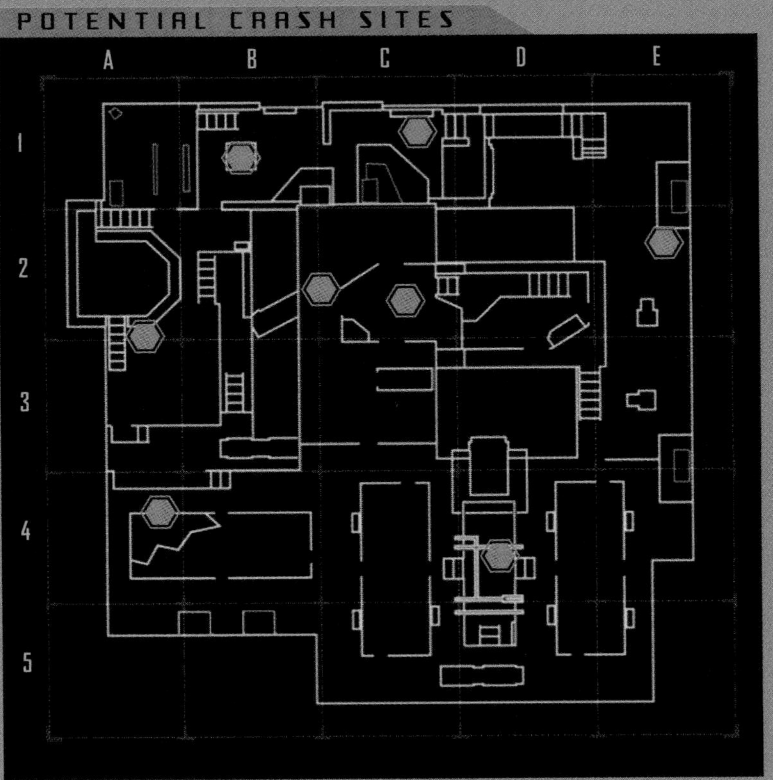

▶ GENERAL TACTICS

Hop atop the small brick structure next to the main greenhouse in the middle of the map and from there run and jump (without sprinting) toward the greenhouse. Jump early enough to enter an extended jump and you can scramble onto the roof of the greenhouse. This provides the best (and highest) view of all exterior sections of the map; be wary of fire through the glass portions of the roof and stay on the metal sections.

Look before you leap! There are many locations on Skyline where you can leap to an accidental death. The best advice is to learn the map and know where you're going before jumping off any ledges. That shortcut you're eyeing may be a one-way trip to a respawn.

The treadmill area in the fitness center can serve as a good camping location as enemies rush down the stairwell above or into the building through the destroyed external wall.

Along the east edge of the map, at locations E1 and E2 and E3 and E4, there are two high voltage perch areas that provide decent cover and sightlines toward the main greenhouse in the center of the map.

▶ MODE-SPECIFIC TIPS

Crash Site: Hop up onto the plant-covered, wooden ledge in the lower-right corner of sector C2 when defending the alien pod in this sector. The metal wall and tree on either side offer cover and concealment and sets you up for some easy kills as opponents rush in to secure the downed pod.

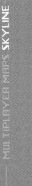

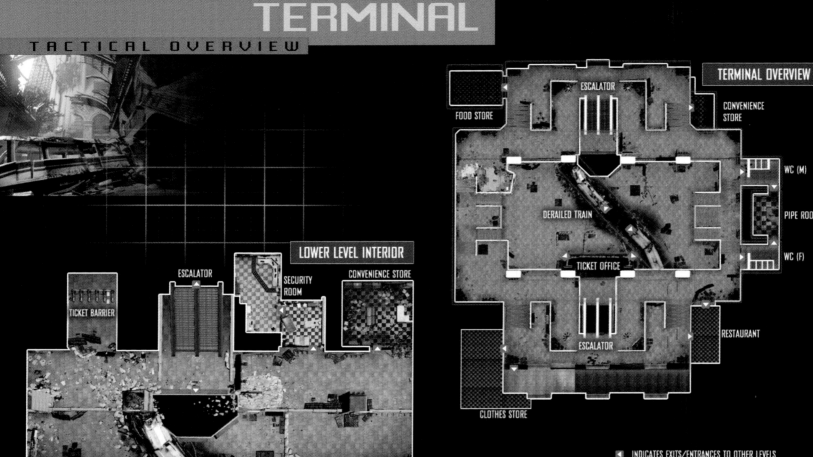

TERMINAL

TACTICAL OVERVIEW

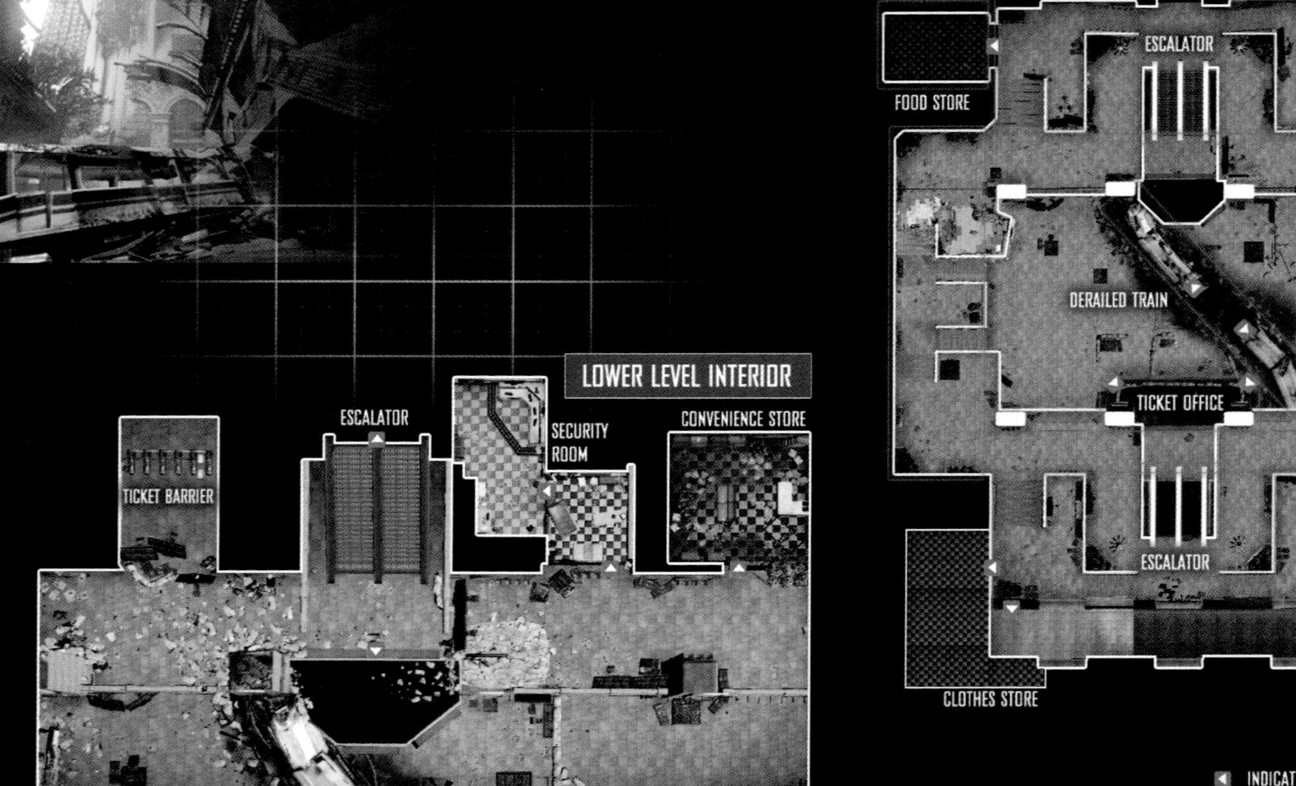

VITAL INTELLIGENCE

RECOMMENDED PLAYERS: 6-10

PLAYABLE GAME MODES

INSTANT ACTION

TEAM INSTANT ACTION

SUPPORT BONUSES

DOG TAGS	SUPPORT BONUS
3	MAXIMUM RADAR
5	RADAR JAMMER
7	MAXIMUM NANOSUIT

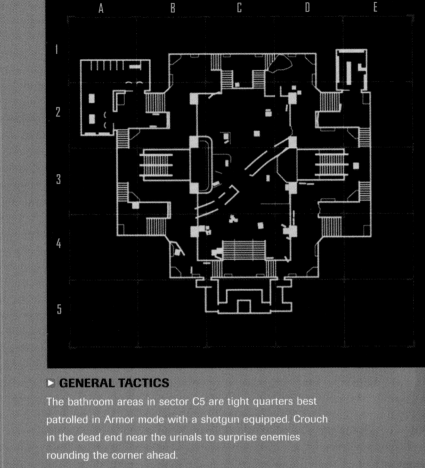

▶ GENERAL TACTICS

The bathroom areas in sector C5 are tight quarters best patrolled in Armor mode with a shotgun equipped. Crouch in the dead end near the urinals to surprise enemies rounding the corner ahead.

Station Security in sector D3 has one entrance, crouch behind the desk inside the entrance and fire on enemies running down the center of the map.

There are several corner planters along the perimeter of the map that provide concealment behind the bushes. Combine these with Stealth Mode to escape from view and fire on passing enemies.

WALL STREET

TACTICAL OVERVIEW

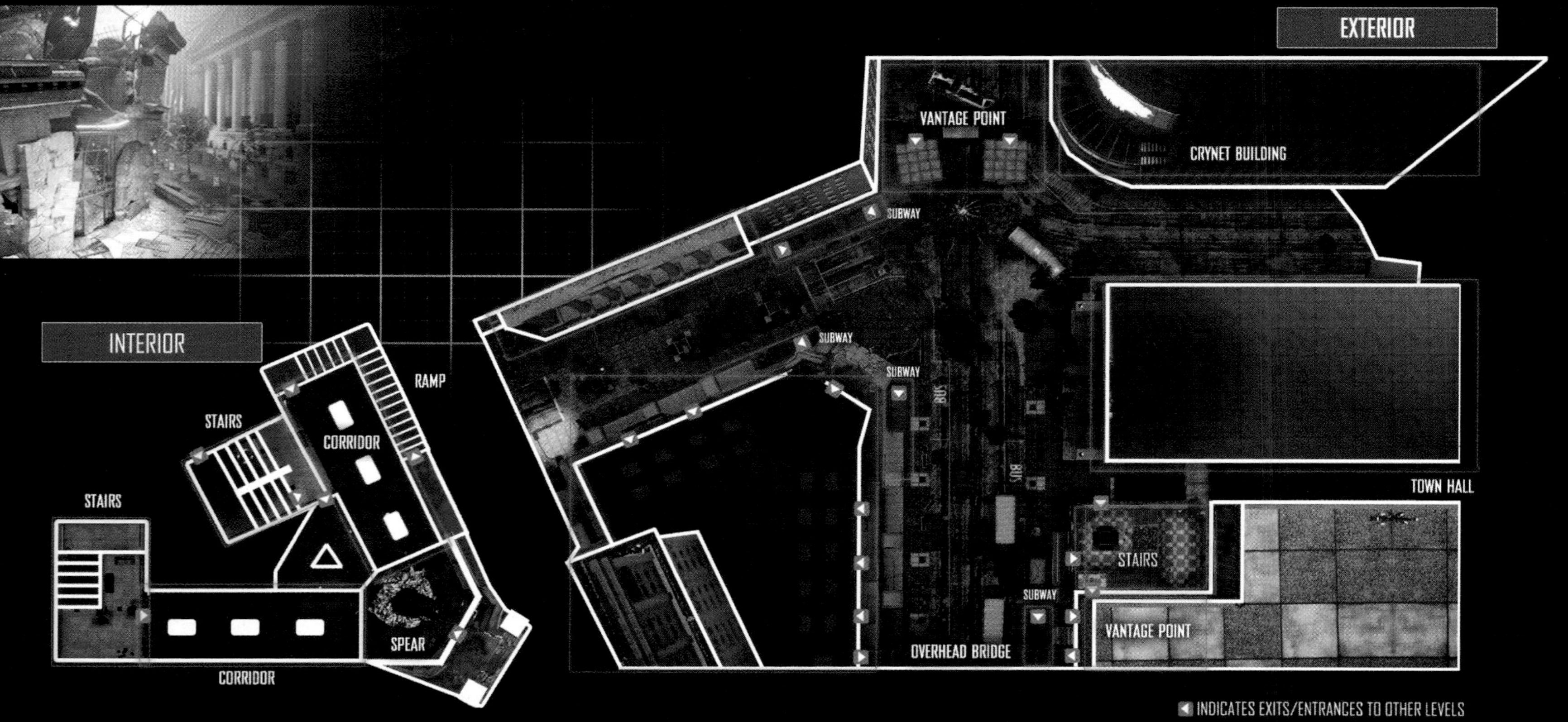

VITAL INTELLIGENCE

RECOMMENDED PLAYERS: 6-12

PLAYABLE GAME MODES

- INSTANT ACTION
- TEAM INSTANT ACTION
- CRASH SITE
- CAPTURE THE RELAY
- ASSAULT
- EXTRACTION

SUPPORT BONUSES

DOG TAGS	SUPPORT BONUS
3	MAXIMUM RADAR
5	ORBITAL STRIKE
7	MAXIMUM NANOSUIT

POTENTIAL CRASH SITES

ALTERNATE GAME MODES

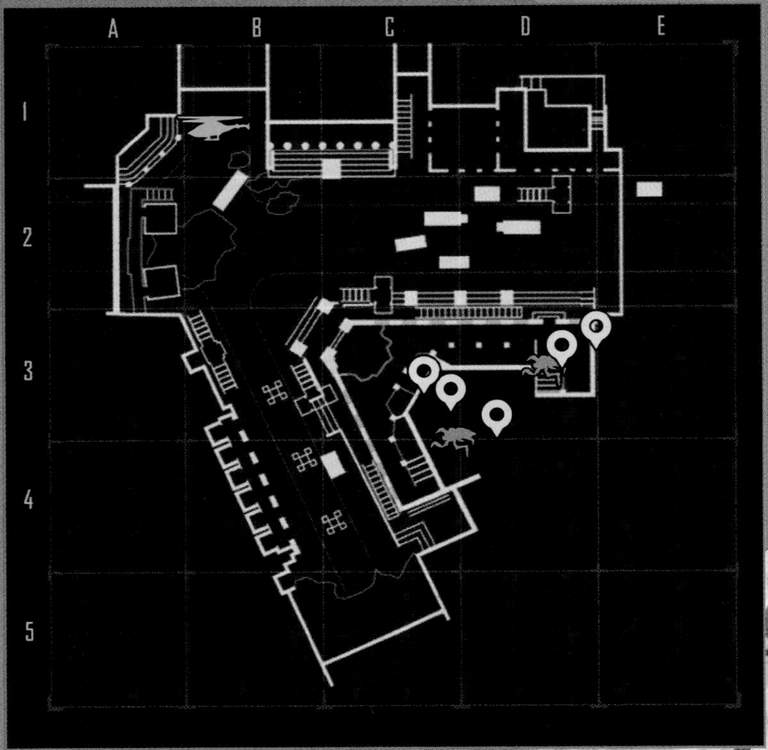

▶ GENERAL TACTICS

The watchtowers in sector A2 provide good views of both streets from their elevated positions.

Crouch in the corner of the 30 Wall Street balcony beneath the Overhead Bridge for a hard to spot location with a good view of the street below.

The area around the Spear in the front of the destroyed building in the middle of the map is provides a good, high vantage point over the main intersection.

▶ MODE-SPECIFIC TIPS

Assault: On offense swing around to the right side of the building and attack data terminal B by mantling up to the windows up the stairs from the data terminal in sector C4.

Extraction: On offense approach the bio-tick in sector D3 via the Overhead Bridge and retreat with the bio-tick via the same route, hugging the right-hand wall of the map all the way back to the extraction helicopter.

ACHIEVEMENTS & TROPHIES

SINGLE PLAYER CAMPAIGN

The majority of bonuses are unlocked during the single-player campaign, both through the normal course of progressing the story and by completing specific combat actions. We recommend simply playing the game through for the first time on the "Soldier" difficulty to get a feel for the game and unlock the bulk of these bonuses. Then use the Replay Mission feature to return to each specific mission and replay it first on Veteran then immediately afterwards on Supersoldier, while the level is fresh in your mind. Combat-oriented Achievements/Trophies and those dealing with collectibles or level-specific actions can be unlocked on any difficulty level.

STORY PROGRESSION

NAME	DESCRIPTION	GP
CAN IT RUN CRYSIS?	COMPLETE "IN AT THE DEEP END."	10
FOREIGN CONTAMINANT	ESCAPE THE BATTERY PARK EVACUATION CENTER.	10
MORE THAN HUMAN	ASSIMILATE ALIEN TISSUE AT THE CRASH SITE.	15
FALSE PROPHET	FIND NATHAN GOULD.	15
INTERNAL AFFAIRS	INFILTRATE THE CELL FACILITY AT WALL STREET.	15
INTO THE ABYSS	INFILTRATE THE ALIEN HIVE.	20
ONCE A MARINE, ALWAYS A MARINE	ASSIST THE MARINES IN MADISON SQUARE.	20
HUNG OUT TO DRY	REACH THE HARGREAVE-RASCH BUILDING.	20
FIRE WALKER	ASSIST THE EVACUATION AT BRYANT PARK.	25
DARK NIGHT OF THE SOUL	DEFEND CENTRAL STATION.	25
CROSSROADS OF THE WORLD	COMPLETE THE EVACUATION AT TIMES SQUARE.	25
THESEUS AT LAST	LOCATE JACOB HARGREAVE.	25
HOME STRETCH	REACH CENTRAL PARK.	25

CAMPAIGN COMPLETION

NAME	DESCRIPTION	GP
START SPREADING THE NEWS	FINISH THE SINGLE-PLAYER CAMPAIGN ON ANY DIFFICULTY.	35
CITY THAT NEVER SLEEPS	COMPLETE 6 LEVELS ON VETERAN DIFFICULTY.	25
EVOLUTION	COMPLETE 12 LEVELS ON VETERAN DIFFICULTY.	25
MEN OF DESTINY	COMPLETE THE SINGLE-PLAYER CAMPAIGN ON VETERAN DIFFICULTY.	45
HEART OF DARKNESS	COMPLETE 6 LEVELS ON SUPERSOLDIER DIFFICULTY.	25
MEDAL OF HONOR	COMPLETE 12 LEVELS ON SUPERSOLDIER DIFFICULTY.	25
SUPERSOLDIER	COMPLETE THE SINGLE-PLAYER CAMPAIGN ON SUPERSOLDIER DIFFICULTY.	65
THE TOURIST	FIND ALL NY SOUVENIRS.	15

LEVEL-SPECIFIC TASKS

NAME	DESCRIPTION	GP
FOOD FOR THOUGHT	KILL A CELL OPERATOR WITH A GIANT DONUT IN LOWER MANHATTAN DURING "SECOND CHANCE."	10
HOLE IN ONE	THROW AN ALIEN DOWN THE SINKHOLE IN "DARK HEART."	10
BAND OF BROTHERS	KEEP ALL THE MARINES ALIVE DURING THE RESCUE IN "SEMPER FI OR DIE."	15
STEALTH ASSASSIN	RE-ROUTE THE POWER IN "EYE OF THE STORM" WITHOUT BEING DETECTED.	15
LITERARY AGENT	SCAN ALL OF RICHARD MORGAN'S BOOKS IN THE NY PUBLIC LIBRARY.	10

SECRET

NAME	DESCRIPTION	GP
SPEEDING TICKET	BREAK THE SPEED LIMIT IN FRONT OF 10 SPEED CAMERAS.	10

Sprint through each of the 10 speed cameras scattered throughout the game. The speeding cameras are mounted above 25 MPH Speed Limit signs, usually on lamp posts and near intersections. Here are the levels they're in and a quick-reference shot to indicate where they are located.

BATTERY PARK: At the last section with Fred's Dinner (Donut).

SEMPER FI: After the encounter with the Heavy, at the start of the vehicle section.

SUDDEN IMPACT: At the street leading towards the underpass at the end of the level.

TRAIN TO CATCH: At the main road leading to the Library.

ROAD RAGE: Inside the tunnel at the end.

UNSAFE HAVEN: At the street next to the Onyx building.

GATE KEEPERS: At the very left road next to the church.

POWER OUT: At the road leading to Times Square.

SEAT OF POWER: At the end of the level, leading up to the slope towards the City Hall building.

MASKS OFF: At the bridge.

SINGLE PLAYER COMBAT

NAME	DESCRIPTION	GP
HEADHUNTER	KILL 4 ENEMIES IN A ROW WITH HEADSHOTS.	15
CLOSE ENCOUNTERS	STEALTH KILL 25 ENEMIES.	15
BLAST RADIUS	KILL AT LEAST THREE ENEMIES WITH A SINGLE GRENADE.	15
TWO HEADS ARE BETTER THAN ONE	KILL TWO ENEMIES WITH A SINGLE BULLET.	15
POPCORN	KILL 20 ENEMIES WITH THE MICROWAVE CANNON.	15
FASTBALL	KILL 10 ENEMIES BY THROWING AN OBJECT AT THEM.	15
DEATH GRIP	KILL 10 ENEMIES WITH GRAB AND THROW.	15
DEATH SLIDE	KILL 5 ENEMIES WHILE SLIDING.	15

MULTIPLAYER

The following bonuses are unlocked by playing the online multiplayer component of *Crysis 2*. Many can be unlocked quite quickly, while others require a high level of commitment on your part. Expect roughly 55 hours of multiplayer gameplay to reach rank 50, depending on your skill level.

MULTIPLAYER CAREER

NAME	DESCRIPTION	GP
MODERN ART	UNLOCK 150 DOG TAG DISPLAYS.	5
TRY ME	COMPLETE 3 ONLINE MATCHES	10
MAXIMUM MODULE	FULLY LEVEL A SUIT MODULE.	20
NOMAD	PLAY A FULL GAME ON EVERY MAP.	10
I AM NOT A NUMBER	CREATE YOUR FIRST CUSTOM CLASS.	10
CRYSIS, WHAT CRYSIS?	REACH RANK 50.	35
DRESSED TO KILL	FULLY LEVEL THE SUIT.	30
TOOLED UP	UNLOCK ALL THE WEAPONS.	30
CRY SPY	GET 30 SPOT ASSISTS.	25
JACK OF ALL TRADES	WIN EVERY GAME MODE.	25
DEDICATION	PLAY ONLINE 6 MONTHS AFTER YOUR FIRST TIME.	25

INDIVIDUAL GAME PERFORMANCE

NAME	DESCRIPTION	GP
LEAGUE OF YOUR OWN	TOP THE SCOREBOARD.	25
THE CLEANER	GET 1 OF EACH SKILL KILL.	25
TEAM PLAYER	BE IN A PARTY OF AT LEAST 3 PEOPLE AND PLAY A FULL GAME.	10
THE COLLECTOR	COLLECT 20 DOG TAGS	15

OFFICIAL STRATEGY GUIDE

Written by Doug Walsh
Multiplayer Content provided by Jim Morey

DK/BradyGames, a division of Penguin Group (USA) Inc.
800 East 96th Street, 3rd Floor
Indianapolis, IN 46240

ISBN-10: 0-7440-1244-9

ISBN-13: 978-0-7440-1244-6

UPC Code: 7-52073-01244-1

Printing Code: The rightmost double-digit number is the year of the book's printing; the rightmost single-digit number is the number of the book's printing. For example, 11-1 shows that the first printing of the book occurred in 2011.

14 13 12 11 4 3 2 1

Printed in the USA.

BRADYGAMES STAFF

GLOBAL STRATEGY GUIDE PUBLISHER
Mike Degler

EDITOR-IN-CHIEF
H. Leigh Davis

OPERATIONS MANAGER
Stacey Beheler

DIGITAL & TRADE CATEGORY PUBLISHER
Brian Saliba

CREDITS

TITLE MANAGER
Christian Sumner

BOOK DESIGNER
Tim Amrhein

PRODUCTION DESIGNER
Areva

BRADYGAMES ACKNOWLEDGEMENTS

First off, congratulations to Crytek for making another astounding game! Thanks to everyone at Crytek and EA Europe that pitched in to help bring this guide together, especially Thomas Ebsworth from Crytek and Chris Brown and D.J. Montgomery over at EA Europe. A special shout out goes to Jens Schäfer for handling all the approvals and making sure this guide was on time and filled with everything all you fans want!